Starwalker 1

INCARNATION:
The Four Angles and the Moon's Nodes

The ancient science of astrology, founded on the correlation between celestial movements and human experience, recognises the universe as an indivisible whole in which all parts are interconnected. Mirroring this perception of the unity of life, modern physics has revealed the web of relationship underlying everything in existence. Despite the inevitable backlash as old paradigms expire, we are now entering an age where scientific explanations and models of the cosmos are more in accord with astrological principles. In such a climate, astrology is emerging from relative obscurity to become once again a serious study offering a greater understanding of our true nature as inhabitants of a living cosmos imbued with sacred mysteries.

Melanie Reinhart was born in Zimbabwe, where the night skies inspired her vocation of astrology more than fifty years ago. She holds a B.A. in Music and Drama, and is an award-winning diploma-holder of the Faculty of Astrological Studies; in 2009 she became one of their patrons. In 2004, she received the Charles Harvey Award, given by the Astrological Association of Great Britain, 'for exceptional service to astrology'. She has been a professional astrologer since 1975; her rich background experience in many psychological and spiritual disciplines draws a worldwide clientele. Melanie has taught for some of the world's leading astrology schools including the Faculty of Astrological Studies, the London School of Astrology, the Centre for Psychological Astrology and Astro*Synthesis. She also offers lectures and workshops at many local and international venues, and runs her own programme, based mostly in London.

First published in 1997 by the CPA Press, London, as part of their seminar transcription series, this newly revised edition contains additional material, from more recent workshops and seminars, which has been woven into the text. The colloquial style of the spoken word style has largely been retained, in order to allow the material to retain the freshness of the original edition.

Melanie's books have been translated into seven languages, and include *Chiron and the Healing Journey* (1989/2010), *Saturn, Chiron and the Centaurs* (1996/2011), *Saturn: Time Heritage and Substance* (2013) and *Chiron, Pholus and Nessus: To the Edge and Beyond* (2014). Visit her website for current schedule of events, audio material and articles of topical interest: www. melaniereinhart.com

INCARNATION:
The Four Angles and
the Moon's Nodes

Melanie Reinhart

Dedicated to the presence of all those astrologers, both known and unknown to me, some of whom have moved on from this Earthly incarnation, whose dedication helps to form the substance of our tradition.

In particular, I offer gratitude to the following people with whom I had the privilege of studying, or meeting personally, and whose life's work immeasurably enriched my own studies in astrology and related disciplines.

Dane Rudhyar
John Addey
Brian Clark
Howard Sasportas
Richard Aisbitt
Charles Harvey
Liz Greene
Rob Hand
Geoffrey Cornelius
Jim Lewis
Joyce Collin-Smith
Heidi Langmann
Christina Rose
Ian Gordon-Brown
Barbara Somers
Fazal Inayat Khan
Frieda Kroeger
Paddy Genner
Sitara Brutnell
Betty Hughes

1st edition: CPA Press, 1997 h/b
2nd edition: CPA Press, 2002 p/b
3rd revised edition: Starwalker Press, 2014 p/b
4th revised edition: Starwalker Press, 2014 h/b
5th edition: Smashwords, 2014 (digital)
6th edition: Amazon Kindle, 2014 (digital)
7th edition: Starwalker Press, 2014 (digital)

ISBN: 978-0-9558231-3-8

**STARWALKER PRESS
BCM Starwalker, London WC1N 3XX
www.starwalkerpress.com**

Design and artwork: Tamara Stamenkovic
Front cover image: Will Parfitt
Proofreading: Jane Struthers

Note: The material in this book is for education, research and reference
only. No part of it is intended to substitute for appropriate professional
treatment of medical, psychological or other conditions.

STARWALKER PRESS

Books for the healing journey

Table of Contents

Part Two: The Nodes of the Moon

INCARNATION

Part One: The Four Angles

This seminar was given on 24 April 1996 at Regent's College, London, as part of the Diploma programme of the Centre for Psychological Astrology. The transcript was edited and this revision (2014) has been augmented with material from subsequent classes and seminars at different venues, woven together with the original text.

Introduction

I'd like to start by giving you some idea of what I hope to cover today. I'll begin with some general material about the angles, both technical and also symbolic, and then we'll consider each angle separately, from several points of view including the modes, elements and ruling planets. Later on we'll also be including transits over the angles. I'm sure most of you already know that those can be hugely important in people's lives, especially if the outer planets are involved. I want to try and leave the whole of the last session for some guided imagery work which will connect the material to you and your own chart.

As always, I would invite any of you who have examples of what we might be discussing, from your own chart or another with which you are familiar, to please bring that in, if you wish to. It is always fruitful to have anecdotes and live information from you about what it feels like to have Aries on the IC, or whatever. So please don't hesitate to chip in.

Orienting Physically

Without more ado, let's start looking at the angles. Some of you at the front may be wondering what I am doing, poring over this strange object on the table. It is actually a compass, because the angles are calculated using some very specific astronomical factors. I want to cover some basic technical information, but I thought it might be interesting to experiment with this by finding our orientation in a direct and physical way.

Firstly, let's recap briefly the difference between the Zodiac and the wheel of houses, which of course is anchored by the four angles.

I like to imagine the Zodiac as the journey travelled by the Sun in its *yearly* 'heroic round', its apparent path around the Earth. In astrology, of course, our main points of reference and description are *geocentric*, or *Earth-centred*. And also, don't forget, the whole solar system is travelling through space at incredible speed! But because the Zodiac is anchored by co-ordinates that relate to the Earth, and the Earth is actually travelling around the Sun, *when we consider the Zodiac, the Earth is always implied.* So the Zodiac provides a way of anchoring and describing the movement of the planets relative to the Earth, therefore to us and our lives here.

However, the angles are something quite different, which relate specifically to our time and place of birth, and to the *daily* rotation of the Earth on its own axis. So, likewise, they symbolise our anchoring here on Earth, making it even more specific. Fortunately, the angles are always consistent but, as you know, there are a large number of different house systems which divide up either space or time, using different co-ordinates, with different results. What they have in common, though, is that they are all measured, dropped down, as it were, on to the Ecliptic.

Firstly, if you think of a chart [draws chart on the board], it is quite easy to conceive of the Asc/Desc axis being the Horizon. I don't have any problem with that, but those of you who remember geography lessons at school and seeing globes of the Earth, will remember that the North Pole is usually up at the top, although sometimes the globe is inclined. So it is easy to get into thinking of the Midheaven as somehow 'up there' [points directly overhead], and north as also 'up there'. They are quite different things, but 'up' and 'north' are muddled together for many of us when we look at charts.

In the northern hemisphere, where we are, the *Midheaven is actually due south* and it is *not exactly vertically 'up there' in the sky* at all. So, as an experiment – and this might turn into total chaos, so be prepared – what I would invite you to do is stand up now.[1]

The Prime Vertical

According to the compass, north is over there ... [points] ... so please turn to face the south. I want you to stretch your arms out by your side, so what you are doing is making a plane with your body. Not an aeroplane, but a plane as in geometry! In fact you are now making an east-west line, with your body and your outstretched arms, and you are facing towards the south, while north is behind you. Just pause, attune, and give yourself some time to get a feeling for that.

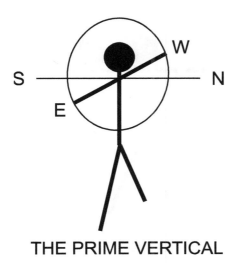

THE PRIME VERTICAL

Have you got it? So east is on your left, west on your right. OK?

Now, this is not a trick question – does anybody remember the name of the line we are making? You are now physically in a vertical plane and with your extended arms you are actually describing right now the **Prime Vertical,** which is the **east-west Great Circle.**

The Meridian

Better give your arms a rest, if you are getting tired, as there's another posture to follow! Next, turn to face west … over there [points]. OK? Now, do the same thing. Put your arms out and make another plane with your body. Does anybody know the name of this plane? It is the north-south plane, **the Great Circle going north-south.** You might want to draw out that circle with your arms. What you are actually describing is **the Meridian**. I have some diagrams which we can look at later but, for now, just get a feeling of it. You are standing on the surface of the Earth and with the plane of your body you are describing this north-south line. You could almost imagine that you are cutting the universe in half, into two hemispheres, your body being the north-south line.

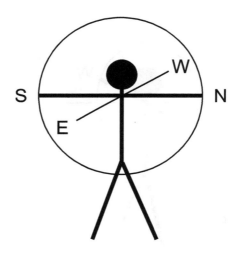

THE MERIDIAN

Now just experiment, if you wish … move from one to the other, marking out the Prime Vertical, then the Meridian again. Try with your eyes closed, too, if you like. This might help you register the axis in your body, rather than with your line of sight which anchors the other directions. Get a sense of the sphere in which you stand being cut by the line of your body from east to west, then north to south.

The Rational Horizon

One more thing! Next, get a sense of an imaginary plane, parallel to the floor, and waist high. You can draw it with your arms to get a clearer sense of it. Now, imagine that plane as a very thin disc surrounding you. Just imagine that plane sinking right down until it comes to rest at the centre of the Earth. You could even do it literally. Push it down with your hands and feel that circle go all the way down. That's what is called the **Rational Horizon,** and that is the horizon that we will see on the diagrams. Did you get a sense of being in a sphere that you were cutting into four?

Audience: Yes.

Melanie: How does it feel?

Audience: I feel an immediate sense of space.

Audience: I feel like I've arrived in the room.

Melanie: It is very interesting living in the city, or driving on the motorways, with your *London A-Z,* and your maps. Probably many of us have no idea where north, south, east and west actually are. I thought I'd bring the compass because when I was preparing for today I realised I had no idea of the orientation of this room that we usually work in! Of course in olden days, and still now to some degree, people navigated by the stars and that's a very useful image for what the angles are – the *navigational points of our life.* Those two axes make our four-way orientation in life, representing *that which anchors us into this incarnation, describing and circumscribing our place of participation in the cosmos.* Our metaphorical north, south, east and west. Having done that, now I want to show you a couple of diagrams, and I hope that the physical orientation we just did will make them easier to understand.

The Horizon System

Here is a very simple diagram of the **Celestial Sphere.** Do you all know what that is? In the middle there, you see the Earth, and this drawing is a bird's eye view of the sphere that would be created by extending the space around the Earth. It can be confusing at first, this 3-D thinking, but hang in there! This diagram simply shows the Horizon system, which we were exploring physically with the planes of our body. So this horizontal ellipse here – the Rational Horizon – is actually a circle, and that is what we were describing when we experienced that circle which we pushed down.

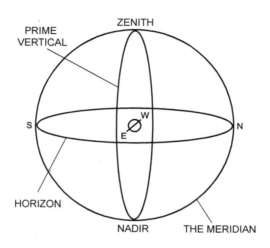

This vertical line, here, is the Prime Vertical. So when we faced south, but were dividing up the sphere east-west with our bodies and outstretched arms, there is the line we were making – the Prime Vertical. The line that goes all the way round the edge – that's the Meridian. We made that line when we faced west, and our body connected the north-south axis. Both are perpendicular to the Horizon.

The Ecliptic

Now here is another diagram, the same, but showing an additional circle. Here again are the Prime Vertical and Horizon lines, and here is the Meridian, all the way round the edge. This extra ellipse shows the **Ecliptic**, which is marked. This is the apparent path of the planets, including the Sun, around the Earth; it is a band roughly 16° wide. All the classical planets orbit within that belt, but Pluto, Chiron and the Centaurs are exceptions because their orbits go much further north or south of the Ecliptic.

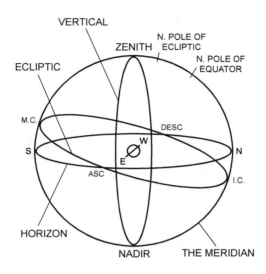

In other words, going back to our physical positioning, if you would stand as we did, facing south, the point called the **Zenith** is always directly above where you are standing, your head is pointing upwards, overhead, above. Conversely, the Nadir is the point through the Earth and all the way out the other side, directly beneath where you are standing. I mention this because sometimes you will see the word 'Nadir' as substituting for the IC when the angles are being referred to, and this is not correct. Equally, the Midheaven is not the same as the Zenith, unless you are living in the tropics, where the Sun passes directly overhead at midday. The further north or south you go, the more divergence there can be.

Referring again to our standing position, this is the Zenith, directly overhead. Now I probably can't do this without falling over, but if I would lean like this … into the angle where my arms are pointing, where we will hopefully see the Sun at midday … I would be leaning into the plane of the Ecliptic. So I'd be lined up with the zone where the planets actually pass across the sky, along with the Ecliptic constellations. That's what's shown on that second diagram, in other words, the difference between the Horizon and the Ecliptic.

OK. Does that help you get a physical sense of how this works?

The MC/IC and Asc/Desc

You see the two angles, the MC and Ascendant, marked in there with their counterparts? So the Ascendant and the Midheaven occur where the Horizon and the Meridian intersect the Ecliptic. I hope that's clear.

Look at the Ecliptic again. See the Ascendant point? Well, relative to that, the signs of the Zodiac will be marked out in twelve equal segments, along the Ecliptic, in sequence. So, for example, if this was a chart with Aries rising, to make it easy, and the person had the Sun in Cancer, whereabouts would the Sun be along this line?

Audience: Somewhere to the right, near the IC point.

Melanie: Yes, exactly.

So I hope you enjoyed doing that. I confess that doing it physically like that was the only way I was able to learn about these things, which otherwise seemed rather abstract to me. Of course they are not at all abstract, really, as they reflect the basic physicality of our orientation on Earth and in the cosmos. I find it useful to remember the actual feeling of how they divide up the sphere. We have been looking at the Celestial Sphere, which you can read all about in any good astronomy book.

But by experiencing it physically, *you can also experience this sphere as the metaphorical 'sphere of your life'*. We even use that phrase in English. We describe someone's speciality, or main activity, as 'their own sphere'.

Orienting Symbolically

The Four Hemispheres

Now that we have looked at the diagrams, and also experienced at first hand the dilemma of translating three-dimensional information into a flat two-dimensional diagram, I'd like to mention the four hemispheres of the chart. [Draws chart on the board.] If you have a good visual 3-D imagination, you can think of yourself inserting a flat horoscope into the space defined by the Ecliptic line on our second diagram. Then you will have the Ascendant on the left, as we do, and all the other points in their right places, and you may find more familiar ground!

Just as a matter of interest, when we did the exercise about the Horizon, what sort of thoughts or feelings did you have as we noted that plane, the Rational Horizon plane going down into the centre of the Earth? What did it feel like, to recognise that you are actually standing on the top half of something and underneath, although you can't see it, under that Horizon, it's night?

Audience: It is funny that you say that because, well, I had the feeling that as the circle travelled down, in my visionary eye, I saw my legs and the feeling that I got was of being grounded.

Melanie: What is on your IC?

Audience: The sign of Cancer, but no planets nearby.

Melanie: I know Cancer is a water sign, but it is ruled by the Moon, which is intimately connected to the Earth; the sign also has good protective qualities that are necessary for life on Earth, like security, nourishment and care-taking. And as we'll see, the IC is about roots, and its 'natural' ruler is the Moon.

Audience: I felt the opposite. Because when it was around me I was contained.

Melanie: What is on your IC?

Audience: Neptune.

Melanie: Neptune is a very boundless energy, watery and uncontained.

Audience: Surely when we stand up, the Zenith is directly overhead, and it is the Nadir, not the IC, which is directly below?

Melanie: Yes, that's correct. That is what I meant by the dilemma of translating from a 3-D system to a flat piece of paper! Providing we know they are not in fact the same thing, we can draw relevant symbolism from this overlap, and think of the IC as also 'underneath', like the Nadir. There are many 'as ifs' in astrology.

Audience: I wondered why it was called the 'Rational Horizon'.

Melanie: That term differentiates it from the so-called **Topocentric** or **Local Horizon**. Here I am, standing in London, at 51°N32'. The Horizon around me is actually something like this … [draws on the board] … it is at an angle, it's a **Little Circle**, the Local Horizon. The Rational Horizon, however, is a so-called **'Great Circle'** and all Great Circles are thus called because they pass through the centre of the Earth. So only a Little Circle can be the Local Horizon, and that's why the other one is called the 'Rational Horizon'.

Back to the chart. The Horizon line divides the top half from the bottom half. Thus it divides the daylight world from the night world of our life. That is easy to remember, but it can yield a lot in terms of understanding. That doesn't mean that somebody born with all their planets in the bottom half is going to be invisible or madly introverted. What it does mean is that the function of interiority and subjectivity belongs in this lower half. In the day half belongs the more so-called objective, manifest, available level. So, for example, if somebody has a lot of planets in the day half, up there, even if they are actually quite an introverted person, they will be very busy, and may attract many intense situations from outside. Because up here, from the 7th house onwards, we are engaging all the time with other people and their feelings, external situations, other beliefs, the world out there. Planets do function differently according to which half they are in, and the Horizon line can usefully be thought of as an axis of awareness.

Audience: I felt rather strange. I was more aware of being like a vertical axis going through the centre of the Earth. One part of me was in the centre of the Earth, with a polarity going out into space towards the stars.

Melanie: We will talk more about that when we talk about the MC. Please remind me if I leave out this image. For now, remember that the Midheaven is not the same as the Zenith, although it also partakes of the symbolism of the overhead Sun. Standing as we are, our heads pointing straight up towards the Zenith, we point to stars off the Ecliptic!

Now what about the east-west hemisphere of the chart? How was it to divide your universe in half that way round? Did it feel different? Somebody is nodding very definitely – would you like to try to put it into words?

Audience: I felt a great sense of peace looking towards the west.

Melanie: Do you have planets near the Descendant?

Audience: No, I don't. I actually have most of my planets in the other hemisphere.

Melanie: So can you connect this feeling with your chart?

Audience: Well, it is my only Earth angle.

Melanie: That's interesting. I'll be mentioning that theme separately, later on ... of how the element which is represented at each angle adds substance and significance to it. Just extend your imagination now and recall a sunrise you have actually seen at some time. Imagine in tandem, if you can, a sunset. See if you can get a sense of the difference in the quality of the light, of the energy and how you feel, and so on. If you can't hold the two just take them one by one.

Audience: It's lighter.

Melanie: Which one?

Audience: Sunrise. An orange-red with fire.

Melanie: For me there is always a forward-looking quality that you find at dawn, and at the Ascendant. Conversely at the Descendant, it is like a sunset, laying to rest a whole daylight cycle of experience, perhaps the end of a busy day, maybe with a lot of work or a lot of stimulation, stress, responsibility. The top half, the journey of the Sun through the daylight hours and everything that has meant, everything that you have experienced in that day, is laid to rest here at the Descendant. There is a reflectiveness about sunset. It is when you pause, turn, and see where the impulse of that day has led, what it has brought. Most of us probably go unaware of the sunset, each day. But if we are watching, this is the mood that probably befalls us. The Sun *rises,* but night *falls.* It's like a releasing.

So in terms of the chart, I would put over here, at the Descendant, the words 'adaptability' and 'response' and 'consequences'. These are words to remind you of images and processes so don't take them too literally.

Over by the Ascendant, I would put 'freedom' and 'initiative'. Dawn is the beginning. There is an incredible freedom in that. It is full of potential. You don't know what's going to happen. Even if you know you've got this or that duty to perform, you don't know the details of what the day is going to be like, or what will transpire. Freedom and consequences.

Audience: Is the Ascendant a place of power and the Descendant the place where we give up the power, or a place of rejection?

Melanie: It can be, but I'm not sure about the association of 'rejection'. We will discuss this angle more when we take each one separately, which I am going to do soon, but first, some further ways of looking at the angles. [Writes on the board.]

Just one more thing about the two halves of the chart. You will see in some books this eastern side described as the half of free will, and the western side the half of fate. When we juxtapose those two particular words, it becomes a very locked and polarised concept. Free will *versus* fate. You probably noticed that I was trying to avoid that. Certainly the art of recognising consequences and the ability to respond to what is given are both qualities that belong to the western hemisphere. Useful gears to learn to move in if you have a lot of planets on this side. By the same token, with the eastern hemisphere, developing a sense of will, initiative and freedom is very important, but I wouldn't see them as starkly opposed. *They are complementary, two halves of a whole.*

Sacred Space

Within most magical traditions, worldwide, and also indigenous religions, orientation to the geographical cardinal points can be an important prelude to ritual work. North, south, east and west are marked out in a variety of ways, but with the purpose and indeed the effect of transforming ordinary space to sacred space. Also, Christian churches, mosques, temples and other places of worship will usually be oriented in this geographical way, with reference to *the terrestrial co-ordinates of the Horizon System.*[2]

Many ancient sacred sites are oriented to the heavens, often to specific stars or constellations.[3] Likewise, in the horoscope, the four angles and the houses derived from them show us the 'location' of the potentials, the energies, the patterns, the gifts, the difficulties that comprise our life story. It shows where and how these are specifically anchored into 3-D ... into the sacred space and time of our lives. *So they are about the soul's incarnation, and are oriented by the celestial co-ordinates of the Ecliptic System.*

If you draw your chart with an Ecliptic style – that is, with all the degrees of the Zodiac shown and planets and house cusps marked along the Zodiac wheel – you don't get the same visual reminder and imprinting of this symbolism, although it is a more accurate portrayal of the astronomy involved. However, I personally always draw charts with the two axes – the MC/IC and the Asc/Desc – exactly at right angles to each other. Then every time I pick up a chart I am reminded of what it's really about, which is our incarnation. That portion of matter (the cross) which is circumscribed by and sourced in spirit (the circle), meeting at the point in the middle, the individual spiritual impulse. The very stuff of life. That's what is symbolically described by the angles.

Consider your own chart for a moment, and try thinking of it as a description of the sacred space of your life ...

This is your sacred space, these are the four directions, personified in a particular way. In many traditions, if you have a request for healing, if you need to make special prayers to ask for guidance if you are in trouble, if you want to worship or celebrate, you begin by creating a sacred space, like an altar. Except here, your horoscope is not an altar before which you go down on your knees, it is the sacred space around you, and you are in the centre. If this idea appeals to you, it is something that you can express for yourself. Find objects, make objects, ask for or buy objects that remind you of your own four angles. Keep them somewhere special so that you can actually set up your own sacred space when you need it. If you have small objects that relate to the angles of your chart, you can carry them around and use them anywhere, like a medicine bag or prayer carpet that describes your personal sacred space. I hope that suggestion conveys what I feel is part of the underlying symbolism of the angles. They are the warp and weft across which the threads of our life story are woven into 3-D, into time and space.

The Elements

What's interesting, too, is that the geographical Horizon System of the 'cardinal points' does link with the symbolism of the four elements. Different cultures ascribe different meanings to north, south, east and west, with different elements, colours, animals or supernatural beings too. There are many different traditions about this, which I think may be partly related to geographical locality and climate. But the energies represented by the four elements do signify the process of creation or manifestation in most systems, except in the Far East, where they use five slightly different elements.

We have four 'cardinal signs', each representing one element. In the wheel of the Zodiac, they represent the position of the Sun as it crosses the Solstitial or Equinoctial points. This refers to the Ecliptic System, and the sequence goes fire (Aries), water (Cancer), air (Libra) and earth (Capricorn).

There is an interesting 'fifth element' which used to be part of the western system, and is still part of the Tibetan system ... that of ether, or space. In medieval medicine, which was directly associated with astrology, the element of ether was sometimes linked with the planet Mercury. However, it is not represented directly by any of the signs of the Zodiac.

But think of the element of 'space' ... what is it? Where is it? Does it have a location?

Audience: It is everywhere?

Melanie: And where is 'everywhere'?

Audience: Maybe 'nowhere'?

Melanie: Lovely! What might be interesting is this ... consider your own chart, or any chart, in this light. What happens when you include 'space', as being 'everywhere' and 'nowhere'?

Audience: I feel more relaxed, more open ...

Melanie: Say more ...

Audience: Like I can just appreciate not really knowing what this chart, this life, this 'me' is ultimately about ...

Melanie: When I am looking at a chart, I like to orient first by de-focusing and looking at the white paper on which it is printed or written. Sort of inviting the invisible element of 'space' to be present, and going from there. The storylines that we discover and explore are held in the mystery of space, inner and outer ...

When you first examine the angles of a chart, check to see whether all the elements are represented on the angles and, if not, which ones are missing. Then see whether the missing two are represented in any other way in the chart because, if not, this may be an imbalance which will show prominently in someone's life. And like any missing element, it will have to be imported from elsewhere, from a relationship, group situation or a job which supplies it. And transits may bring it along, too. For example, if all the cusps are only air or fire, then you want to see where other anchors for earth and water are found, if any. For example, if the person has several earth planets or a lot of water planets, then that is a great blessing, but it can happen that they don't. So then you will have to look elsewhere in the chart to see where these anchors, these elemental energies, are located. In this example, you would look to and explore Saturn, being the earthiest planetary energy. Also, see if there are any planets in the other earthy houses – the 2nd and the 6th houses. Of course the MC, being the 10th house, unless you are using the Equal House system, is an earthy house anyway.

Following this example, if water is not represented on any angle, and there are no planets in water signs either, then consider the condition of the Moon and also Neptune, both being connected to water, and check the watery houses – 4, 8 and 12. Similarly, with no fire angles, and no planets in fire signs, you would consider the Sun, Mars, Jupiter and the other two fire houses, 5 and 9. Likewise, with no airy angles or planets, look to Mercury, Jupiter and Uranus, plus the 3rd, 7th and 11th houses. Do you get the picture?

Extreme Latitudes

If we parallel the angles with the cardinal directions, of course the Ascendant is east, the Descendant is west, the IC is north and the MC is south. This is reversed in the southern hemisphere, with the MC as north and the IC as south. Prototypically, there is one representative of each of the elements on each angle, but it doesn't always work out that way in practice, particularly towards the more extreme latitudes, north or south. The further a birthplace is from the Equator, the more likely it is that you will find charts with angles only representing two elements. And of course, above 60° north or south, the chart looks very distorted, sometimes with one pair of houses covering several signs.

Audience: How would you read a chart like that?

Melanie: Good question. There are many places, for example in Russia, Alaska, where you'll see this issue cropping up. However, I've found that the astrological symbolism speaks anyway, and what looks 'distorted' to us may describe accurately an emphasis in that person's life. I remember a spectacular example of this, where a woman born in Russia had all her planets in the house axis of 3 and 9. She was multi-lingual, as expressed by her many planets in the 3rd house of communication. She also ran a school for the children of Russian migrants in her host country. So for 'foreigners', a 9th house theme! Very interestingly, she was also passionate about restoring the permission for people to have a personal spiritual life, after the oppressive atheism of Communism, or perhaps we should call it the 'worship of the state'. So she wanted to help transform the beliefs and dogma of the past. More 9th house!

You can approach these charts in other ways, too. Simply using the Equal House system will mean this problem doesn't arise because the houses are created by measuring out twelve equal segments along the Zodiac from the degree of the Ascendant. I usually draw up three charts when reading for people born at extreme latitudes – the natal chart in Koch, which is the house system I use, the natal chart in Equal House, and then also the natal chart relocated for where the person is now living, if they have moved away from their birthplace. Cross-referring the three, *based on what is obvious from the person's life*, will give you more than enough information to work with.

Conversely, the closer a birthplace is to the Equator, the more likely it is that all four elements will be represented on the angles, and also that the actual degrees of the respective signs on the angles will be similar. Meaning that they are more likely to be about 90° from each other, like the prototype of the cross within the circle. I have often wondered about this, in terms of the collective psyche of a place … what does it mean if most of the people in a given area have their angles at 90° to each other? Or the axes not in a major aspect relationship? You can see a certain dynamism in the life of an individual whose angles are at 90° to each other, because every time a transit touches one of the angles by conjunction, all four become involved, by square or opposition. There is a lot of energy, intensity and activity.

The Modalities

Similarly, it is useful to check which mode predominates. If the angles are roughly squaring each other, there will only be one mode represented, and it will obviously be emphasised. But there could also be two, more likely as the latitude gets further away from the Equator, as I already mentioned. The cardinal signs – Aries, Cancer, Libra and Capricorn – are the generators of a particular elemental energy, and are themselves powerful initiators. So cardinal angles can make for a life of personal dynamism, momentum, creativity and a desire for manifestation and achievement. If the rest of the chart doesn't support this pattern, it can create conflict.

Audience: Can you give an example?

Melanie: Anyone in the room have this?

Audience: Yes, I do. I have Capricorn rising, but Sun, Venus and Mercury in the 12th house. I don't feel very worldly, but I seem to have to meet endless challenges professionally, and I often feel terribly burdened. I love solitude and reading, especially things spiritual or philosophical, but I seem to be pulled further out into the world than I really like!

Melanie: Where is your Saturn?

Audience: In the 10th house, very widely conjunct Neptune, which is in the 9th. Life just feels too fast and too busy sometimes.

Melanie: I think that illustrates it very well. Thank you.

Fixed angles tend to create patterns just like the word says – fixed! Change is difficult, but there can be great strength and persistence. Likewise, this can feel very slow and sticky and frustrating if the rest of the chart consists of mainly mutable or even cardinal planets. Mutable angles give flexibility and an ability to flow with change, but again, if the rest of the chart contrasts with this, there can be difficulty anchoring things, and a tendency to blow with the wind and be too easily influenced by circumstance, moods and other people.

Audience: I have mutable angles, but the fixed signs predominate in the rest of my chart. I keep feeling that life is asking from me more flexibility than I have to give!

Melanie: So what do you do?

Audience: I used to get stubborn and resentful, but I've found if I can negotiate a slower pace, that helps. It's not always possible, but I can try.

Audience: For me, I have all my angles in fixed signs, but lots of mutable signs where planets are placed.

Melanie: How is that?

Audience: Sometimes the mutable energy becomes agitated and restless because the fixity of the fixed angles seems to go way too slow, as you said. But there is another side to it, for me. I feel so fluid and formless much of the time that I'm grateful to these fixed angles, as they definitely peg my life down, like a tent in the wind!

Melanie: Lovely, and thank you for reminding us that in natal astrology nothing in the chart is 'good' or 'bad' of itself. These words are mostly descriptions which the mind overlays on things, according to whether they feel pleasant or not.

The Rulers, Indigenous and Individual

Let's explore the sequence of planets that 'naturally' rule the angles. I'm calling these the 'indigenous' rulers, for fun! If we parallel the signs of the Zodiac with the circle of the houses, some interesting themes emerge, like this:

The Ascendant is Aries, so Mars rules
The IC is Cancer, so the Moon rules
The Descendant is Libra, so Venus rules
The MC is Capricorn, so Saturn rules

Do you see the story there?

The primary impulse (Mars) is nurtured and gestated (Moon), then socialised (Venus), in order to be useful to the world (Saturn). Or the sperm (Mars) penetrates the egg (Moon) and this union results in a nine-month relationship (Venus) before the baby is born into the realm of worldly clock-time (Saturn). The first three rulers are all personal planets, then the MC is ruled by Saturn, the outer boundary of the inner solar system. *Note there are no signs with transpersonal rulership.* I find that very eloquent. It's like we are bound into incarnation by the angles.

Notice also that these four signs describe the 'domicile' of Mars. I was very struck by this when I noticed. Almost as if we incarnate here, on Earth, in order to learn about the energy of Mars ... its beneficial potential as well as its hazards.

> Dignity in Aries
> Fall in Cancer
> Detriment in Libra
> Exaltation in Capricorn

Audience: What do you mean by 'transpersonal rulership'?

Melanie: Well, Scorpio, Aquarius and Pisces, if you use the new rulerships, are ruled by Pluto, Uranus and Neptune, respectively. They are all outer planets, so their themes concern that which is larger than the individual. But the angles are very specific, very personal. Likewise, it is interesting to consider the sequence of planetary rulers of your own angles, because unless you have Aries rising with Capricorn on the MC, your actual rulers will be different. However, the sequence that is trying to occur I think remains constant, and the overlay of your own rulers might show you how your own process meshes with the archetypal sequence described by the 'natural' rulers.

What is your own individual storyline, from impulse to manifestation? How do your angles describe this process?

How do things start for you (the Ascendant)?

What do you need in order to nourish and gestate creative impulses (the IC)?

What qualities do you seek, or find, in relationship (the Descendant)?

What does the world ask of you (the MC)?

As an example, if you have Uranus natally conjunct the IC, or ruling it because Aquarius is placed there, you may have residual insecurity from a home life where you moved a lot, or where the family structure was broken up through divorce or unexpected events, possibly involving your father. That may mean it is difficult for you to allow enough time for creating a nurturing space to gestate ideas, prepare for new stages of life, and so on. On the positive side, it may also mean that you don't hesitate to uproot and move on when things get too entangled emotionally, or where there are too many demands being made of you. Like the snail, you get used to carrying your home with you, on the inner levels.

The Asc/MC Midpoint

If you bisect the distance between the Ascendant and the Midheaven, you will get the direct Ascendant/Midheaven midpoint. If you further take all the hard aspects to this point, you will also have the so-called 'indirect' midpoints. These are very interesting points, showing where some very strong themes manifest. A planet there, especially on the direct midpoint, will often be emphasised in a person's life, although it may not otherwise be so obvious in the chart. It will usually fall in the 11th house, our place of ideals, desire to improve society, and so on. It is the deep initiative of our being, the Ascendant, but also combined with the ambitions and aspirations of the MC.

Also the symbolism of the Asc/MC axis, with its attendant squares falling in the other quadrants, is rather lovely because it divides the circle into eight. In the Christian Church there are eight sets of prayers said throughout the day. Certainly sunrise, sunset, noon and midnight are marked with prayer, and then other times in between, although I suspect that these times may have become synchronised with clock time rather than celestial time. They all have names and were called 'hours' or 'watches'. A medieval book of hours will have prayers to be said at each of those points, so it was a way of recognising the sacredness of the passing of time. There is also a strong connection with the number eight and the Sun, or the gods and heroes. In Vedic astrology Surya, the Lord of the Sun, was said to ride across the sky in a chariot drawn by eight horses, the animal often associated with the Sun, and we see this same image associated with other gods too. Apparently it also takes around eight minutes for the light of the Sun to reach us on Earth![4] So just as the Sun symbolises the Source of the light that is our own individual centre that we are here to reflect, to incarnate, you can see that same eightfold system also underpinning the angles and the Asc/MC midpoint.

Do remember, however, that because you'll use very small orbs with midpoints, *it only makes sense to use the Asc/Mc midpoint if you are reasonably sure of the birth time.*

A Question of Existence

You can also explore the angles in terms of questions. This is particularly useful as a contemplative device for looking at your own angles, but it can also be a useful way to focus on the chart of a client. They are semi-rhetorical questions, ones that are meant as a focus of exploration, rather than any simple answers or definitions. Here are four fundamental questions posed to us by existence ...

> For the Ascendant, the question is 'Who am I?'
> For the IC – 'Where did I come from?'
> For the Descendant – 'Who are you?'
> For the MC – 'Where am I going?'

I'm not entirely sure about this last one, so let me know if you can think of a better one! Another one I like is 'What is the world asking of me?' Of course, you can make up your own questions. These are simply the ones I have found most useful, so far. They were partly inspired by the work of Dane Rudhyar.[5]

Around the angles these 'questions of existence' are posed in a very concentrated way. Remember the symbolism, the cross within the circle, the manifestation? What you find is that the closer a planet is to an angle, the more likely it is to manifest extremely strongly in that person's life, as a person or situation. It is not a 'take-it-or-leave-it' theme, a background theme. It is potent and powerful, sometimes troublesome and sometimes helpful, and it is useful to pay close attention to it. With this image of manifestation, either we will make something happen, or it will manifest anyway, as a 'given' or a necessary development, sometimes in a way that feels beneficial, and sometimes not.

Audience: How about 'What is my connection?' for the one at the top?

Melanie: Yes. I like that. Thank you.

Before and After

When considering the angles themselves, it can be useful to consider them dynamically, taking into account both the angular houses and the ones before them, the cadent houses. This is especially useful if the birth time is in doubt, and also because a planet can be considered 'angular' when conjunct an angle, on either side, up to 12° or so in orb. In natal astrology, I find it useful to think of an angular 'zone' when looking at how planets are placed.

Finally, one more symbol for the picture in general ...

Squaring the Circle

In alchemy there is a process where they talk about 'squaring the circle'. It is a particular alchemical image, frequently illustrated throughout the writings of Jung, which is about taking the wholeness of spirit and 'squaring' it. The number four relates to manifestation, earth, putting something into form, giving it a shape, giving it a destiny in real terms. The image of squaring the circle, if this crops up in dreams, is a very important one, because it is the stage of taking something that is latent and birthing it, giving it shape in the world. The 'roundness' of uterine existence, like the uroborous, all flow and instinct, becomes the 'squareness' of life in the world, with its polarities, conflicts and dynamism.

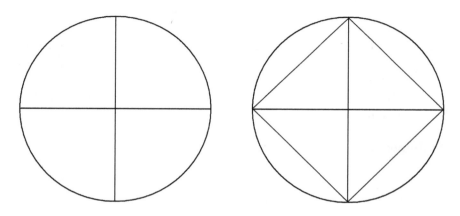

In astrology, the symbol of the cross is said to represent matter, while the symbol of the circle is said to represent the wholeness of spirit. So on a horoscope, you have exactly that. The round chart, containing the cross of the two axes made by the four angles, which make a square when joined up.

The Ascendant – Who Am I?

Now let's focus specifically on the Ascendant. As we go through the four angles I will focus on different levels of their expression. Firstly, there is the external, environmental and physical level. Next is the relational or psychological level, and then thirdly, the most deeply internal, metaphorical or spiritual level.

Birth and Beyond

Now because the angles relate to the precise place and time of birth, that beginning, our Ascendant, is very literally about birth. It divides the great 'before' from the great 'after', the ending of the 12th house from the beginning of the 1st house. We will return later to the 12th house theme, but let's first consider the Ascendant as the beginning of the first house. The degree of the Zodiac at the Ascendant rises with you, as does any planet near it, accompanying your physical arrival on Earth. The Ascendant, together with the aspects to it, and the condition of the ruling planet, will very often give a lot of information about the actual physical circumstances of birth. And it is sometimes amazingly literal. It can give you some idea of what kind of beginning is suggested by a person's chart. You know that phrase 'As you begin, so you go on'? That seems to be depicted around the Ascendant. It is our physical style of entry into the world, from the womb-like state of the 12th house.

That translates into the way we start things, how we initiate things, how we begin things. That can be little things, like what is the first thing you feel in the morning? Sagittarius rising may feel very different about starting the day than Capricorn rising. Sagittarius rising probably gets up, turns on the radio immediately, bounds out of bed, and does fifty press-ups! There is a sense of promise and optimism and joy about starting new things. However, if the Ascendant is ruled by Saturn there might be an unwillingness to get going, which if explored might reveal strong feelings of dread. 'Oh no, another day! Phew, what burdens will I have to carry today?' Or perhaps getting up and immediately attending to the duties and responsibilities, the tasks at hand – opening the bills before breakfast! Gemini rising may be talking on the phone, online or listening to a chat show first thing in the morning.

I am caricaturing, but I think you get the picture. The Ascendant relates to both the immediate level of new beginnings, as well as the big threshold crossings: new stages of personal growth and development, new relationships, big new projects. Although birth is the biggest one until we die, we cannot simply say that birth is *the* irrevocable hidden foundation which sets the tone for the rest of life. This would be to espouse a form of materialism which is not 'spiritually correct' … we need to expand our notions of causality! However, it can be useful to know about the circumstances of our birth, because these may recapitulate when we are 'giving birth' to something new. That could be a physical pregnancy, but also a symbolic one, like starting this course and wanting to give birth to your future work as an astrologer.

So the Ascendant is a place of initiative, of initiation, an impulse towards something as yet unformed, but coming from very deep inside. It almost seems that the more aligned one's own impulse, the more likely it is to evoke material which relates to birth. If this is something that you haven't considered before, I can assure you it is well worth the effort. If you want to follow this up, the man to read is Stanislav Grof. He has written a number of extraordinary and pioneering books, and I would recommend the one called *Beyond the Brain.*[6] Grof refers to the process of gestation, birth and the immediate afterlude as the 'perinatal matrix'. Initially this work was done as a research project in the early days after the discovery of LSD, before it was made illegal. Stanislav Grof is a psychiatrist who was working at that time in Czechoslovakia, where they were testing samples of LSD in clinical trials with mentally ill patients in hospital. He was mainly Freudian in training at that stage, and the experiments yielded results which he couldn't understand at all. Eventually he had to completely remap and remodel his entire way of understanding the psyche, bringing into it all this material to do with birth. He has outlined the different stages of birth and the different kinds of consciousness which they relate to, which can also be seen by astrologers as relating to the themes of the outer planets and also Saturn. Significantly, Stanislav Grof has studied astrology and is a close friend and colleague of Richard Tarnas, whose work many of you know.

We come into the world through a 'life-and-death' situation ... birth. Even a relatively uncomplicated birth may sometimes be fraught with peril for both mother and child. That fragility is imprinted, and rests at the Ascendant. Hence, this is where we start on our journey of wanting to make our mark on the world. We impulse ourselves out, or we are impulsed out. It can be either.

You may find this is relevant if somebody has transits going over the Ascendant – we will talk more about that later in the day. Any transit going over this point is like a mini-birth, ranging from an experience that is fairly quick and transitory to something which changes your life for ever. If it is Mars or Venus, it may be over in a week, but if it is a slower moving planet – any from Saturn outwards – it may be a very long transition. Months or even years, as in the case of Neptune and Pluto in particular.

Having some understanding of that link can be incredibly helpful, because it is also a way of being able to contain our experience. As the experience is not only physical, it is also a metaphor which applies to the Ascendant – the imprinting of our own first beginnings. You know that phrase, from the computer world (although of course it originated elsewhere!) – 'What you see is what you get'? I connect this also with the Ascendant. Because how you look out on life is first of all conditioned by your own arrival. In other words, is this a hostile universe? Do you have to fight to survive? Are you welcome in it or not? Is it interesting? Is it oppressive? Are you going to get what you need? These are all the fundamental accompanying questions that are patterned very deeply according to the circumstances of your actual arrival.

However, from the astrological point of view, our first arrival itself may be seen to reflect what is on the Ascendant. So there is a two-way situation posing the question as to which comes first, the chicken or the egg!

The Chicken or the Egg?

Audience: What did you mean, 'expand our notions of causality'?

Melanie: Thank you for asking that question – I was trying to skip by it! The question of causality does open up an enormous area of consideration, which I'll try to condense. I am referring to the 'cause and effect' view within our thinking in general and the therapeutic field in particular. If you are limping because you damaged your leg in an accident, that appears to be a fairly simple cause and effect. However, if you engage in some introspection, you might see that the 'cause' of the accident was a set of invisible pressures on you and those around you, perhaps, which are actually unfathomable if you go deep enough. At the surface level, you will find personal issues, but the deeper you go, the less personal they are. The mind so wants to have reasons for things, but part of the problem is that guilt and blame get attached to causality, once it seems to have been located, and then we get stuck.

Another hazard is that when we are in therapy, the mind keeps thinking that it has found the big 'IT', the reason for our suffering which, once dissolved, will leave us free. But I think this deeper kind of causality cannot be appreciated by the denser levels of the mind which seek to 'fix it'. Newtonian thinking works best in external reality, describing mechanical processes. However, the realms of the psyche will continually confound our mechanical thinking!

So ... how does it happen that the Ascendant describes birth? Does birth make the Ascendant, with all its patterning, or does the Ascendant make birth? In other words, does the experience shape who we become, or does the invisible 'shape' of what we are carrying within us, the seed of our becoming, find its expression in the manner of birth? This is like the conundrum about which comes first – the chicken or the egg! And you can see how treacherous this kind of thinking can be if it becomes attached to judgement. Then 'bad' experiences are 'my fault'. Not just difficulties that I must deal with, or behaviour I must adjust, or processes that happen, but indicators of my 'wrongness'.

So, how do you enter the journey of life? Do you go willingly, or are you dragged out kicking and screaming? I mentioned the 'chicken and egg' theme already. Howard Sasportas once said that basically if we were all chickens, then the Ascendant shows your style of pecking your way out of the egg! He had some hilarious examples, a couple of which I can't resist repeating. He would say, for example, that if you have Scorpio rising, then pecking your way out of the egg is a life-and-death drama. If you have Leo rising, then you have to be the finest chick to be hatched, and you don't come out unless there is an appreciative audience watching. If you have Gemini rising, you'll come out cheeping and looking around curiously. If you have Capricorn rising, it takes forever and is very difficult. It goes on ... you can make up an 'egg story' for yourself from your own Ascendant!

So it is the way we hatch, perhaps that's how it's phrased! The Ascendant says something about our initial impact on the world and its impact on us. Think back to birth. That's about how the world first impacted on you, as you separated from your mother.

So the Ascendant in that sense is how we manage that first imprint. Go back to the Scorpio rising. If you felt the world was unsafe, or perhaps it was a difficult birth and you nearly died, you may be carrying the imprint that this is a very dangerous place, so what are you going to do to counteract that? Anyone?

Audience: Protect yourself.

Audience: Be invisible, be suspicious.

Audience: Don't trust other people, and be powerful.

Melanie: Yes, exactly. Also, a certain trust in your own capacity to survive difficulties.

There can be a compensatory quality around the Ascendant, where it is like a persona, a mask, an act we put on deliberately, or sometimes we just do it without even realising. Usually this is a protection for our vulnerability, and the sign on the Ascendant shows the nature and quality of this mask, or defence, to give it the psychological term.

So because the Ascendant is what you are bringing in, it is also what you see when you look out there, at other people and society. 'What you see is what you get.' And so you also encounter, even seek, deliberately or otherwise, those experiences that reflect the Ascendant. I think that may be why the Ascendant is described by some authors as the soul, or the journey of the soul. It is not the same as a planet. It is not like the Sun sign or Moon sign, and yet the Ascendant shows us something very fundamental about the quality of our life journey. If you have Taurus rising, regardless of what your planets are doing, you are on a Taurean journey. I think you can get a sense of what I am saying there. It describes your first threshold crossing, the way you start your quest, and indeed the road you travel. And if you enquire persistently within yourself as to who is arranging the journey, you will encounter some very deep areas of your being.

The Physical Appearance

It is also said that the Ascendant is the overall physical appearance, and you sometimes see written in the older textbooks that the Ascendant *is the body itself.* I don't think that's completely true, as strong physical characteristics can also express dominant planetary themes which are not linked to the Ascendant. Perhaps the Ascendant is more about *the impulse seeking to be embodied.* However, with some people that does indeed show itself very clearly at the physical and behavioural level.

I have sometimes done a chart for a client where the Ascendant is in the first or last couple of degrees of a sign, and there is no guarantee of the accuracy of the birth time. Sometimes when they arrive, their whole demeanour is so obviously one sign or the other that there is no mistaking which sign is actually rising. Then at other times it is not so clear at all. To familiarise yourself with the physical descriptions of the rising signs is very useful, although not so many modern textbooks pay attention to that. You would have to research into older publications. I found some very good concise descriptions in Vivian Robson's book *A Student's Text-Book of Astrology.* You'll probably find it in the Astrological Association library, and it has also been reprinted by Ascella Publications.[7]

An example comes to mind, of a man who had 29° of Gemini rising, according to the time of birth given. However, when he arrived, his whole face and body type were very obviously lunar. He had light silvery hair, pale and moist skin; his face and general body tone were quite fleshy. And as if that wasn't enough, the very first thing that he said when I greeted him at the door was 'I've brought some sandwiches for my lunch. I hope you don't mind if I eat them while you are talking.' So he wanted to be sure that he was going to get nourished. Saturn was also in Cancer in the 1st house! One might assume that the world into which he came into didn't feel nourishing enough, so later on when going out into life he had learned that he must be sure to take his own sandwiches. On a deeper level, life may be met like an inadequate mother, for whom one must compensate, or even an outright bad mother who must be warded off and placated. Sometimes people with Cancer rising are compulsive caretakers who must look after the whole world, and sometimes they ask by their demeanour to be taken care of. In that case there was absolutely no doubt, but unfortunately it isn't always that clear cut.

So to summarise the Ascendant with those three levels – the first level is birth. It is also the physical body or appearance, sometimes. The relational or psychological level is like the impulse to initiate, the impulse out into life, what motivates us to start things, to appear, and to imprint ourselves on life. It is also therefore what we receive into our life, or rather how we see it and the impressions we form of it. Our imprinting by life. The metaphor is the beginning of the journey, or the chicken coming out of the egg. Then the internal level of this is the will to discover 'Who am I?'

Momentum and Motivation

The Ascendant is naturally the beginning of the first fire house. Through physical birth we get our own air and breathe. Fire needs air in order to burn, as well as some flammable substance. The word 'inspiration' means 'to breathe in', like catching your breath. So how do you generate fire? What fuel do you consume? What moves you out into the next stage? This will be shown by the sign on the Ascendant. There, it is as if we have the breath of life which ignites the fire of becoming. So if we add in some elemental symbolism for the angles, this is the place of fire. Obviously people with fire signs rising will generate and demonstrate fiery energy in a fairly pure way, as this is the natural place of fire. They are often fairly easy to recognise, as well. Aries rising will begin things as a challenge, a conquest, and if nothing tempers the energy, will also not want to stay around once the initial impulse is spent. Nurturing and duty are just not 'their thing'. They can also have a way of turning even quite simple things into conflict situations. There is a 'get-up-and-go' quality. Sagittarius rising will approach life with enthusiasm, good humour and hope, Leo with generosity, heartfulness and a need to be centre stage.

Another element will show a different motivation. Water signs rising are moved out through their feelings; this is the fuel that drives their motor. Relationships or deep feelings cause one to move country, change job or start a new life. Pisces rising may be deeply motivated by compassion for others, or for a desire to escape from the harshness of the world. Earth signs are pushed out, or go out willingly, in a very practical way. For Taurus rising, good Venusian things are the motivational forces – comfort, money, material prosperity. And one pursues them stubbornly, patiently and, all being well, with pleasure and devotion too. Air signs rising are drawn out 'head first', through curiosity, relationship, ideas and ideals – connections of all kinds.

Singleton Element

A particularly interesting situation occurs when the Ascendant is the only representative of an element. This is true to some degree of the other angles, but of the Ascendant and the MC most obviously. It can be very difficult, because the quality of one's life journey seems such that you travel a path for which you do not feel naturally equipped, so there can be the feeling of always firing on one's weak cylinder, or often encountering experiences which force a high level of surrender into the unknown. It can be very exhausting.

Audience: Can you elaborate … I don't understand the thing about surrender.

Melanie: Yes. If you have planets in an element, they act as containers and also agents of that elemental energy. If you haven't, then you are at a loss to know how to be with experiences represented by that element. So your ability to trust in something greater, something unknowable, is stretched to the limit and beyond, as the more ordinary means of being with those experiences is not easily available.

I am thinking of an example of someone with Capricorn rising, and nothing else in earth. She has a strong Neptune, opposite the Sun, and several planets in Pisces; you can see this sensitivity in her eyes and her manner. But she works very hard, running a family of three children, and is like the 'Rock of Gibraltar' for not only her immediate family but a wide circle of people she comes into contact with. She has a powerful sense of duty that motivates her: Saturn is in the 7th house, and is anchored in a strong relationship with her husband. She has also had to learn a lot about setting limits. The qualities of measure, proportion and right timing are all things she's had to learn. So she even appears very earthy, if you judge her by her activities and the life she leads, but if you sense her energy, she is obviously not.

Audience: What if it is water rising and no planets in water?

Melanie: Then the journey is a very emotional one, but in this case the water doesn't flow to order, like out of a domestic tap. You encounter the force of the ocean, or a tidal wave, and it is necessary to learn to sit patiently with the chaos, the spillage, the drama, until your own feelings distil out of it, so that you know what you are feeling, and then what action must be taken, if any. The risk is that feelings will just be acted out, with little or no consciousness. The gift is that it can stimulate a capacity for introspection which brings awareness to the feelings, so that they are not only instinctual but also conscious.

Before the Beginning

If we think of the houses sequentially, the Ascendant can be considered as the 'end of the end' as well as the 'beginning of the beginning'. And the 12th house is the preparation for the 1st house.

Audience: There is something that I've always been confused about. I know that if you are born at sunrise, the Sun is at the Ascendant, and if you are born at noon, it is at the MC. Which means that the time in-between should be symbolised by the activity of those houses, I mean 12, 11 and then 10. But it doesn't seem to fit. Could you say something about that?

Melanie: Firstly, on the symbolic level, I can see some resonance. I know if I rise just before dawn, and stay tuned inwardly during the first couple of hours of the day before having to enter the world, I find that there is something very magical about this time. A sense of stillness before we enter the density of our day-time activity.

In monastic traditions, and other spiritual paths too, people rise sometimes long before dawn for this reason. If you are anchored in this sense of connection before you start the day, it can make a big difference. Secondly, on the technical level, if you think of the Zodiac 'clock', the degrees do rise in forward sequence. So if you have a chart with, let's say, 10° of Leo rising at 10.30 a.m., as time passes, you will see the Ascendant degree 'move forward' through the Zodiac. A few minutes later it will be 11°, and so on, through the day. Remember the angles move according to the daily rotation of the Earth.

Audience: What orb would you use when looking at whether a planet is conjunct an angle?

Melanie: Initially, about 7° or 8° – within that range, you can expect a strong manifestation of the planet in the person's life. Remember the image of the cross of matter? Things materialise, become matter, when they are conjunct an angle, and the closer they are, the more likely that is so. However, you need flexibility when assessing whether to consider a planet conjunct an angle, especially as the birth time may not be reliable. A planet may be considered rising even when 12° away from the Ascendant. I think it does also depend on the significance of the planet.

For example, if someone has Aries rising with Mars in Aries in the 12th, you might see the Mars rising qualities even if it is 12° away, although it will be affected by the 12th house tone of diffuseness, unboundedness and invisibility. Therefore, this could be a Mars that endlessly gets itself into trouble through not taking action quickly enough, letting resentment go underground or giving initiative over to others and getting confused and angry as a result. Positively, this can also be the fire of Mars tempered with the ability to wait, sense the moment, read the subtle signs and be informed by intuition or dreams. The further back it is in the 12th house, however, the more you will see it partake of typical 12th house themes.

This is also true as a general principle for other angular planets, but perhaps especially noticeable at the Ascendant. A 12th house planet really does feel different, and function differently, from a

1ˢᵗ house planet! For example, when the Sun is in the 12ᵗʰ house, even if it is only 3° behind the Ascendant, there is often that sense of diffuseness, vulnerability of boundary and unsure personal identity which is quite different to the more definite, expressive and obviously radiant Sun in the 1ˢᵗ house. Sometimes, this difference can even lead you to question the given birth time.

The 12ᵗʰ house is like the womb, or represents the womb-like experience. It was traditionally called the 'house of hidden influences', and can be a very undifferentiated area that relates amongst other things to what I call the 'deep past'. This refers to the deeper layers of the family tree, beyond but including the first couple of layers of grandparents and great-grandparents. So planets there represent parts of us, impulses, which are profoundly connected with these hidden layers. Here are the gifts, problems, issues, unfinished business, that have a longer history. It is also where your own family matrix blurs into history, the 'big picture' of the flow of culture and human experience. I sometimes think of it as the ancestral bottleneck or traffic jam!

In other words, if somebody has an angular planet there, it is going to be quite a loaded one. In addition to the labour pains of birth, being close to the Ascendant, so what is seeking to be embodied, seeking personification, this planet probably has an ancestral trail behind it. Sometimes it's also not possible to know the details of that, because we don't have the information consciously. However, the deep psyche knows, and may try to inform us through dreams, symptoms and other intuitive means. Some contemplative skills or familiarity with dream work, meditation and other processes which honour the deep psyche are very important for planets in the 12ᵗʰ house. There is a Zen question 'What was your face before you were born?' which I think applies to this area.

In traditional astrology, this house was called the 'house of self-undoing', the abode of hidden enemies. And although sometimes this turns out literally true, it is also useful to regard the statement symbolically. The 'hidden enemies' can be our own blind spots, where we are very vulnerable, or powerful in a covert way which others experience as undermining or invisibly threatening; archaic remnants of primal ego structures may live in the 12th house. These 'enemies' within can also leak out in the form of experiences we attract, from which we must learn to differentiate ourselves from the collective. It is what stands behind us, behind the beginning, and so can profoundly influence our sense of motivation. Also, the 'self-undoing' process is a necessary part of our spiritual awakening, in the sense that the false self-images which obscure our true nature must be 'undone'.

As regards self-undoing, think again about the question 'Who am I?' In the 12th house, the separate ego does indeed seek to 'un-do' itself, to unknot the tightness of its struggles within the world, its narrow view of reality, and to be released. Our responses to the question 'Who am I?' might sound very different, depending on whether we consider the Ascendant as the end of the 12th or the beginning of the 1st house! The Ascendant is the place where the deep Self or our true nature takes on individual form.

Planets conjunct the Ascendant, but in the 12th, may show a specific ancestral theme, an unfinished story, skeletons in the cupboard that need attention, or creative gifts looking for expression. It's our deeper heritage, and may be referring to what was suppressed or not honoured, and thus a balance needs righting, or something given form. A conjunction to the Ascendant will give urgency to that theme. This little corner of the chart, the last few degrees of the 12th house, is also where everything is diffuse and seeking to go beyond form, to go beyond the boundaries, to be dissolved, to release itself and to surrender individual selfhood. It is the place of the mystic.

So if there is a planet there, just behind the Ascendant but conjunct, it may have a very archetypal quality to it. If it is Venus then that person will go for relationship, and this isn't by conscious intent either, because things that are just behind the Ascendant drive us from behind, we can't see them. It is like they are veiled from us. Remember that this is the house of hidden influences. Whereas that doesn't need to mean anything sinister, it can certainly feel sinister to sense the force of something pulsing through you, and you don't know what it is or where it comes from. Sometimes it is possible to find out and sometimes it isn't. To go back to the example of Venus just behind the Ascendant, it is like the person with that Venus placement may go for and attract relationships with a very high level of emotional symbiosis and merging, almost like a 'Babes in the Wood' syndrome, or a 'back to the womb' scenario, where the urge to merge is far stronger than the wish to remain separate, often with very complicated results. It can also be the life of fantasy and longing, preferring illusion to reality in relationships. Or a very refined feeling sensitivity, a capacity for worship and devotion which if directed solely towards a human partner can bring enormous suffering. Any planet there can also literally absorb psychic content from others without even realising it, especially if the Moon is there, but that is true for other planets as well. Any planet just behind the Ascendant has blurred edges, leaky boundaries, and it merges into the archetypal.

It is very difficult for 12th house planets to just be ordinary – that is more the province of the 6th house. Maybe that's why this is the biggest sector in Gauquelin's study, because planets manifest in a larger than life way if they manifest from the 12th house. It's as if they sometimes sweep the rug out from under your feet. His study was with people who had excelled in their field, become heroes or icons of the people, not with ordinary mortals like us. Did you have your hand up?

Audience: I'm just wondering, does that go for all the planets in the 12th?

Melanie: What exactly?

Audience: The tendency to manifest in an archetypal way …

Melanie: No, not necessarily. I am mainly referring to planets which are conjunct the Ascendant, but in the 12th house. Some of that quality will apply to planets which lie back in the 12th house, but, without being anchored into the Ascendant, they can remain below the surface of the great ocean, unless or until a transit occurs. Then it's like the cosmic fisherman coming by, and 12th house planets are like fish hooked or caught in the net and brought ashore for a while. Suddenly up comes a Venus or there goes a Mars. There is this completely alien quality, like strange sea creatures coming up out of the depths. Sometimes covered with seaweed or barnacles too!

Usually, there is no pressure to manifest, without a transit or progression activating a 12th house planet, but this can happen via relationships, where the synastry provides the fishing line. But planets connected to the Ascendant have an innate pressure to manifest. Then it can feel like trying to pour a torrent of water through the spout of a very small teapot, because there is the great archetypal realm birthing into form in the world, and it is all so constricted compared to the 12th house perspective.

Sometimes you will find significant intrauterine experience depicted by this last bit of the 12th house. From 'grass roots' research – in other words, examples from my practice – I think you can view many things on the chart in terms of prenatal experience. However, it seems that the 12th house can contain very specific information about this area. For example, it can show whether we came from a realm of peace and tranquillity and relative safety, into something else when we crossed that great divide. Or we were glad to get out of there, came out fighting, and have been taking the world head-on ever since. Sometimes with Mars and/or Pluto in the 12th, it was like that. The 12th house, the womb, was a hellish place, and a fight to get out of, and you need to continue fighting, even though you do it invisibly.

Audience: Is it like planets in the 12th don't want to be seen?

Melanie: Yes, sometimes. To contrast with that, planets in the 1st house *do* want to be seen. They want to be visible. They are just coming out, rising. Think of sunrise again. In fact that's a beautiful image because the first thing you see, before you see the Sun, is the rays. So perhaps planets in the 12th house conjunct the Ascendant are visible more like those rays, announcing, heralding, rather than being actually seen. Implying rather than stating.

If the Ascendant is what you radiate, planets conjunct it will also want to be seen to radiate out into life and into the environment. So if it's Venus, the person will step across the threshold in a Venusian manner. Now obviously what kind of Venus that is will depend on the sign of Venus, and the condition of its dispositor. Everybody know that word? No? OK.

Let's say Venus is in Scorpio. Pluto and Mars rule the sign of Scorpio are therefore called the 'dispositors' of Venus. The house and sign positions of Pluto and Mars will in turn say something about what kind of Venus this is. Is this a veiled Venus? Is this an embattled Venus? And so on. I am thinking of an example, where Venus was rising in Scorpio, but in the 12th house, and was disposited by Pluto in Virgo in the 11th house. You can see some of the potential difficulties with this, around subterranean rivalries, conflicts and jealousies in group situations (11th house).

Think of the difference if it is Venus in Cancer rising in the 1st house, and the Moon is in Libra in the 4th. This person's journey has the quality of homeliness, the aesthetic, the emotionally intimate, the nourishing. It is also anchored in the 4th house, which is naturally the Moon's house anyway. Here difficulties may revolve around being too flexible or indecisive and taking cues all the time from others. Do you see?

Audience: But one way or the other, the Venus manifests strongly.

Melanie: Exactly. Perhaps even embodies. Some of what I have just been saying about this Venus would apply to any Venus in the 1st house, more so if it is in the same sign as the rising sign. But when planets are conjunct the Ascendant, the obvious manifestational quality is increased. If there is a shift of sign involved, it seems to water it down a bit.

Audience: Going back to the other example, what if Pluto was in Leo in the 9th house?

Melanie: This is a journey where what is valued is depth of encounter, and also Truth; what may be encountered are extremes. You bite deep with Venus in Scorpio. It is not a light-hearted, entertaining Venus. With Pluto in the 9th house, some of this intensity is located in the search for meaning, the need to find a philosophy that backs up one's personal sense of values and that must include the depth realms.

Audience: What if that was Libra rising?

Melanie: You mean with Venus still in Scorpio?

Audience: Yes.

Melanie: So this Venus rising in Scorpio will be the Ascendant ruler, located in the 1st or 2nd house. With Libra rising, the person will be on a journey of trying to embody, discover and evoke harmony, beauty, fairness and justice. This balancing act will be forced to include the Scorpionic things that nobody wants to know about, and with Libra rising, the person will also seek to proceed through life cultivating diplomacy and harmony. So a great deal of patience and grace may be called for, as well as emotional honesty, because the intensity of Venus in Scorpio will sometimes upset the aesthetic balance of the airy Libra rising.

Audience: So 1st house planets all want to be seen, but there is an added intensity and tendency to manifest literally, when they are conjunct the Ascendant.

Melanie: Exactly. And 12th house planets which are conjunct the Ascendant have a connection to visibility in a way not characteristic of other 12th house planets.

Guardian of the Threshold

The Ascendant shows what is trying to be personified and embodied. Let me think of a real example … OK. This is the horoscope of somebody who has Gemini rising with Saturn just in the 1st house, a very close conjunction, also conjunct Uranus, which is in the 12th. She has Mercury in Libra in the 5th house. Can you visualise that? [Draws on the board.] In fact the Mercury in the 5th is in the middle of a large stellium. What is wanting to be personified or embodied?

Audience: Communication.

Audience: Intellectual curiosity.

Audience: Networking.

Melanie: Yes. All of the above, but what about the Saturn?

Audience: The need to structure is combined with Saturn.

Melanie: Yes. This person has a very reserved demeanour, as you would expect. Saturn is actually right on the Ascendant. In fact her birth was very long and through her life she had various trouble with her knees and spine, which are both ruled by Saturn. Other Saturn in Gemini troubles include hesitancy in speech, the experience of a lot of restriction and burdens in her life. So, in naturally extensive Gemini, especially with Mercury in the 5th, the playful, the intellectually curious qualities have been dampened. This has all been inhibited and deepened, which is a function of Saturn, and interiorised as well. So in fact this is somebody who has never pursued any direct intellectual study. Her mind is very introvert, introspective and intuitively absolutely brilliant, with the 12th house Uranus conjunct the Ascendant. Now in her younger life she did a lot of acting – that is the stellium in the 5th house. Recreational, creative, artistic expression, together with other people, helped to free up some of that energy. But over time, one of her most powerful facilities is a kind of contemplative inner communication. She is the sort of person who will phone a friend just when they are in crisis, be in the right place at the right time, say the right thing, and although she is usually rather restrained, she has also taken huge risks for the sake of relationship. An interesting expression of Gemini rising. Multiple connections, fuelled by intuition – that's Uranus rising in the 12th.

Another way of thinking about planets conjunct the Ascendant is that they are the beings who directly accompany our birth. Like guardians of the threshold of beginnings. Sometimes they seem obviously helpful, and sometimes they have a fearsome demeanour, like demons that have to be encountered in order that we learn to see beyond the obvious. The example I just quoted, with Saturn rising, shows a life pattern of delays and obstacles being patiently negotiated, and profound lessons learned over time.

So a planet rising in the 1st house is like one's constant travel companion through the whole journey of life. In terms of birth, it's the dominant quality of the experience, perhaps the incomplete *gestalt,* or what greets you on arrival. I know someone who has Pluto within 2° of the Ascendant. Now she knows that if she is really going to invest energy in something, taking an initiative that she really wants to follow up, the first thing that will happen is catastrophe. When she was younger, she used to think 'Oh my God, I must be seriously on the wrong track because everything is going wrong and this is terrible.' Now the way she frames it is something like 'Aha, there's Pluto again – what's the lesson this time?' It is like Pluto tests your will, saying 'How serious are you about this impulse? Are you going to survive this one? How pure is your intent? Is it OK? We are testing you.' That's the feeling.

Audience: What if you don't … I mean carry the impulse through?

Melanie: If you don't then it goes back inside. It is like an impulse that gets half-born, is halfway out of the birth canal, and then gets pushed back in again. If that happens enough times you build up a huge amount of pressure. Often with Pluto rising, action and initiative occur after a great build-up and release of pressure.

Audience: … fighting to get out …

Melanie: Exactly. You'd be impulsed by that.

Audience: What if there is no planet on the Ascendant?

Melanie: To some degree this image of the guardian of the threshold can apply to the planet ruling the Ascendant, although it is not quite as obvious or as intense.

Audience: What happens when the Ascendant is in one sign and in the 1st house there is conjunct to the Ascendant a planet in another sign?

Melanie: That's like the Venus example I mentioned – but of course it depends on what the signs are. I am thinking of another example, of Pluto rising in early Virgo, although Leo was on the Ascendant. This person said that she always begins things in the dark, in extreme darkness, and also, new stages of her life are often heralded by major loss, upheaval or bereavement. In this case, Pluto and the Sun are actually connected via Mercury in Gemini in the 10th house, as the Sun, ruler of the Ascendant, is conjunct Mercury, which is also the dispositor of Pluto. This theme showed itself strongly in connection with work-related issues. Leo rising would like to be able to bounce into life and shine, but Pluto sometimes seemed to say 'It's not going to be like that. Can you get through this one and still smile?' One way that her creativity shows itself

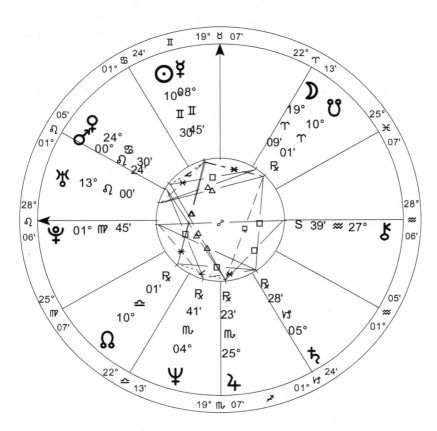

1 June 1959; 10.38 PST; Seattle, Washington

strongly is in her capacity to organise, manage detail, communicate clearly and be loyal and responsible, although she does not easily appreciate herself in this. In her work, she has also successfully dealt with various administrative nightmares, by which she felt sorely oppressed, but which she also saw through to the bitter end. This included the suicide of a business partner and being left with all the complex legal and financial dealings to see through to completion, as well as the emotional process of coming to terms with his death, all of which took many months.

A planet in the 1st house conjunct the Ascendant will either help or hinder us from manifesting or embodying something. It is more obvious than when a planet is simply in the 1st house. If you think of it as a journey, then planets conjunct the Ascendant are like life companions that accompany you everywhere, and that you always have to take with you. They can help or hinder and they can trick you, but you have to include them somehow.

Audience: What about a mutual reception with the Sun and Moon?

Melanie: So that would have to be Moon in Leo and the Sun in Cancer. Is Leo rising?

Audience: Yes. Moon in the 12th and Sun in the 11th.

Melanie: So the Ascendant is ruled by the Sun. The Sun is what is seeking embodiment, wanting to shine. Now, when you follow this mutual reception you discover a very unifying theme. Look at this … the Sun is in the 11th house, in Cancer. So here is an emphasis on groups of people, networks, subgroups in society, people who are focused around a common ideal, a common aim, a common search for knowledge. This is the place of ideals, and also the 'non-blood' family. It is the place where we refine our contribution to society. It is in the sign of Cancer, so this is very much about feelings, about nurturing and about the feminine principle, in whatever form.

That is amply supported by the fact that the Moon is in the 12th house in Leo. This is a Moon deeply in touch with all kinds of invisible currents; in Leo it wants to express those. Now the worst scenario with this could be that this is the kind of person who picks up everything that is going on in the group under the surface, picks up all the unconscious seepage, and expresses it privately or floods it out into the group. Even as we are all sitting here focusing on the angles, looked at from a 12th house point of view, our own energy fields are interacting, seeping and leaking even, with the residue of all kinds of things – what happened yesterday, the dream we had last night, deep anxieties, worries – we carry them all around all the time in our energy field. So a Moon in the 12th house person feels those. So the worst scenario would be that they felt compelled to express that, and get injured as a result, because then you are the person who says the thing that nobody wants to hear. The best scenario is somebody who expresses themselves within groups in a caring and nurturing way, by drawing on instinctive information – that's the Moon – picked up invisibly, and expressed through activity that is caring, sharing, raising the consciousness of the group.

Audience: If the Ascendant was Virgo, with that same mutual reception?

Melanie: If the Ascendant was Virgo? An Ascendant ruled by the Sun is certainly a rising sign that wants to express itself, wants to be the fiery centre, and to be appreciated for being this. But Virgo is the Virgin, who wants to be veiled, wants to hold back in order to discern and discriminate, be more detached. She is the eternal observer, sizing up and analysing. So the approach will be analytical, practical, cautious and sensible. Now, here, to follow the trail, we would need to know where the Mercury was.

Audience: Mercury is in the 9th in late Gemini, conjunct the Midheaven.

Melanie: Then here may be somebody whose way of approaching others and life becomes intimately connected with their public life, their professional life, the Midheaven. It is also needing to be based in the sense of philosophical quest, meaning and intuitive rightness. A practical idealist. The gathering of practical information, communication and its expansive use are in emphasis. Also, Moon in the 12th is often very interested in the past, in archaeology, in charitable work in hospital or prisons.

There's lots more questions. The Ascendant seems very alive today!

Audience: What would you say if the Node, or Part of Fortune, were at the Ascendant?

Melanie: I do not usually pay detailed attention to the Part of Fortune, because it is only one part of whole system, and also, like anything which uses the exact Ascendant to calculate it, there is a significant margin of error if the birth time is not sure. Because you use the Sun, Moon and Ascendant to calculate the Part of Fortune, and if it is conjunct the Ascendant on the 1st house side, you know that the person was born shortly after a New Moon. So the Part of Fortune does serve to alert you to the phase of the Sun-Moon cycle, and as that cycle is laid out round the houses, so to speak, it will additionally emphasise an area of life experience. So if it is conjunct the Ascendant, meaning the person is born around New Moon, that adds further weight to the theme of beginnings, new impulses and the vulnerable phase of starting a journey. If the Part of Fortune is in the 1st house, although this indicates the New Moon part of the cycle, it is still 'dark of the moon', as the Moon would not have yet been visible at the time of birth.

The other very important axis on the chart is of course the Nodes. I am not going to say much about this because there will be a whole day on them later in the year, but suffice it to say that if the Nodes of the Moon do line up with any of the angles, then they do add extra emphasis. Now if the North Node is conjunct the Ascendant in the 1st house, if you keep the orb narrow, over a lifetime of progressions it may well progress all the way back into the 12th house. This can of course happen with any of the angles. As regards the Ascendant, though, this is extremely interesting because that is describing a life where at first there is a very strong emphasis on the things we have been talking about to do with the Ascendant – initiative, going out there, forward motion, impulse. Yet over time one seems almost required to surrender that and release it back into the 12th house. The locus of the 'Who am I?' question shifts from the personal and emergent to the transpersonal and universal. So the sense of connection with some greater purpose is very important with the Nodes conjunct the angles. It can also mean very important relationships with a karmic feeling about them, or also relationships where there is an element of a shared spiritual path.

If the Node is conjunct the Ascendant and in the 12th house it adds a contemplative flavour to the question 'Who am I?' So there is a need, a drive, a kind of requirement in that life to explore the very deep inner terrain of the 12th house. That can be through dreams, through meditation, through contemplation. Through some means whereby the process of surrender and release into the larger whole, into the formless realm, can happen. That can also be through artistic work, or through service. The axis of the 6th and 12th houses can be seen as the axis of service, and it seems important, if the North Node is conjunct the Ascendant, for the person to find positive ways of doing that because otherwise it can be quite erosive because it may be a direction that is resisted, unless the rest of the chart supports it.

Then the feeling is 'Well, as hard as I am trying to go forward and initiate things, I always feel something pulling me back and I can't seem to get clear and I get in a muddle and I lose my keys, get chaotic and everything seems very difficult.' You go into chaos. In other words, finding appropriate ways to somehow embrace chaos seems to be important as part of the birth process.

The IC – Where Do I Come From?

Before descending to the IC, I wanted to mention some etymology. The 'C' in MC and IC stands for '*Coeli*', Latin for 'the heavens'. 'M' is for '*Medium*', which translates as 'the middle, the public eye, the community, and the common good'. Isn't that interesting, for the MC? Now 'I' stands for '*Imum*', and itself means 'the lowest, the bottom, the deepest, and the end'. It also links with other words meaning 'from below, the lower world, southern'.

Cosmic Origins

I am going to consider the IC now. I have an image here, which I love, for the IC, but before I say it, I must warn you that it can be astronomically misleading! The potential confusion would arise from mixing up the Rational and Local Horizons, like I mentioned this morning. So let's refer to the diagram again. There is the Rational Horizon, and where the IC occurs, as marked, it is below the horizon. So far so good. Symbolically the lower half of the chart is thus also 'under the Horizon', in the night part of the chart, and the IC is carrying also the symbolism of the Nadir, opposite the Zenith overhead, remember. So it is 'under the Earth', somewhere out in deep space.

Now if we still thought the Earth was flat, that would do nicely. You have probably seen old diagrams of this, with the hell realms depicted as under the Earth. If all you know is that the solid Earth is under your feet, then further under would be more of the same, but perhaps more dense. But once you get the idea of something round, a spheroid Earth, then the idea of 'underfoot' implies the idea of 'centre', because it actually goes into the centre of the Earth.

Once, when I was preparing a class on the houses, I had what I felt was a major revelation, and I then discovered the very same thing in the writings of Dane Rudhyar, which I had certainly read before, but obviously did not really grasp its profound significance![8] Anyway, here it is – think of a globe, our little globe we live on, the Earth. [Draws on the board.] That's the Earth, and there are people standing all over it. I suddenly thought 'My God! Everybody's feet all point in the same direction – to the centre of the Earth.' Imagine that. So this is like the Local Horizon. But your head points somewhere completely different to everybody else. That is the MC, symbolically.

So under where you stand is this underground, invisible, unreachable point of unity, and you extend upwards towards your particular star – at the Zenith, directly overhead. Amazing, really. The fact we are not born actually standing upright is symbolically enshrined at the MC, which we grow towards fulfilling, partly on the basis of what we have been given (the IC). To me that is an incredible symbol of what the vertical axis is about, and also about the two different levels of the theme of 'origins' as represented at the IC. One level is about our human, terrestrial origins, our family, clan base and tribe. The other is about our unknowable cosmic origins.

If we take this MC/IC axis as a pair for now, then the centre of the Earth represents the invisible point of human origin and unity from which we develop at the IC, and up here at the MC is our individual self-expression for real, for 'the common good'. In other words, it is well and truly in form up here – this is Saturn's house. Our offering to the world. I think that is where the idea of destiny comes in because – think about it – your head points to a particular star up there! That is like your individual guiding star, metaphorically speaking. At many levels we are all the same … our bodies are all roughly the same structure. And the same elements which are found in our bones and our blood are also the material that the stars themselves are made of.

So, in that very profound sense, the IC is the place of unity. It is like the womb, the matrix of belonging, on different levels. I have started on the cosmic level here, so I will continue a bit with that. After noting certain transits over my own IC, I decided it should really be called the 'I don't see'! Because this is a very hidden area of the chart, in a different way to the 12th house. In the 12th house at least you have got visible or inner chaos, or you are collapsing or getting into addictive patterns, or whatever it is that you do with your flood. But 4th house themes can be so private and personal as to be virtually invisible. Like 'Does the fish feel wet?' sort of thing.

So let's take those three levels that I mentioned earlier: external and physical, relational and psychological, and internal spiritual. We have started exploring the IC with the deeply internal and spiritual level – the image of the unknowable centre located in deep space. It is almost impossible to plumb the depths of the IC because of the huge leaps of consciousness that you have to make, once you contemplate the fact that some of the chemical ingredients in your own body are also found on the most distant stars. You have to go back in time beyond the 'Big Bang'. Some people believe that there are other civilisations in other galaxies, or in other dimensions in the universe. By the way, the famous philosophers Kant and Swedenborg also thought so, although this is not perhaps commonly known.[9]

So if we talk about origins in the IC we may need room for that kind of feeling of origin. I have occasionally seen clients who have said something like 'I'm not from here'. If you say this kind of thing to the wrong person, you end up on a hospital ward, or with a prescription for Lithium, but who's to say it's not true? Seriously. Even now in science, beyond the Superstring theory and the theory of everything, they are now working on this proposition that everything in the universe happens in ten dimensions. Most of us have trouble being aware of what's happening in our normal 3-D, let alone ten dimensions!

This is not such an unusual idea. In traditional cultures down the ages there has been acknowledgement of other dimensions of reality, other kingdoms than the obvious ones visible on Earth: the mineral, plant, animal and human kingdoms. But our Earth is also part of a larger system, and who knows what other kingdoms might be there in other dimensions? We are probably not the top of the evolutionary ladder, but believing that we are is a distortion that has run riot for the past two hundred years in Western culture, at least.

But the IC is something about the feelings that bring you in contact with the sense of belonging that is both place-specific, and also cosmic. I made this task difficult for myself by starting with the biggest possible picture. I meant to do it the other way round, but never mind! So, 'in the end', who or what is it that we belong to? What brings this sense of deeper participation? Remember the IC is 'the end of the matter'. Forgive the pun, but what takes over when what seemed to matter doesn't matter any more, or it's gone?

Personal Origins

The more traditional interpretation of the IC is that it represented the parental axis, the father, the clan base, the tribe. 'Who is your tribe?'

Ah, that's a nice IC question! The nature of your family, including your extended family, whether or not you actually live together in the same place. So it is also the security base of the family, or lack of it. So to some extent things like national identity and racial identity all belong to the 4th house as well. That's a 'grey area', however, because that theme does spread into 12th house issues. But I think the 4th house is more immediate. It is like how current national and racial issues impinge upon you in this lifetime. The 12th house equivalent has to do with the deep and hidden past, like 'Were your parents or grandparents, perhaps one hundred or two hundred years ago, involved in land deals or wars or whatever for which there is still blood wanting to be spilt, or reparation made?' Or was there an unrealised talent or spiritual vocation? So it has a more archetypal, long ago and far away quality. But the 4th house is more immediate, lunar, naturally ruled by the watery sign of Cancer. It is the place of the immediate parents, the clan, and the feeling climate within the home.

Father – the Hidden Parent

Taking the more traditional interpretations of the IC, it is also on the parental axis. This end is usually considered to be the father, but there is often controversy about it. I personally find it useful to think of the MC/IC axis as the parental axis, and then you don't waste time worrying which is right! But to consider the IC as father makes a lot of sense, because here is the hidden parent. Today we can have paternity tests, but there was a time when it was very difficult to prove, and a woman could secretly be carrying a child conceived with someone other than her official partner. So the theme of the mystery and power of origins is symbolised here, both literally and spiritually.

Totem and Taboo

The totems of your tribe are shown at the 4th house. Many indigenous people have totem animals, sacred places or totem plants which form a part of the spiritual basis of their clan identity. And remember the word 'Zodiac' means 'the circle of animals'! For example, in Zimbabwe where I come from, there are numbers of clans named after different animals. Although they all belong to the same tribe, each subsection, each clan, has a special animal, and there are all sorts of taboos which relate to this animal. Like if you are in the clan of the Fish Eagle, then you must not hunt that bird and if you see it fishing in the river you must not fish there, because you don't have permission to compete with it for the fish in the river. You may not wear its feathers as trivial decoration although they máy be necessary as sacred objects for ritual purposes. Now, that might all seem a bit quaint and rather inhibiting to us, and yet it expresses some principles which are very important at the IC because this totem system is partly about acknowledging the oneness of all life, and your place in it.

The totem is not only central to the core identity of the clan, but also may be invoked for protection. So the IC shows this – from where, from whom, do we seek protection, blessing and personal guidance, as regards deeply personal matters to do with family relationships, belonging and security? For in our Fish Eagle example, it's not just that the bird may be seen fishing or flying, but its spirit also animates the people of the clan. Thus the IC is like your totem, or that spirit animating you from the depths. Parallel questions might be 'What is it that gives you a sense of security? What do you need in order to feel safe?'

Audience: Or 'Where do you feel at home?'

Melanie: Yes, the IC is connected with *where* you feel at home, at the external level, and *how* you feel at home, on the inner level.

The totem of the Fish Eagle clan, with its taboos, when translated into psychological factors, is a metaphor for those beliefs, patterns and injunctions which come from our familial origins, which initially we dare not go beyond. For to do so would be to cast ourselves out of the tribe. The Cancerian, lunar quality of feeling is geared towards creating and maintaining bonds that mean security, belonging and continuity of the matrix of the family, group or nation. And for some people the issue is not about breaking these links, but how to live creatively within them and honour the need for the continuity of tradition. For others it may be about radical departure and its consequences.

I think it is perhaps through 8th house experiences that taboos are broken, and we experience separation and loss. This house is the next of the water houses from the 4th house. Someone dies, we give birth to our own family, or we lose our innocence and are propelled out, often through emotionally embattled experiences. However, at the IC we will find the hidden messages, the shoulds, the oughts, the dos, the don'ts, that say, 'If you don't comply here, if you don't hunker down with us, you are not going to be safe.' That's the message. Up here at the MC it is like 'If you don't conform, society will make you an outcast', or 'You won't get self-respect in terms of professional work.' But here at the IC it is the threat of being cast out of the tribe, adrift in a vast world peopled by potentially hostile strangers who are not familiar kith and kin, and therefore do not have the same obligations towards us.

Audience: It is our reaction to the unknown?

Melanie: Yes ... but maybe the IC describes what kind of nest we need, our place of safety to return to, where our immediate reality is sort of circumscribed, protected from the unknown. How we protect ourselves from the unknown.

Hearth, Home and Hospitality

Certainly taboos which register around the IC might be things that we simply have to find the courage to shed and take the consequences because in a tribal setting if you break taboos you are in big trouble because it is like you have hacked your way out of the etheric web which contains a tribe and a clan spiritually and emotionally, and perhaps even physically, in terms of the land. You see, that is what 'home' really means. Today, our whole idea of what 'home' means is rather different and we don't necessarily experience home as a place of embedded connection where we are in touch with the rest of life and other planes of existence. But I think, archetypally, that is what 'home' means. It is the sacred core, the hearth, the altar, the place where the gods who protect your life and your home are welcomed, and you feel welcomed in return. It is the base of operation around which you orient all these points which relative to this are all very external actually. They are outside the gates of the city wall or outside the sacred circle, or on other edges of it.

Even if you were a nomad, travelling all the time, and your possessions were camels and carpets, you would engage the 'homing instinct' every time you pitched your tent or lit your fire. To 'make home' is the IC task: 'What do you need in order to make home? How do you orientate yourself in space, in tune with the energies of the environment, with the people around you? How do you get to feel at home, literally, physically, on the planet?' In my youth when I was travelling if I had in my rucksack one sacred book, a candle and some incense, I felt that wherever I was I could make a temporary home, even if I was in a seedy hostel!

Audience: What is on your IC?

Melanie: Jupiter! So I'm at home when wandering … or dwelling on things philosophical. I just thought of the pun there! 'Dwelling on something' is quite a 4th house, lunar kind of thing to be doing. It is a mental activity which circles around and chews over something already known.

Then there is the sense of being at home with oneself. That's an even more subjective level, but the two are often connected. If you don't feel at home in your actual home, then the IC question is 'How do you make home? What do you need?' For instance, somebody who has Libra on the IC obviously needs to be surrounded by beauty and needs peace, harmony and balance. In an environment where there is too much discordant noise or maybe neighbours who are rowing until 3 o'clock in the morning, they'll really suffer.

I'm thinking of somebody I know who has Gemini on the IC with Mercury in Scorpio in the 9th house and needless to say this person is a bit of a wanderer, but has an incredible gift, a Mercurial knack for making himself feel at home and indeed making others feel at home. That's the other side of the IC, 'How do we make others feel at home?' There are traditions within which offering hospitality to travellers or strangers is a sacred duty.

Going back to the theme of home, the IC is 'me at home', in a very private space. So the IC is also how we are when we feel completely safe. It is what emerges when we are feeling really at home, and with people who are familiar and who we trust. If you have a good relationship with your family, where you can really 'let it all hang out', then the IC is that feeling of 'at-homeness', whatever that means to you. Whether it is not getting dressed all weekend, or leaving dirty dishes in the sink, or just hanging out talking with people, the IC is where you really come down home and what emerges when you do that. Sometimes it is quite a surprise, what you find when you get to know somebody really well, or see them for the first time in their familiar surroundings. The themes of the IC will come out, and the private, the personal, will be revealed.

The 3rd House Connection

Audience: What about planets conjunct the IC, but on the 3rd house side?

Melanie: Ah, yes. Well, like anything conjunct an angle, it will tend to personify, and it will usually be connected with the father. However, a planet there can also signify a sibling with whom we have a particular connection, and who played a significant role in our early life, or indeed later on too.

Another significant 3rd house theme, lying behind the IC, is about beliefs. In the 3rd house, which is Gemini-ruled, we are perceiving the world and conceiving thoughts about it, extending our sensory and perceptive ability by exploring it. We are concerned with the use of language, communication skills and information: how we take it in, give it out, process it and what we make of it. The conclusions we draw, too. So the taboo aspect of the 4th house comes from this.

Audience: I always associate Pluto with taboos …

Melanie: Pluto is certainly about taboos, but I think it is more about the terror that accompanies either the process of holding tightly on to a taboo, or indeed the breaking of it. The taboo itself is a collective thought form, a set of perceptions and beliefs, which is held together by the emotional glue of the tribe or family. And there is an interesting connection of levels, because in many tribal societies the disaster threatened by the breaking of taboos is not only about personal clan disaster, but spiritual disaster, which is a 9th house connection, relating to the MC. In the 3rd house, though, we can sometimes find the nature of the thoughts and beliefs which underpin the family system. If the 4th house is a nest, the 3rd house beliefs form part of its structure, like the twigs and leaves it is made of, glued together by bonds of belonging, emotional needs and security.

Womb and Tomb

In traditional astrology, the IC is considered as 'the end of the matter'. In psychological terms, the IC is about the womb of roots, home, security and tribe. However, too much emphasis on the IC can become imprisoning, like a tomb, where we fear to extend ourselves beyond the narrow confines of our origins, and become turned in on ourselves with it. It is said that the IC reflects the end of life, and although I have some anecdotal evidence which would seem to affirm this, I have not sufficient personal experience of this to know whether or not it is generally true at the literal level. Given that there is something so deeply personal about the IC, at this level, it might not register literally.

The Midheaven – Where Am I Going?

I was going to do the Descendant next, as it follows in the sequence, but I will go on instead to discuss the MC with you, as I think it is useful to contrast it with the IC . That means we will have woven a figure of eight around the chart – remember the imagery around the figure of eight?

The Public Front

The MC is the most public end of the chart, and this is where we meet the world head-on. We meet the world at the Ascendant too, but as an impulse seeking form, in the raw. Up here at the MC, it is like we are out there in the world and the world is also beaming in on us, impacting on the forms that we have created with that impulse. So the Midheaven is the place of mastery and achievement, whereas the IC is far more a place of being. The Ascendant is fire, initiative, the IC is water, feeling and being, but the MC is earth. Up here is the place of mastery, where the challenge of the density of the material world is met. We must put something into form.

Planets conjuncting the Midheaven register that pressure very strongly. It is like the test is 'How well integrated are we personally (the IC) and also with others (the Descendant)?' The challenge is 'How can we actually hold at the Midheaven level the kind of power and authority that may be asked of us?' The question up here is about how you relate to the theme of authority: your own sense of authority, or lack of it, how you react to the authority of others, how much authority to attribute to society, and who you ultimately answer to. Do you answer to your own conscience, the norms of society, or a particular set of religious beliefs? Your career, your partner?

Destiny and Duty

Consider again that image of the IC with everyone's feet pointing to the same centre, but each individual's head pointing to a different star. That symbolises the unique sense of personal destiny that seeks form, up here at the Midheaven. So it describes what individual impulse we are seeking to embody (the Ascendant); it will begin enclosed in a sacred space (the IC) so that it can, with due consideration for others and in connection with them (the Descendant), be offered to the world at the Midheaven. So in that sense the MC is an offering to the world. It is a consummation of our existence at the level of form, what we both come to embody for others, but what we might also need to labour dutifully to create and offer.

Mother – the Obvious Parent

The interesting thing also about the Midheaven, taking those different levels, is that it is traditionally about career, profession and place in the world. It is also on the parental axis, and is usually mother. Simply put, mother *is* our first world. We spend a whole nine months inside her body before we emerge at birth.

Audience: But the Ascendant is also to do with the body, isn't it?

Melanie: Yes, but this is somewhat different. Remember I gave the example of Scorpio rising, to do with birth, and how some of the compensation patterns get embodied, or locked into behaviour that describes a basic approach to life? At the MC, it is more about what you have to prove, fulfil or earn in the world. It is the form that you are called to, and in that sense which you embody, but it is also 'outside' you or an expression of you, visible in the structures that you have created, which interface with the world. It is Saturn's house, remember.

It is very interesting to see how these themes are interlinked – mother, career, profession and place in the world. For example, if someone has transits to the MC, although their presenting issue when they come for a reading might be about their job, or power struggles with their boss, it very often links directly with deeper issues involving their early relationship with mother. In astrology, there is a magnificent lamination of the layers of symbolism, so that things which are not apparently connected are shown to be so, at a deep level. And you can see this by noticing how the energy moves when you 'join up the dots' correctly.

Audience: What do you mean, exactly?

Melanie: Well, the soul knows about the deeper levels of consideration which might be invested in our troubles, our symptoms or our suffering. I can remember once saying to a client, 'In the horoscope, the 6th house is the house of small animals.' As I heard myself say this, I was also thinking, 'C'mon, Melanie, can't you find something more interesting to say?' However, I was aware that the client, about whom I knew nothing, had Uranus conjunct Pluto in Virgo in the 6th house. She also had some major Pluto transits, activating her 8th house. Knowing how powerful Pluto transits can be, and how carefully one must tread around 8th house themes, I was at a loss for what to say, and so I was sort of fumbling around, verbally.

This mention of 'small animals' produced an immediate reaction of very vocal grief, and my client began to sob, and to tell me how she had fallen apart completely when her much-beloved dog died. I had the feeling that this experience also contained displaced emotion from another loss, perhaps of a mother or a father, thinking of the Pluto transit. I also knew that I did not need to probe or question, as the link embedded in the astrology would provide the context, should she wish to speak. Which is what happened. She proceeded to tell me how she had felt 'frozen with grief' after her mother had died and how it was the loss of her pet which had opened the floodgates.

Sometimes, there is no need to 'interpret' things on a chart. It is enough that we have noticed something, are curious about it and able to hold the space. This enables our client to speak. This is also a very 'IC' way of going about a reading, where a lot is hidden from view, but connected in to places which are very deep. An 'MC' way would be more active, where you say, and tell, and give information. Your relationship with your client will inform you as to which is more appropriate and when – this is the Ascendant/Descendant axis, of course.

Authority, Success and Failure

The MC shows our attitudes towards success and failure, and also issues to do with authority. And these themes test the ground we stand on, which is the IC. Somebody who had a very turbulent home life who was perhaps always in conflict with one or other parent, or perhaps even abused, is not going to have an easy time up here with the whole theme of authority. They are either going to fight authority, or strive to *become* the authority, so that no one can ever do that to them again. But it doesn't necessarily work. If in the past we fought our parents and society, for whatever reason, it may be difficult for us to allow ourselves to grow into a sense of authority which is balanced because it takes relationship and personal need into account. Authority based on self-defence is usually very precarious and therefore vigorously protected. However, authority based on a willingness to serve others has a strong base in what is greater than the personal ego and therefore needs no protecting.

The theme of success and failure is an interesting one, as Bob Dylan's famous lyrics express! Interestingly, the etymology of the word 'succeed' has the implication of 'following'.

Great Expectations

The IC is like the foundation, and here at the MC is the fulfilment. The IC is very private, while the MC is the public end of the axis. So the MC is *what the world expects from you*. That is one way of looking at the MC. For some people that feels like an enormous burden, and for others it is not. To have Saturn on the MC, for example, to take an obvious one, often feels like heavy pressure from the world. You can't just take on a small amount of responsibility, because when you do everybody comes and asks everything of you, and pretty soon you are buried in obligations! That's the feeling and you need to learn where to put the boundaries, otherwise the world can seem like a very demanding place.

The Midheaven may also show what we project onto the world … it is a demanding place (Saturn), or a scary and oppressive place (Pluto), or an endless array of exciting possibilities (Jupiter). It is also how the world sees us, and what is asked of us. So to refer again to a 10th house Saturn conjunct the MC, the person with that placement is offered the opportunity to grow into the kind of authority and sense of respect which will make them an embodiment of Saturn for the world in some way. So planets up here are meant to be offered to the world. They are meant to be formed and shaped by your own life force, like breathing life into them. It is the product of your own life force; your own being is also shaped and offered at the Midheaven. It is both of you, and also not you.

Sometimes the MC shows how we like to be seen by others, not individuals so much, but the world at large. That is an interesting one, because if there are a lot of contradictory themes there, or if the MC themes contrast strongly with the rest of the chart, it can leave you feeling that you don't quite know how to present yourself, because you are not quite sure what you want to be or do out there in the world. I've just remembered a really clear example of that. It was a woman who had Jupiter in Sagittarius conjunct the Midheaven on the 9th house side. The MC was late Sagittarius and, although rather wide, it was also conjunct Saturn in Capricorn in the 10th house. She had sometimes experienced great tension, because of wanting to do something really expansive, and wanting to seek freedom and broaden her professional horizons. Then she would have strokes of good luck, and either go too far (Jupiter), or try too hard (Saturn), and then she inevitably met the Saturnian blocks and delays and so on. It wasn't until after her Saturn return that she realised that she had to do the setting of creative limits and the circumscribing of her own energy, or the world would do it for her in a way that was unpleasant. She worked in a travel agency, and although she organised exciting journeys for others, she went through a stage that, when she travelled herself, everything seemed to go wrong! So with Saturn up there, if you don't find the appropriate shape and limits for your impulse, the world will limit you. That's the kind of balance that's looking to happen.

Aspiration, Vision and Vocation

Up here in the 9th house is the vision and possibility which seeks to be grounded in form and offered to the world at the MC. It is like 'OK, this is the possibility; now let's see what can really happen with it. Let's see if it will stand the test of time, the challenges of society and the world and so on.' The quality of aspiration also belongs to the MC, and there is also a vocational quality. The 10th house is about what is meant to be put into form, what is meant to show. Yet if that is to be more than grey conformism, it must be based on a greater sense of vision. If we consider the really interior level of the MC, as the border between the 9th and 10th houses, then we are talking about something very difficult to define. This is the place of our highest aspirations. The 9th house is traditionally linked with meaning, purpose, higher education, the search for knowledge, understanding and higher learning. It is also the place of intuitive wisdom arising from one's own deeply personal experience (8th house), that has the sense of being able to connect in a visionary way with what is greater than personal. The 10th house is the place of manifestation in the world at large, where the vision is tested and grounded.

For many people the MC can be connected with actual profession, career and their obvious place in the world. But for others, it is more subtle. It is more qualitative, even though this is the earth angle. But what if you've got Neptune in Libra on the Midheaven? How do you 'earth' Neptune in Libra? Basically you can't. You can create many different kinds of forms where Neptunian energy can flow in and flow out, but you can't 'earth' Neptunian energy, or any of the outer planets, as they are greater than what one individual can hold. You are a servant of Neptune, with this placement, and that is a paradox too, because the MC is the place of mastery.

Audience: I don't understand the difference between 'earthing' energy and giving it a form.

Melanie: Let me try and explain it another way. If you are a musician and working with Neptunian energy in that way, you craft over time a channel through which that energy can flow. But you can't control it. It will come and go as if by magic, offering exaltation, and perhaps sorrow when it leaves and the spell is broken. But if you don't have a suitable means of expression for it, with Neptune on the MC, you will find yourself under pressure from the world to *become* it. An example comes to mind. A woman with exactly this placement was in management training consultancy. She did very well, but was constantly exhausted, because the people in her trainings would often seek to use her as a wet shoulder. It was as if they saw the Neptune up there, which she was actually trying to hide in her work, by being very Saturnian. It became so extreme that she started to feel like the other pole of Neptune – the victim. Because her chosen profession did not really provide a suitable enough vehicle for the Neptunian energy to flow, she was herself pressured into becoming the vehicle herself.

So, for some people this is the place of vocation, in the sense of career, profession and something you do in the world, but for others this may be a more invisible vocation. I remember years ago I had a friend who was in this category. You know how in your passport you have got to write what profession you are? Well, he wrote 'Student of Life'. Needless to say that covered a whole variety of skills, roles and professions he had done, as well as describing his purpose. Guess what sign was on the Midheaven?

Audience: Sagittarius.

Melanie: Yes! He considered seriously and deeply this to be his vocation, to be a student of life. He was on a path of knowledge, and orienting himself around that was the most important thing. Whether he was working as a waiter, or bricklayer, or whatever country he was in, was of secondary importance to this interior sense of vocation.

Because this is Saturn's angle, we often feel easily judged in this area. Up there at the MC may be fear about doing it right, getting accepted by the outer world, effort to meet standards – your own or others. These can simply be a transposition of early issues to do with your relationship with your mother, which may leave you vulnerable to conformism, but it can also be your own moral effort to live up to your own standards, which refers back to the 9th house themes. So the question is 'What god or goddess or vision (9th house) sustains you when the going gets tough (10th house)?'

Audience: I know someone who has Neptune on the MC and he is very ambitious. He wants to be the man who's really 'made it' in the world, but he seems all the time to miss out or not really get there. He is a writer but there is some kind of guilt with this planet.

Melanie: Where is Saturn?

Audience: In Scorpio in the 10th, more towards the 11th house.

Melanie: I don't know about this person, obviously, but sometimes there can be guilt about having success. If it means we outstrip a beloved parent or sibling, it can feel very lonely, and we may opt for the pain of struggle and failure, rather than this aloneness.

Audience: You have to wait for the cosmos to tell you with Neptune.

Melanie: That's a lovely way of putting it – you are the servant of something conjunct the MC.

Audience: Sure, I can grasp that, because I try to be a writer myself, and I write novels and other things although I've not been published yet. I carry a cassette, trying to get inspiration, and I have periods of great activity, and then lose it. But grounding?

Melanie: I have another image which may help here, as it brings in the theme of control. When we are talking about planets on the angles, then it is like you can't ground the energy by hoping to control it. You are in service to it. This is especially true of the outer planets. Let's switch to a really easy example ... someone who has Venus in Taurus on the Descendant, as long as there are no other major complications, you can be pretty sure that person is going to be able to have and to hold a partner in their life, who will also, if possible, put money in the bank. So it is like the earthiness of loyalty, stability and committed partnership will be likely to manifest. It is something that you embody and ground just by how you live your life. But you just can't do that with any of the outer planet energies. You are in service to them, and that can mean a whole variety of different things. Like with the example of the musician, or indeed your poetry, you develop your skill with words so that the Neptunian energy can flow through you and inspire you and prompt the words and so on. But you can't *have* them, or *be* Neptune, if you understand the difference.

Audience: Yes. It is not for me to have it because I know things come at the right moment. When I get this feeling, everything is all right.

Melanie: But if you were then to try to capitalise on that inspiration, trying to control it, and fix it, then it doesn't work, which is the difference. You can serve by paying attention to the form level, so that when the spirit of Neptune or Uranus moves, it has something of a container to move through, but you can't own it.

Audience: So you never really feel like you contain it, and maybe you have difficulty with a world that seems to own it. Perhaps that is why I sometimes can't grasp ideas and ground them, because I feel they don't belong to me.

Melanie: Yes. On one level, they don't!

Audience: Can I just ask about Pluto at the MC?

Melanie: Wherever Pluto is, we are going to meet some very potent processes of transformation that we need somehow to engage with, even if it feels like an area where our life is at stake and it is too scary to go near. But guess what? You are pulled there anyway! Where Pluto is, that's where the doorway to the underworld of your cosmos is located. So to have Pluto up here at the Midheaven is a very exposed place for it to be, and you cannot afford to go out as one of life's innocents because, if you do, you may get abducted, metaphorically speaking. You probably all know the story of Demeter and Persephone and the abduction of Persephone by Hades-Pluto? Yes? Well, that's what happens if you go out into life as little Miss Shiny Eyes picking the narcissus flowers! Because that stance will attract abduction into the underworld.

Audience: You can't do that with Pluto on any angle.

Melanie: That's true. But the MC is particularly exposed, and involves our relationship with the world at large. The alternative to this innocence is no safer. This would mean always being attuned to what's going on underneath, that nobody else is looking at, doesn't want to know about. Then you find yourself either carrying those perceptions alone, which can be a great burden, or if you try to do or say something, you get branded as the one focusing on the negative side of things.

Audience: What if Pluto is in the 9th house, but conjunct the MC?

Melanie: The transformation of our intuitive understanding, our philosophical orientation, is suggested. You can't afford to espouse philosophies that are basically pie in the sky idealism. You need one that encompasses the dark side of life, that helps you make sense of, or at least accept, the absolutely unthinkable, and something that really does include and incorporate the underworld of your experience. So if you encounter your own negativity, or that of others, you need to have some context that encompasses the process, or you will feel like you fell off the edge of the flat Earth! In order for that to happen, the transforming of a lot of collective beliefs may be necessary – the breaking of more taboos, like we mentioned when we discussed the IC.

Pluto conjunct the MC may mean that you experienced your mother as oppressive. Indeed, her own experience of motherhood may have been terrifying, like her own underworld threatened to open up because of your presence and the intensity of her own feelings. So you began life carrying this projection, and may feel the need to hide from the world, finding it too scary or oppressive. So what follows later on is that if you unconsciously expect trouble, if you are programmed to be Pluto for the world.

Audience: Pluto's a catalyst.

Melanie: Yes. When I said that you cannot afford to go out into life as one of life's innocents, I meant that very seriously. If the transformative energy of Pluto is looking to find expression through your professional life, or your role as a parent, and if you can acknowledge that and find a place for it, the question is, perhaps, 'How do you serve that energy without getting blown away in the process?'

When Pluto is on the MC, this has to do with authority, position, profile and authenticity. Very often the baptism of Pluto is about feeling powerless, which in turn will reveal itself in issues to do with power, carrying power, being powerful and feeling powerless. So if it is at the Midheaven we may feel powerless in the face of the world, with overwhelming responsibilities that we feel we will never manage. And sometimes with Pluto these are invisible, like Pluto's helmet of invisibility. These can be the invisible emotional burdens from our mother, our deeper parental lineage which will get triggered by situations in the outer world, to do with profession, career, place in the world. Then I think you have to learn how to release it or to ask for help. Which raises the question of who it is that you answer to in the end. Who is the ultimate authority in your life? Perhaps that could be another MC question.

Pluto conjunct the Midheaven may feel like a sense of being mightily oppressed by a huge task that somehow you know you've taken on and you may not even be sure what it is. Often it is a task on behalf of one's mother, her unfulfilled ambitions, or unresolved feelings to do with her mother before her. Then, initially, you cannot easily enjoy the fruit of your own labour, because you are never sure who you have done it for – yourself and your destiny, or that of your mother. With Pluto conjunct the MC, a high degree of authenticity is asked of you, because if you do what you do to comply with mother, the world or the great 'they', you will build brittle structures that will topple, because you don't really believe in them. At the MC, there is the need for achievement to be consecrated to something higher than yourself and your ambitions, but if that 'something higher' is your mother, or the norms of society, you may feel somehow cheated. It is a precarious place. In some books you will see this aspect described as a 'fall from power', and I think this is what lies behind that interpretation.

Audience: That's it! That's my mother. She was a housewife who wanted to do lots of things that somehow always came down on me. Huge expectations. 'Why don't you do this?' and I used to think 'Why aren't *you* in charge of doing this?'

Melanie: That's a really clear example, but sometimes it's not so conscious. I think with Pluto on the MC, we are asked to transform our whole idea of what success, ambition, profile and responsibility might be. You cannot easily just follow in the footsteps of someone else, or you topple, and to do that is one way of returning to the 'Me in here'. That seems to be oddly characteristic of planets in the 10th house in general. It is naturally Saturn's house, Saturn's angle, working towards forming and crystallising and shaping something. It does not flow or change easily, so sometimes has to be broken apart, or overthrown dramatically, or left behind in a radical way.

Audience: I've got Saturn and Pluto there.

Melanie: That must be a Leo Midheaven, yes? So the desire to conform and the need to transform live side by side. Perhaps you would have liked to be able to conform to your mother's picture of you, but actually it didn't leave you enough room to move?

Audience: Yes, exactly. Neither place is comfortable at times.

The Descendant – Who Are You?

Going on to the 7th house cusp, the Descendant, and taking the obvious and external level first, we are talking here about other people and our interactions with them. It is the place of the 'Other': the partner, in marriage or business. Where we 'level' with people, where equality of some kind, or negotiated agreements concerning role and behaviour, are an issue. This axis, the Ascendant/Descendant, remember, is the Horizon, so it is likewise about 'horizontal' relationships, not parent/child relationships, which have more to do with the MC/IC axis.

The Descendant and the 7th house are also the place of our enemies. In traditional astrology, this is the house of open enemies. Over here in the 12th house are the hidden ones! So here are found open enemies, who can sometimes be our own shadow in disguise. Here we get into some very interesting territory, which is profoundly inward as well as impacting strongly on our relationships. Let's expand on some of those themes.

Separateness

Paradoxically, the Descendant is both an important place of relationship and also of separateness. This angle is where we meet another person, a *separate* other person, a stranger, and the challenge is to somehow find a way of relating to them. It is not about being merged. The Descendant is the beginning of an air house, naturally associated with the sign of Libra. You are out of the clan over here. At the IC, you are looking for ways to blend in and connect with your tribe and your cosmos, whether that consists of a block in the neighbourhood in the middle of a city, with a single parent or a 500-acre farm with lots of relatives nearby. It's home.

But at the Descendant, you are away from home, out of the nest. We could perhaps expand our question here to 'Who am I when I am on my own, *and* in relationship to another person?' I am not on familiar ground, and I can't be 'just me', because there is somebody out there who I am affected by, and who is affected by me. That's the 7th house, and its territory encompasses the whole transactional field between two people, with all its nuances of love, hate, appreciation, rivalry and mutuality.

Equality and the Noble Rival

The Descendant is the beginning of the battle for equality, and I use that word advisedly! Some people play dirty, some play clean, some get others to do their dirty work while some always manage to come home from the playground with their noses bloodied! Some are subtle, some tactless, some keep things smooth and others make waves. Obvious or not, this is battle terrain. At the deepest level, this is a place where we are apprenticed to Venus, goddess of love, which is precisely why the unlovingness of our transactions can show up here. We are battling with ourselves, as much as anything, to develop the skills which enable us to relate to another person in an appropriate way. The 7th house is the place of the lower courts, set up to try and resolve disagreements between the parties concerned so that the issue doesn't have to go to the High Court! Also the Venus connection implies values, and in the 7th house we value someone enough to continue in relationship with them, whether through love or even in rivalry, or a mixture of the two.

Rudhyar points out something very interesting about the 7th house. He says this is where socially sanctioned relationships happen, those relationships that form an important part of the fabric of society, i.e. the MC. There are many areas of the chart that also concern relationship, like the 5th house, which is about affairs of the heart, romance and recreation, or the 11th, which is about friendships, or what I call the 'non-blood family'. Then the 8th house is the real emotional and erotic depth of relationship, which is nothing to do with being socially acceptable. It is what happens in the bedroom, and also in the bank accounts, and will usually be hidden from others, although it may go along in tandem with the more socially acceptable side of relationship.

What Rudhyar is emphasising is that today a lot of relating is happening only on this horizontal axis, because the structures of society and the shape of family life are changing, so we no longer know where the goalposts are, collectively – the MC/IC axis. This puts a great strain on one-to-one relating. So it is me-you, woman-man, woman-woman, man-man in love, and also in rivalry, looking for new ways to relate, and without the security of cultural and social customs. Even who goes first through a doorway can become a loaded issue!

This doesn't affect the 8th house, because 8th house truths and experiences come from the underworld. They come from a very visceral level, which may or may not be contained in a courtship ritual.

The Mating Game

But at the Descendant, you play the mating game, not just to get somebody into bed, but as a courtship ritual, like peacocks. This phrase comes from the work of Antero Alli. He points out how you can't engage the Descendant unless you can 'drop your act', the Ascendant, in order to embrace who you are meant to be with others, and to discover that precious polarity of yourself within your relationships.[10]

Audience: I can't really get rid of my Ascendant.

Melanie: No, exactly. I think what Antero Alli means by being able to 'drop your act' is perhaps about becoming familiar enough with who you are at your Ascendant, so that you have a bit more leeway. Then you are not compulsively attached to the image you are presenting to the world, without even realising it.

To me, a useful image for the 7th house is a fencing match, because it is a potentially deadly game which is also terribly aesthetic – there's the Libra and Venus connection. It is stylised competition, even ritualised, with many rules and regulations, but people can get injured anyway. You can get run through if you don't watch it! So the 7th house is about relationships with social consequences. How we manoeuvre, negotiate and mediate, so that some greater purpose is served. Not a big philosophical vision, but the humanitarian principles of right relationship which form part of the fabric of both our individual lives and also of society as a whole. So the mating game here means a dance intending to move towards establishing of relationship, with consequences: a household, a family or, in the case of a business partnership, an enterprise which also has profile in society.

How you begin and end relationships may also be shown here. For example, someone with Uranus on the Descendant, or Aquarius there, might have relationships begin or end suddenly, so fast that feeling is suspended and cut off for a while. Indeed, this might be necessary for a while, to gain insight or take stock afterwards. A variation on that theme might be a relationship starting or continuing under unusual circumstances.

Projection

The Descendant is also a place very sensitive to projection, although any part of the chart can be experienced in projection, meaning something that we don't recognise about ourselves, either because it is very much outside the kind of context in which we were raised, or the society in which we live, or because we have some kind of belief about it. Whatever the reason, the Descendant can be like our 'blind spot'. On the other hand, planets conjunct the Descendant are *meant* to be discovered in connection with other people. We cannot 'do' our Descendant on our own, and it will very likely show what qualities in you are evoked best in connection with others, at least initially, and especially if that quality, that element, is somewhat weak. For example, if this is your water angle, you need others in order to be in touch with your feelings. If it is fire, others will stimulate your imagination and creativity. If it is earth, the presence of others stimulates your physicality and your capacity for practical action, and so on.

Remember that this actually is an air house, so although it is also a place of feeling, because it is about relationship, it will also show our capacity to reflect on what we learn from our interactions with others, how we process experience in relationship, what basic attitudes we carry and which may be challenged. So there is space around the interactions. We learn a lot here by discovering what we thought we were not, and having it proved otherwise!

As the Descendant is prototypically square both the MC and the IC, it is also the place where we meet the residue of our relationships with mother and father. The committed quality of the 7th house (remember Saturn is exalted in Libra) will bring to the surface the patterns, expectations, role models and unfinished business of our past (the IC). The perception and management of this material is very much a 7th house/Descendant theme, although the transformation will occur through 8th house experiences of surrender, letting go, loss and intensity of feeling. A person strong at the Descendant will be able to manage very complex emotional situations smoothly, as they will have highly developed skills of relating, in the sense of keeping things socially acceptable, functioning and smooth. Remember the 6th house precedes the 7th, where we are trying to be efficient, maximising our resources and keeping the show on the road. But remember different relating skills are required in the 8th house area.

The struggle for equality that I mentioned also has to do with parental projections, where suddenly our partner seems to be turning into the condescending father or the manipulative mother. Or the idealised brother or sister. Perhaps we find ourselves becoming the frightened child, the rebellious adolescent. Watching this happen and finding ways to deal with it is the province of the Descendant. The phrase 'It takes two to tango' applies to the Descendant and the 7th house. Meaning that a transaction is like a rope, with two ends. As long as both people are holding it, a tense push/pull situation will sometimes occur. Perhaps the greatest hazard of this area is negative judgement – Libra's symbol – and the greatest art is to learn how to let go of the rope and see what happens!

Audience: It is really hard if you have a very stressed Descendant because you place too much focus out there. You start idealising the projected part.

Melanie: Yes, projecting your 'goodies' on to others, too. That's when it might be useful to consider the Descendant as one end of two axes, or one of four points. If you have a loaded Descendant, that means a great deal of energy reaches you from other people, and your interactions with other people are indeed extremely powerful. That's how it is meant to be. That's a feature of your life pattern, not a symptom of something wrong with you.

But you can refer back to the other angles for balance, sometimes. Take the IC – if you have a good ability to make a home, make a sacred space, then this helps the process of turning events into experience, and experience into nourishment for the soul. Down here it is womb-like and gestatory and, at the deeper levels, the IC addresses our relationship with the cosmos, including other people, but is not focused exclusively upon them. We feed our souls down there, and we chew on experience like cows chew the cud. Then self-awareness can be generated, reflecting back onto the Ascendant, providing you give it enough time, like the cow going 'munch munch' on the experience. If you think of all the angles as connected, and explore those connections, that might be more useful.

The Partner

Audience: Does this angle show us our partner?

Melanie: So some of the books say! This is obviously a question which needs careful consideration. As I mentioned, the qualities around the Descendant are meant to be discovered partly in connection with someone else. The Descendant is also the place where relating to another challenges us to shed the residue of our relationship with our parents, the patterns represented at the MC/ IC, and to find a measure of equality and harmony sufficient to make a partnership that has social viability. But to go as far as to say that it literally describes the life partner? It can do, but I would hesitate to consider it as an absolute. That kind of thinking can set up destructive thought patterns and expectations, of a negative 7th house variety – comparisons – where either you or someone else is being set up to be judged. Something much more profound is what brings people together as life partners. That is not to say that there is *no* truth in this statement, but I think it has more to do with the 'inner partner', which may or may not manifest in a person out there who resembles him or her.

In other words, the Descendant is clearly one's *own* other half. However, some people know and live that dimension of themselves, while others do it vicariously through another person. Neither is right or wrong. Taking an obvious example, if you have Capricorn rising then there is a Saturnian approach to life in general, so you may be somewhat cautious, reserved and hesitant in expressing your personal feelings. You value things that have mileage in them, that last, and that you can build on, and you don't let people close without giving it due time. You take a serious and somewhat paternal approach as you peck your way out of your egg, with serious intent. But over here, at the Descendant, is your underside, Cancer. That too can be very self-protective, but when you 'drop that act' you are like a soft-bellied crab with no shell, a crab which absolutely wants intimacy, absolutely wants merging, and wants to be inside that shell, not on the outside trying to get in. You can see, I think, how these fit together.

Preparing to Meet

Audience: What about planets conjunct the Descendant, but in the 6th house?

Melanie: Yes, thank you for asking that. The Descendant is the end of the 6th house, just as it is the beginning of the 7th. I think of the 6th house as the place of preparation. It is associated with the sign of Virgo, thus ruled by Mercury, and is connected with the process of ordering material resources like time, energy and money, and creating routines and following rhythms that make for productivity. Things must work for real here, and also be useful to others. It is on the axis of service, associated also with servant/master or employer/employee relationships – in other words, *unequal relationships*. It's the place of apprenticeship, learning and perfecting skills; it is about dedication, self-improvement and discipline. It is traditionally linked with the healing arts, too, especially where the interface between the mind and body is specifically addressed. It is one of the areas connected with both illness and that which supports physical health.

So planets conjunct the Descendant, but in the 6th, are intensely committed to service, self-improvement and being useful. There is an additional demand, to do with the relating style, because it is only at the Descendant that this theme of equality comes in. The hazard of the 6th house is the sense of always being in preparation for something, and for losing sight of what it is all for. Therefore there can be a very devoted quality shown by this placement, where another person becomes the object of one's devotion, and before whom one feels inferior, unworthy and needing to improve. Or the devotion can show as dedication to one's work, to the activity of service, to the process of self-improvement.

Questions Thus Far

Melanie: Are there any questions at this point, any loose ends that need tying up?

Audience: I was thinking about the 3rd house as the immediate environment, the neighbourhood – can you say more about this in connection with the meaning of the IC?

Melanie: Yes. Amongst other things, the 3rd house describes the kind of impressions we receive as we begin to crawl, walk and speak for the first time, and the 'conclusions' we draw from this. Is our immediate environment (our 'world') quiet, noisy, dirty, clean, lonely or full of people? We will gradually learn these labels, and associate our own experiences and value judgements with them. I also think of the 3rd house as therefore describing the 'mental environment'. This is particularly interesting today, because the mental environment, at least for urban dwellers, is of unimaginable complexity. So the 3rd house is also what beliefs we absorb online, or from the media in general – radio, newspapers, TV, billboards, as well as the traditional meaning of neighbours, gossip, hearsay and so on. The immediate impact of ideas, not their grander implications. So the mental environment includes things like whether you lived in a home that had a television in every room, or one with no television. Did you read as a child? If so, what? What were your mental connections with the outside world, including education and schooling?

From quite an early age, most people spend more than half their waking hours outside the home, in school. So education doesn't only teach you facts. It may also be the first place outside the home where your views of the world are formed. You see, if there is not enough containment in the lunar IC sense, you will be more vulnerable to being influenced by collective ideas. In that sense, because of its fragility, being only the first air house, the 3rd house is the place of the conditioned and as yet undiscriminating mind.

Audience: Could you say more about the Ascendant/Descendant – with the image of the mask?

Melanie: Yes. Perhaps we could apply that image to all the angles. So the Ascendant would be the mask that initially you might not realise you are wearing, but may be how others see you. The IC would ideally be where it is safe to unmask, while the MC would be the mask that is created by you according to the demands of the world, and your need to manifest the impulse that you are carrying, as who you are to become. Then the Descendant ... remember the metaphor of fencing, and the struggle for equality? A fencing mask has holes in it, so you can see through it, but your face is also protected.

Audience: How do the angles relate to the Gauquelin sectors?

Melanie: Some people think they don't, but I think they do, and I'll explain why. Some of you may know about the work of Michel Gauquelin. He was a famous French researcher who did large-scale statistical work. He started out deeply sceptical, trying to disprove astrology, and over the decades consistently came up with results in his work that didn't disprove astrology at all, but convinced him of its validity, and he dedicated the rest of his life to this research. One of the most well known aspects of his findings revolves around what are known as the 'Gauquelin sectors'. These sectors were found by examining the horoscopes of people who were shining, obvious examples of planetary motifs, and noting where the main significator fell. Traditionally, planets were said to have been strong near the angles and in the 1st house.

This was one of the areas of Gauquelin's research that appeared not to tally with the tradition, because a peak of activity would be found in the house area immediately behind the angle, in the so called cadent houses – 12, 3, 6 and 9. Needless to say, this finding resulted in considerable debate.

I would like to mention something on this subject for you to consider. Note that even though they do record accurate birth times in France, the question of what time is actually recorded is an open one. Even if recorded by a doctor on a birth certificate, there is no guarantee that a time is correct from the astrological point of view. The birth moment is actually the cutting of the cord, because that is the first physically independent moment, the first separate breath. That is the rationale for it. At least that is how Dane Rudhyar describes it, and I'm sure he's not the only one. The chances of that moment being written down are extremely small, unless someone is aware of this and clock-watching as the cord is cut. It is very difficult to get a chart with that level of accuracy, unless you have the good fortune to have parents who understood this, or you have had your chart rectified.

However, the interesting thing is that *even a chart not completely accurate in this sense can be adequate for the purposes of doing a reading.* There is an X factor, a mysterious divinatory or oracular function at work, which serves to remind us that astrology is a living art or science, and perhaps to protect us from trying to get too smart! At least, that is my view, and I'm not alone in this.[11] The question as to how this obvious margin of error, this 'grey area', might distort attempts at statistical work is an open one that to my knowledge has not been properly considered.

The peaks of the Gauquelin sectors occur just past the middle of the Equal House sector 'behind' the four angles. Depending on the time of year of birth, giving the birth time a leeway of as little as twenty minutes could make a big difference to where those peaks would show. I have also taken the opportunity of asking doctors and midwives about this, and they usually say that the time recorded is often a bit later than the time the cord was cut, and is averaged out retrospectively in the duty book. Or if the cord is cut early on in the process, that's not considered either. Unlike in India and other eastern countries, the importance of the birth time to the future life of a person is not understood.

And here is a true story about birth times which raises more questions than it answers. A man, born in India, had his birth time deliberately adjusted by the family astrologer in order to try and avoid the 'bad fate' which was foreseen for him, with Mars conjunct the Ascendant. This was also backed up by extensive (and expensive!) ceremonies presided over by a priest. However, the adjusted birth time put Neptune in the 7th house, opposite Mars, still in the 1st house, although further away from the Ascendant. The reason this person consulted me was to do with a very painful, confusing and compelling relationship situation. Now bearing in mind that the family astrologer did not use the outer planets, as is traditional with Vedic astrology, some very interesting questions are raised here. Did the family astrologer really save him from anything? Did the prayers and pujas do anything? Or did he create a worse fate for this child of his client with the new time? Or was it my client's 'fate' to have this kind of 'intervention'? And did it make any difference? When you really think about the kind of questions that the practice of astrology confronts us with, you really have to admit to a lot of 'unknowing'. Which in my view, is no bad thing …

Audience: I'm interested in the two different kinds of relationship, the 6th house and the 7th house, with the Descendant in-between. Can you say more about that?

Melanie: Because the 6th and 12th houses are the axis of service, the question could be 'Who, or indeed what, are you serving?' With planets conjunct the Descendant, but located in the 6th house, this can become important in relationships, because the tendency to put yourself 'one down' is strong. Now, the positive side of that is the activity of service, putting your skills, your resources and indeed *who you are* at the service of something greater than yourself. But I think that 'something greater than yourself' is meant to be coming from the 12th house, from the archetypal or spiritual dimension. If it is coming from the 7th house, from another person, it can mean oppression or subjugation. Then we have slave/master dynamics going on in a relationship, rather than any kind of service which is more reciprocal.

Equally, people who have got that 6th house/Descendant emphasis may well gravitate towards activities that are service-related, and also dealing with people. Perhaps the healing professions. Perhaps working for somebody in a very supportive role, like perhaps being a personal administrator, assistant or secretary, where one is holding the practical details of the earthy level for somebody else. Depending on the signs and planets involved, of course, when something is conjunct the Descendant but on the 6th house side, it will bring that odd dimension of inequality into a relationship area which is really about the movement towards equality. Does that clarify things a bit for you?

Audience: Yes. I have the Sun in Aquarius conjunct the Descendant, which is actually in Pisces, and I have often found myself giving and serving in a way that I end up feeling ground underfoot!

Melanie: With Aquarius, the desire to serve on behalf of the group or of strongly held beliefs and principles can sometimes obscure individual feelings and needs. And Pisces rules the feet!

Audience: If the MC/IC is the parental axis, are the grandparents also shown on the angles?

Melanie: Yes, they do. I am glad you mentioned that. If we take the IC as father, then his mother and father will be represented by my Ascendant and Descendant, respectively, because the 7th house is the 4th from the 4th, and the Ascendant is the 10th from the 4th. So the Ascendant is also the place of my father's mother, and the Descendant is the place of my father's father. Then it is the other way round for the mother's parents, so her mother is my Descendant and her father is my Ascendant.

What's interesting is that through the generations it reverses on the axis, from vertical to horizontal and then back to vertical, and so on, like the wheel of fate or a vortex of incarnation. It's often said that grandparents get on better with growing children than parents do and, while there are obvious reasons for that in terms of immediate pressures within the family, it is interesting how that shows in the chart. In other words, the vertical axis is parents, the horizontal is grandparents, so the feeling of authority is perhaps less pressured. Grandparents live on the axis that is fundamentally about 'Who am I?' and 'Who are you?'

This is often very literal. It is in my case. I have Scorpio rising, and my grandmother on my father's side was a Scorpio Sun; her husband, my grandfather, although he was actually Sun in Libra, had a very prominent Saturn in Taurus, and I certainly remember him with a very strong Taurean energy around him. He worked with the earth, and ran a nursery where he grew plants.

Audience: Where is the mother's mother again?

Melanie: On the Descendant, which is the 10th house from the 10th house.

Audience: Do you think this has relevance for our own relationships?

Melanie: Yes, it does. After all, our first relationship is with mother, and how that goes is influenced by how her mother before her related to her. And certainly, echoes of this will be found in some of the patterns that we typically run in our 7th house relationships.

Audience: Another question – what is the face without a mask?

Melanie: The face without a mask? Sounds like a Zen question! Well, as I mentioned, the IC is the place where ideally we feel safe enough to go without a mask. But I imagine you may be hinting at something deeper?

Audience: It must be in the chart.

Melanie: Not with an obvious astrological significator, perhaps – but this reminds me of something I wanted to clarify, to do with this idea of sacred space and the four directions. I did mention the metaphor of setting up an altar, with yourself in the centre. The four points, the four angles, are thus always relative to the centre. So when you make your sacred space *you stand in the middle*, and maybe that is the face without the mask. So perhaps the questions, 'Where am I going?', 'Who am I?', serve to pull in our consciousness, instead of action simply going out. The answer to all of them is the same, from the centre. It is just 'I am'.

Maybe this centre is the place of the 'I am'. Well, remember that the circle is the image of the potential wholeness of spirit. The glyph for the Sun in the chart is a circle with a dot in the middle, like the lens of a camera which is like an image of consciousness.

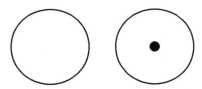

It is the small beam of light for which you are meant to be a prism, or a transformer. It is what you are meant to express. So the chart as a whole is like a larger version of the glyph for the Sun – a central point, usually empty or tracing out the aspects, and surrounded by a circle.

Transits to the Angles

It goes without saying that transits over the angles are very important, especially transits of the outer planets, as they tend to correspond with whole stages of life beginning and ending. This is not necessarily about your biological age, with its particular threshold crossings, nor your connection with society. It usually goes deeper than any surface or visible structure, although there are often significant changes also in the outer world, in jobs, relationships and so on.

Also, consider that the outer planets do not complete one transit round your horoscope, except Uranus, assuming you live past eighty-four years old! You get Neptune going round less than half your chart, and Pluto only transiting one quarter or so, although some people will live long enough to experience Pluto opposite its natal place.

The Last Few Decades ...

So, assuming a lifespan of eighty-four years, and considering where a planet is natally, everyone will get Neptune over one, probably two, angles. But there are people who will not get a transit of Pluto over any of their angles; not many people will see it cross two, with the exception of people who are born at extreme latitudes or with natal Pluto closely applying to an angle. Of course, we do not know the lifespan of an individual, but it is nevertheless worth bearing this in mind when you look at a chart, as the houses, signs and angles recently traversed by the outer planets are often areas of turbulence, present and past.

Think about it – from the 1960s, until about the year 2000, all the outer planets have been moving through the signs from Virgo up to Capricorn, and recently on into Aquarius. So over the last three decades, that segment of the Zodiac, therefore also someone's chart, has seen all the major transit activity.

Sensitised Degree Areas

During this period, there have been a number of powerful planetary conjunctions, particularly in late Sagittarius and early Capricorn, where Saturn made conjunctions with Uranus and Neptune in the late 1980s. They were also conjunct each other in 1993 at about 20° Capricorn. Note that area includes the Galactic Centre, currently at about 27° Sagittarius. This zone is sometimes described as a vortex of energy through which new souls are said to incarnate. As there is nothing new in the Universe, from one point of view, perhaps this refers to souls incarnating on Earth for the first time, although they may have been 'elsewhere' before. This area seems to have a connection with religious direction and vocation. The notion of it representing a 'deeper centre' around which our solar system revolves is very evocative, and it makes me think of Rudhyar's book *The Sun is Also a Star*, where he refers to the 'galactic dimension' of astrology. So the Galactic Centre reminds us that our familiar and central Sun is but one of many stars, beholden, as it were, to a greater context in which it is embedded. This late Sagittarius area also includes the infamous '13th constellation', Ophiuchus, which is associated with information that challenges existing models of the Universe.[12] It was also traditionally linked with healing, especially of plagues, and its image, often associated with Asklepios, the pupil of Chiron, shows a man carrying a snake.

The mid-to-late Virgo/Pisces axis is also significant, as the Uranus-Pluto conjunctions took place there, and were opposed for a while by Saturn and Chiron in Pisces. There are other degree areas, too, like around 27° Libra, which is where the Saturn-Pluto conjunction was exact in November 1982.

Note also that, by transit, Pluto is trailing behind the other two outer planets, which means that all Pluto transits will also be activating previous transit points of Uranus or Neptune. This is particularly important if an angle is concerned, as many people will experience *all* the outer planets crossing any angle located in Scorpio, Sagittarius or Capricorn!

It would be a useful exercise to go through the last few decades and list all of the major conjunctions, squares and oppositions of the outer planets, so that you become familiar with them. If you can get a copy of *Tables of Planetary Phenomena* by Neil Michelson, go through it and mark all those aspects.[13] Or make a list using your astrology software. You might want to first get familiar with the main conjunctions, which will be the most powerful, and which may also take a long time to process, and then include the other aspects like oppositions and squares between the outer planets. I personally would include Chiron and the Centaurs as well. Although Chiron's cycle is only just short of fifty-one years, Pholus has a cycle of about ninety-two years, and Nessus about one hundred and twenty-four years, so half a Pluto cycle.

In addition to checking when or whether someone has had an outer planet cross one or more of their angles, it is useful to get familiar with these sensitive degree areas, because should one of someone's angles fall on any of these areas, oppose or square them, you will know immediately that something very important occurred back then, or will occur in the future. Also, in my own practice, I've noticed that people often seek astrological guidance when they have an outer planet on one of their angles. So the deeper your understanding of this process, the more useful you can be in reassuring your client, giving them some idea of what can be expected, and the timing of it, as well as assisting them to draw on resources they have for the management of the inner turbulence, creative change or other intense manifestations that are occurring. If the transit has already occurred, your compassionate articulation of its themes and meaning might really help your client process any difficult experiences which happened then, or establish themselves more firmly in their new situation.

It's as if the depth of transformation, trauma or threshold crossing that these sensitive degree areas symbolise cannot be absorbed all at once, and the energy becomes 'stored' in that degree area of the Zodiac. To briefly extend our focus – it can be useful to reckon where any of these past major conjunctions took place within the chart as a whole, angles or not.

Audience: How can something be 'stored in the Zodiac'? I mean, it is a man-made construct, isn't it?

Melanie: I do not really know how or why this happens! Also, is the Zodiac man-made? Completely? Is a revelation really the word of God, or it is fabrication of man's imagination? I don't know that either. When I say that information is 'stored' in the Zodiac, I'm speaking metaphorically, of course, but empirically, from observation. As an analogy, if you were wearing Chanel N° 5 when you had a car accident, every time you smell that perfume afterwards, you might be reminded of the accident, even to feeling inexplicably panicky. So is the memory of the accident 'stored' in the Chanel N° 5? Not exactly, but that resonance, that particular stimulation of the sense of smell, has become linked in our brain with that bad experience, the car accident. I think it is likewise with the Zodiac. Perhaps the Zodiac is like a repository of human experience. But I think its sacred images which reflect human experience at an archetypal level also facilitate a raising of consciousness, which in itself 'gives space' and thus promotes healing.

The reason for exploring these sensitised degree areas is that, later on, minor and quick planetary transits across those same areas can trigger a process of recollection, recall or even the repeat of an experience. This is for the general healing purpose of coming to terms with or processing the changes that happened, or didn't happen, and the experiences of that time. This will often be dramatically so when it is on or near an angle.

The Outer Planets by Transit

Transits across the angles do often clearly manifest the meaning of the angle, so I will be concentrating on the most intense aspect, the conjunction. You can extrapolate the discussion to include the square, which will produce an intense drive towards manifesting something, and sometimes conflict between the two ends of the polarity involved. Something will be wanting to happen. Remember also that if a planet makes an aspect with one angle, the opposite angle will also be involved, and sometimes the locus of intensity of the conjunction even appears to be more obvious at the opposite angle.

The direct contact, the conjunction, to whichever angle, will be preceded by a period of very intense pressure and internal or external chaos as the planetary energy accumulates into a push for change. The length of that pressurised time depends on the speed of the planet. In other words, Chiron and Uranus are the two faster moving outer planets and Neptune and Pluto are the two slowest ones. Jupiter and Saturn are faster still. There will be between one and five exact aspects, depending on the speed of the planet, and also how many periods of retrogradation it makes during the sequence. In addition, *the following times of year will be significant for a considerable time before and after a planet is applying to or separating from an angle ...*

1. When the planet stations and turns direction.
2. When the Sun makes its annual conjunction and opposition to the planet. This is useful, because there can be times when the thrust of an energy is blocked during the actual transit, and released gradually during these periods, over the following few years.

For example, the build-up to Pluto crossing an angle goes on for as many as four years beforehand, and sometimes the concrete results of the process do not show in manifestation for another two to four years after the exact transit, depending on how fast it is moving. So when the aspect is separating by about 4° or 5°. If you are working with clients it is useful that you …

1. Know about this time frame, and
2. Find a way to convey that information to the person without getting into what I call 'doom talk', because it is no fun to realise that something that you feel like you are barely surviving in is going to go on for another few years. Of course the intensity will wane, but the need to stay carefully with the process remains.
3. Be aware of the detail, as mentioned above – the dates of the stations, and conjunctions or oppositions with the Sun.
4. Be aware of the 'almost exact' transits which can happen in the prelude and postlude – the year or so before and after they are exact. A lot can happen at these times, which will not show in an exact transit list made on your computer. Using a 45° ephemeris can help with this, or just your common sense!

If you can be with that information in the right way, it is incredibly useful. Then you can focus on assisting your client to find creative ways of settling in for the ride, and handling the process that is going on. Like getting the kind of help you need, or just shaping your life around the process. In a sense all transits 'take as long as they take' on the level of the psyche, because although the obvious astrological timing can be easily seen, and shifts and events occur, the digesting of experience or adjusting to external change can take a lot longer. Remember also that this might be the only time in someone's life that Pluto will transit an angle, so it is an enormous letting go, transition and threshold crossing. Something will leave our lives forever, inwardly or outwardly.

With Neptune transits, the experience itself may not be very focused in time and space, and may be characterised by low energy, nostalgia, daydreaming or the desire to escape, as the longing to refine and spiritualise tries to find its way into the area of life where

Neptune is located. I would consider the main transition to be of about four to five years in total.

With Uranus, a quite different energy kicks in! I use that phrase advisedly, as the pressure build-up and release is often rapid, intense and jagged in feeling. Very few people get through these transits without some insomnia, hyperactivity and uneven energy flow, alternating between speedy and inspired activity, especially mental activity, and then periods of exhaustion as the exciting energy leaves and we face the dishes in the morning! Uranus transits can either be times of intense seeding of ideas for the future, or also times when changes that have been in the offing for a while, on the drawing board, are suddenly precipitated into 3-D! Also, the intensity and speed of events gets to feel 'normal' and it can be quite a let-down when we realise how much donkey work certain changes   may require. So it's sometimes difficult to get a sense of the following:

1. The timing, meaning how long things may take to be manifested, and
2. Whether things are 'meant' to be acted upon now, or gestated further for the future.

Uranus transits to the angles, however, are usually the most accurate in terms of timing, providing the time of the chart is actually correct. In fact, one useful preliminary stage in checking the accuracy of a birth time is to see if any angle has had a conjunction of Uranus to it, and then explore that period of a client's life. Beginnings and endings can be made rapidly when Uranus is active, and the timing is quite remarkable sometimes.

Also, when considering any transit over an angle, remember to also refer to the house and sign position of the ruler of that angle, and also the natal location of the transiting planet. For example, if there is a transit over the Descendant of an outer planet which is natally in the 4th house, you might meet, or re-meet, someone from your home town (the 4th house), or marry someone (7th house) who looks like your father (4th house). You might go into official partnership (7th house) in the family business (4th house reference to the family).

The possible variations are endless, but you'll find that considering the planet's natal position will serve to signify elements of the actual life situation, as well as indicating possible resources with which to deal with difficult situations.

Transits over the Ascendant

Because each of the angles is like an anchor into incarnation, transits over any angle are like a birth, in terms of their process. However, those crossing the Ascendant are very specifically linked with this theme. Remember I mentioned this when we spoke in general about the Ascendant? Well, in addition to the likelihood that residue of our own actual birth will become activated as a planet crosses the Ascendant, each of them also has a unique quality. Like different kinds of birth process.

So, with the Ascendant, whether it is the electrifying, speedy quality of Uranus, or the long drawn out painful quality of Pluto, there is a birth process which sometimes also references the natal position of the planet making the transit. It is a profound emerging from a 12th house period of chaos, internal and/or external, where the trails of the ancestors are finally ploughed over, where bigger cultural and historical themes are encountered, and where the archetypal psyche is met. Then we have to release all that and return to a more individual focus, allow forward motion to develop and new impulses to generate. For some people, the 1st house feels very precarious compared to resting in the ocean of the 12th house, while for others it will be a welcome release. So the question 'Who am I?' is meaningful. We are not what we were, and we do not yet know who we will become.

In order to locate the new aspect of self which is forming, look to the area of the chart where the ruler of the Ascendant is located. Very likely you will find there the activity, new step, innovation or choice that is reflecting the new self. So things may be happening that are powerful, new, challenging, welcome or unwelcome, but it may take time for the new sense of self to catch up with the outer manifestation of it.

In addition, as I mentioned, the themes of any transit will usually include a resonance to where that planet is located in the natal chart. To mention an example, in a chart with Sagittarius rising, and Jupiter in Cancer in the 8th house, Saturn and Uranus both crossed the Ascendant within a fairly short space of time. A marriage ended and a new relationship began, fairly quickly. It was initially difficult for the woman in question to believe in the new person that she seemed to have become within the new relationship, thinking that her newfound confidence was probably just a 'flash in the pan', not a reliable development in herself. Jupiter was the only water planet in this chart, and in the marriage which she left, this woman seemed to carry the deeper feelings for both she and her husband. It was always she who did the expressing, and this was not always welcome. She also had Saturn conjunct Uranus natally, in Gemini in the 7th house, and so this transit was also the birthing of what was already a natal theme. So instead of enduring the feeling of being 'fobbed off', emotionally and sexually, and always being the generous one (Jupiter in the 8th), she asked for a divorce!

Another example is coming to mind, of somebody with late Capricorn rising, and Neptune now approaching to cross the Ascendant. This person has Saturn conjunct Neptune in Libra, and it is in the 10th house, with Neptune exactly on the Midheaven. Now the person has already had Uranus cross the Ascendant. As it is Capricorn, it feels very knocked about by change. It doesn't go 'Whoopee, I've been waiting for this all my life!' It gets brittle and rigid, then breaks and falls apart. This person's Uranus is in the 6th house, in Cancer. So this was the terrain of operation, the locus of the 'Who am I'? question. It was all to do with work, and also some things to do with his family. Because if you don't know who you are, then no work you do 'feels right', and Uranus in the 6th hates routine anyway! The person shifted from creative work which involved a lot of travelling, glamour, stress and excitement, to a more settled life, and initially could not feel comfortable.

With the slower planets crossing the Ascendant, you will have more than one crossing, including periods when it will retrograde back into the 12th house. The feeling may be one of nearly getting born, or of just seeing light at the end of the tunnel, but during the retrograde period you may be drawn backwards or inwards for further preparation, reflection, or indeed the work of changing of structures on the external level.

So, the first crossing is usually when the cards are laid out on the table, as it were. You can often see what the forthcoming sequence of events, inner and outer, is going to be about. Then during the retrograde time, it may be a much more interior process, or a time when that sense of forward motion is gone.[14] So when the emphasis is interior, going back into the 12th house can feel like you have really lost it. This is often a time when people will seek a reading, as it sometimes very disorienting, and you can even feel physically a bit feeble too, with crossings on the Ascendant, which directly affect your sense of embodiment, clarity and confidence. For example, if it is Neptune crossing, and we feel energetic and clear after the first crossing, it is important to pace carefully the creation of new structures, because if we act too soon or try and 'push the river', there will be further disintegration and we will have to start again. It's like sandcastles on the beach, getting washed away because the tide is still coming in.

So the art of 'managing' big transits across the Ascendant is something like what they tell women who are in labour – 'Breathe, don't push!' That's the rhythm of how it goes, and the process requires us to allow something to be birthed in its own time, as well as the external changes which we might have to deal with.

Transits over the IC

Now it is a bit similar when it gets to the IC. The traditional thing you think of with big transits across the IC is that you will move house, or cut your ties with your family. However, having watched my own and other people's transits to this point, what I can see is that the issue is not necessarily anything to do with moving house in a literal sense, although it might be. What I seem to have noticed is that it takes a while, sometimes, so the transit may be just a bit past the angle before you either do the action or make the decision. Or, if circumstances have catapulted you along, like if it's Uranus making the conjunction, then it takes a little while to catch up with yourself and to reorient yourself in the new stage. It was while I had Uranus crossing my own IC that I came up with a pun, and decided that the IC should be called the 'I don't see'! I had no idea how deep these transits would go, and also how illuminating it would be.

So, transits over the IC go right down into that tribal base, clan base and sense of our origins. Often, if it is an outer planet, what actually happens is a loss of roots, or rather a loss of what you previously thought were your roots, which gave you emotional security, and from which you drew nourishment. So for some people that might mean losing a tenancy on a flat they love, it might mean losing their dream house, or being forced to move because of work, or a new relationship will force them into a new living situation where they feel a loss of the previous sense of security. People move country, or leave home, in an enforced uprooting from the things that you thought were going to give you security. This can progress into deeper and deeper and deeper levels of it, until you really get to something pretty formless and mysterious when it is an outer planet crossing the IC.

Remember that this area is naturally ruled by the sign of Cancer, and has a lot to do with feeling and being. So the subtlety of what may emerge can be surprising. It is not necessarily about your bricks and mortar, and often during a big transit across the IC you will have the opportunity to learn how to 'make home' in the midst of insecurity. The emotional level of these transits can initially include feelings of chaos, insecurity, unknowing, lack of direction, discomfort, feeling displaced. And this may or may not correspond with a move of actual location. But often the sense of being uprooted from the past will go on for several years, and present the need for completion, resolution and exploration in these areas. Often the relationship with father is featured, too.

Audience: What orb would you give the transit?

Melanie: As for the Ascendant, it depends on the speed that the planet is moving, but I would certainly consider it within orb when it is 5° or 6° applying, and the same separating. It also depends on the person, and also how accurate is their given birth-time! Some people clearly register their forthcoming transits well ahead of when they are exact. So there is no hard and fast rule, especially in the consulting situation. Usually you can tell through dialogue with your client whether something is registering consciously. Or sometimes through events which are already underway.

With any of the angles, as any planet is approaching conjunction to it, there can be a feeling of intense pressure. That is the time it is most tempting to prematurely or inappropriately externalise something just to take the heat off. Of course this is different from one individual life to another, but probably if you are desperate to make a career move, or to move house, for example, and it is simply not working, the 'action' or rather the 'non-action' may be trying to occur on another level, and what is needed is acceptance and reflection first. I have seen many examples of that in my practice, and indeed in my own life. There the phrase 'Breathe, don't push!', which I mentioned in connection with the Ascendant, can be useful for any major transit to any angle!

Audience: What would that look like in practice?

Melanie: In practice, it would mean finding ways to facilitate deep relaxation, which is not the same thing as collapsing into indifference or resignation. It is a receptive state, actively receptive. So, for example, find somewhere where you can be comfortable to sit and literally breathe! Follow your breath with your awareness. Take it on to another level. That is a very interesting spiral thing to observe with transits to the angles. When the pressure gets really hot, or if you are misdirecting the energy, it will make incredible tension in your body. I think this is particularly true of the IC and the Ascendant, but I'm not sure. It will manifest, somatise, very strongly. It may also be that it is precisely by attending to symptoms that you access sufficient interiority to anchor the next step in your life, whatever that is to be.

Transits over the Descendant

Big transits across the Descendant will often manifest in actual relationship situations, and this can be very turbulent. It can be the time in somebody's life when a long-standing relationship disintegrates rapidly or blows up, when we can no longer be in partnership with someone with whom there is no more mutual growth. Another question for the Descendant is 'Who am I in relationship?' Many expressions of this are possible. One which comes to mind is of someone who swore they would never get married a second time. She was once bitten, twice shy, reached the ripe old age of forty-three, let go of that decision made in her early twenties, and got married again. That was Uranus over the Descendant! Uranus often brings 'the last thing you would have expected'!

So it is not correct to think that Uranus crossing over the Descendant is inevitably going to mean the breaking up of relationships. What is true, however, is that the transit will accompany a strong challenge to your habitual patterns and a prompt to awaken to a new level of consciousness. In the example I just mentioned, this woman gave up the limiting decision she had made in her twenties and got married again. Needless to say, it was a kind of unusual situation with a lot of unusual features, and it was a very individualised and heartfelt decision. It can also be that people who personify Uranian energies will come into our life, to shake things up! This is a curious manifestation of transits in the 7th house. If it is transiting Uranus, this could also be group of people – like astrologers, political activists, those with revolutionary intent and strong ideals.

Remember that at the moment, if you have Uranus crossing an angle, Neptune is following closely behind. That stretches out the period of transition considerably, and blurs some of the issues. However, taking Neptune singly, you might find yourself meeting either one person or a group of people who are very Neptunian. So this could be poets, musicians, artists, drug addicts, healers, people who are attuned to an invisible world of inspiration, ecstasy and spiritual longing. As well as the deceptive side of all this. In other words, you might find yourself coming into contact with Neptune's energy via a relationship with another person, or people.

Thinking again of Uranus on the Descendant, I remember many years ago doing a reading for a lady who had Sagittarius on the

Descendant and Uranus crossing it. She actually had natal Uranus in Gemini, but it was in the 12th house, conjunct Saturn. It was therefore very hidden and she didn't live it out externally. In fact she was rather conventional in her life-style. When Uranus was crossing her Descendant, she went to the pub one night with some friends, had more to drink than usual, and ended up taking home a young man she had just met. He was less than half her age, with green streaks in his hair, safety pins in his ears, leather jacket and trousers, and all the rest of it! They had a wild night in the family home. Her husband had left some time back, so that was not the issue. But she was a very dutiful person, a single mother to four children, and this personification of Uranus entered her life at that moment and put her in a state of shock. It was really touching. She had no desire or intention to pursue any kind of long-term situation with this fellow, who was totally inappropriate as a life partner. But it had the desired Uranian effect! It rocked her structures from top to bottom and literally she was never the same again, because it gave her the courage to step out of other habits. She was able to give equal value (7th house) to a side of herself that had not been lived out – being quirky and expansive and taking risks.

If Pluto is involved with the Descendant, then there can be some pretty tricky things happening in relationships, and a loss of innocence or 'blind faith' in someone can occur. Personal relationship issues that either unfold or begin when Pluto is crossing the Descendant often have a significant element of power struggle but, as Pluto is an outer planet, the situations arising may have collective significance too. I am thinking of an example of somebody who, through all sorts of bizarre coincidences, became aware of serious shady dealings going on in an organisation that was purporting to be whiter than white, and supposedly all about healing and benefiting mankind. He put his own life and resources at risk for several years, acting like an unpaid detective, gathering information, trying to set the record straight. Remember that the 7th house is the place of the lower courts, so sometimes transits to the Descendant will involve dealings with the law.

When Pluto is there one can get gripped by issues to do with justice and rightness, because everything that is not quite right or is downright unjust may be more obvious than usual. That can be on a collective level, but if it personifies in a relationship it may well be a situation where everybody's dirty laundry hangs out and there is no getting away from it! At the same time, it can be deeply transformative. I have known a number of people who have started therapy when Pluto was near their Descendant. So their life-path took them into a transformative and therapeutic relationship with another person. There are different ways in which that can happen. A therapeutic relationship is one way. An intimate partnership is another way. And it can be that deep changes begin occurring within an existing relationship that either destroy it completely, or transform and regenerate it. Or a mixture of the above. That sort of process may go on a long time, with a build-up of intensity as Pluto gets to the end of the 6th house and moves to conjunct the Descendant. Often the 6th house prelude will include strong body tensions, and physical issues will start showing the way. As it moves into the 7th house, another stage opens up.

Often, where we have been 'taking everything upon ourselves', which is a 6th house tendency, or putting ourselves 'one-down', there may come a huge equalising thrust as a planet crosses the Descendant. Then the relative ease of one-up/one-down relating, which occurs in the 6th house, just will not do, and we enter the battleground. In the 6th house, we can sometimes get ill rather than confront things interpersonally, but when the Descendant is stimulated, a doorway opens into a new and exciting territory, where we discover who indeed we are in relationship.

Transits over the Midheaven

Remember that the 9th house is the place of possibility, so transits to the MC comprise a very interesting shift. Note that anyone who has Uranus and Neptune making this transit will of course have had many years of 9th house stimuli preceding it, including the conjunction of 1993. I have seen a number of examples where this sequence eventually became massively ungrounding, because there was too much focus for too long on the potential, the possibility, the inspiring vision of the future, to be able to ground in a way that satisfied the MC requirement of putting things into shape and form. Too much luck, opportunity and enthusiasm can be as difficult to manage as not enough! With intense 9th house transits, it may be like living in the future, or in the realm of possibility. People who do well with this energy seem to be the ones who have found some sense of philosophical and spiritual meaning, either deeply personal or perhaps also echoed through some particular teaching, possibly 'foreign', another 9th house theme.

Now because Uranus and Neptune dissolve or explode forms, part of this journey can be the changing and rearranging of philosophical structures and major beliefs. If you have any cherished yardstick of meaning which you hold too tightly, you may need to relax your grip, otherwise you might lose it. So incredible flexibility is demanded of us in this 9th house area. You may have to give up long-held beliefs, or you may finally shed some ideas in which you only half believed, but didn't have the momentum to think out for yourself. You have got to think it out for yourself when Uranus hot-wires the 9th house. To call Uranus 'individualistic' can be misleading, because after all it is an outer planet. I think of it as a voltage, a resonance that supports the breaking away of our individuality from the density of our collective and Saturnian structures.

So this pressure, as an outer planet transit approaches the MC, can be enormous. Some people find it depressing and strongly resist the shift, which is from potential to form, into the real 3-D world, into what's actually possible. Some of you will have heard me use this phrase before – 'After enlightenment, more laundry!' Obviously the 'enlightenment' is the 9th house phase of the transit, and then the 'laundry' happens in the 10th house, because it is where you get down to making something happen. Where you land. So the MC is also about landing from fire to earth, from potential to actuality, dealing with the limitation of the fact that although potential is unlimited, it is not possible to manifest everything.

So, as planets cross the Midheaven, you have to let go of all that potential, for the sake of manifestation, focus in the world and fulfilling your purpose and ambitions. Some people really enjoy this, and find it satisfying and energising. That doesn't mean you can't also enjoy a sense of possibility at the level of 'Wouldn't it have been wonderful if ...', but once the planet has crossed the MC, if you indulge in that to the point where it drains energy out of your commitment to the present, then a backlash may happen. Backlash in the form of depression, or unexpected obstacles, delays, restrictions. Saturnian lessons that are designed to bring one into the present, really, and out of the future.

Audience: If somebody has their Pluto square and it is transiting the MC, but natally just at the beginning of the 7th, that is like a 'double whammy', because then all the angles are involved.

Melanie: That's a good point, thank you. Did you all follow that? At the midlife transition, Pluto squares Pluto, Neptune squares Neptune, and Uranus reaches the opposition to natal Uranus. Now if one or more of those outer planets already sits on an angle, then you are going to get some very potent activity during that time. That also reminds me of something else – if the angles themselves are roughly square each other, all angles will be picked up each time any planet transits the angles. That means the nearer you are born to the Equator, the more likely it is to happen.

I have also seen a number of charts where people have had, say, Pluto on the MC and Uranus-Neptune crossing the IC. Or variations on this theme, with other angles. Births fairly far north, which have one angle in Capricorn and the preceding one in Scorpio, may have had this. Needless to say, when outer planets touch two or more angles at the same time, it usually means big changes, sometimes a radical ending of many things at once. An entire chapter of life may close, and may be a time of huge loss and also huge gain, but it is a long and often stressful transition to negotiate, and it may require a long mourning period afterwards, although for some people this will have been mainly felt beforehand ...

Audience: You don't see the gain immediately.

Melanie: No you don't, necessarily. You sound like you are speaking from experience of this?

Audience: Yes. I have had exactly this sequence, which is not over yet. It has been about ten years already.

Melanie: What have you found that has helped you the most?

Audience: Well, I have Taurus on the IC, and I had to learn to mobilise myself from my inertia and 'make home' as you put it, on my own. I had the laissez-faire attitude of Taurus, and it was financially convenient to continue living at home.

Melanie: If it works, why fix it!

Audience: Yes, but when Pluto opposed this point, conjunct my MC, I started to see more deeply into what was happening, and how this was a trade-off that actually had a high price tag attached. I could no longer afford to be there, because of the price I was paying in other ways.

Melanie: I love the Taurean way you have described this process, in terms of money and value.

Audience: As Uranus and Neptune began to stimulate my Ascendant, I realised that I could not sacrifice my need to find my own way in life and to build structures that were mine. It was all very graphic. Even the theme of authority, too. I realised that I had to become my own authority.

Melanie: Thank you. Anyone else?

Audience: I have 13° Scorpio rising, so Pluto crossed my Ascendant a few years ago, and after that squared my natal Moon in the 9th house. It is all a process.

Melanie: Can I ask you – what transit Pluto is now making?

Audience: It is square my Sun, which is in the 4th house in early Pisces. I actually emigrated. I have just sold up my house and I am moving to the States.

Melanie: So there's the 9th house Moon connection.

Audience: Yes. The process of seeking further afield and looking for where I should live began when Pluto squared the Moon. Now that it's contacting the Sun, I have made myself temporarily homeless. It feels as if this planet was heralding disruption even as it crossed the Ascendant, but the action is only coming now.

Melanie: Your story is also an example of how long the process can be. It takes a while to really learn the lesson, get the teaching, get used to whatever it is that this new shift has been about.

Audience: What I am actually doing now is experiencing the loss. Leaving my home has been a painful process and now I must let go of that – like leaving the loss. My experience when I actually left the house, and gave away everything, was like being born.

Melanie: That's a wonderful experience. Thanks for sharing that. Anyone else?

Audience: Your example of trying to do something in the material world and it not working was part of my process. What I have done is similar, but different. I gave away all my clothes. You can buy new clothes. Everything didn't fit, so it had to go.

Melanie: The Ascendant as the self-image was being transformed. To follow that example, if you had a fixed idea in your mind that this should be an internal process, then you would have been less able to deal with the things going on around you.

Audience: May I add something? It's as if the process happened on other levels first, but the interior process is happening now that I have sold my house.

Melanie: This is an example of having planets that are picked up in sequence just after a planet has finished transiting an angle. So you can also look to the first hard aspect made by a transiting planet once it gets over the angle.

Audience: Before, it felt like preparing the ground. And the word 'compulsion' is so true. You are pushed into a world you don't expect.

Melanie: Yes. It is like you are being birthed into something when the angles are involved.

A Guided Imagery Exercise

Introduction

To shift gear now, this last part of the afternoon will be focused around a guided imagery exercise which I will do with you. First, I want to check if there is anybody here who has never experienced guided imagery before? Several. OK, I'll explain briefly. What I will be doing is a semi-guided journey with you. It is like participating in an imaginary story which will be based on the work that we have done on the angles.

What I will do first is a simple relaxation exercise. It will be a sitting up exercise, but done with closed eyes. Then I will talk you through a sort of guided journey. What is very important with this work is that you don't try and force anything. There is no 'right way' to respond. Allow my words, the images and the metaphors, to provide a kind of container for your experience coming from within you in the form of images, sensations, thoughts, feelings.

Now, visual images are not necessarily something that you see in Technicolor behind the lids of your eyes. Very few people see images in that way. More often it is a felt sense of something, or a fleeting thought, or a memory, that comes into your mind. It can also be a felt sense in a very physical way. Don't ignore any of those signals and remember that, whatever happens, you can't fail at this exercise! It is just an opportunity to see how your own interior process might respond to the images and the storyline which I will talk you through. So just allow the experience, and let it unfold as it will.

I will talk you through the exercise and out the other side, and then I will leave some time aside immediately afterwards, when I would encourage you to write as much detail as possible about your experience. It is a funny thing, when you do guided imagery, or any closed eye work, things may seem obvious at the time, but when you are at home tonight you may realise that the whole thing has disappeared from recall, which can be frustrating. Or you might drift back out and think 'Oh, yeah, I found myself thinking about this tree. Oh, well, I don't suppose that is very significant,' and dismiss it. Later on you may get a glimpse of an important meaning, but you may not be able to recapture it!

So, think of this exercise now as a way to enter your own sacred space and trust that what happens in there is what is meant to happen at this time, this place, this here and now. If the structure of the exercise really makes no sense to you, then no matter, just dwell in your own space, but stay tuned in if possible. Keep your senses internally alert. To withdraw from the experience at any time, just gently open your eyes, and take care not to disturb the person sitting next to you. Nobody should get up and leave the room until the exercise is complete. OK? Any questions? No?

Audience: You didn't have time to mention Chiron crossing the Ascendant.

Melanie: No, I didn't. I am not sure whether I will, but I will try. It may come up in the course of the processing afterwards, but I actually meant any questions about the guided imagery! Here we go ...

The Exercise

OK, let's begin.[15]

I would encourage you to sit with your feet and legs uncrossed. Put the soles of your feet on the floor and get yourselves as comfortable as you can. For some of you that might mean leaning back into your chair, while others might want to sit up. Either way, get yourself feeling as neutral, as physically neutral, and as relaxed as you possibly can … and begin the process of changing gear now, by becoming aware of your breath …

Experience the weight of your body on the chair and begin releasing any areas of pressure or tension in your spine that might have collected over today with the concentration. Allow yourself to gently take a couple of deep breaths and focus more on the exhalation, by allowing it more time …

Exhale further and further and further … breathe out residual effort and concentration. Let yourself sink into a comfortable and relaxed position in your chair. Make the choice, if you will, to be present now with yourself in your inner sacred space. So turn your attention inside …

Let yourself just enjoy the experience of sitting right in the middle of your own sacred space …

Now I'd like you to imagine that you fall into a light sleep, a pleasant, drowsy sleep that makes you think of warm summer afternoons or evenings. So you fall into a light sleep, into a kind of reverie, and when you stir from that reverie you realise that you have woken up in the same place but it is no longer the same place. You are now in the magical landscape that lies behind the world of form. You realise that in that magical landscape you are sitting in the centre of what seems almost like a crossroads. There are four paths that lead from the place where you are sitting …

Now, somehow you know that there is a gate, or a door, or some kind of entrance at the end of each one of the paths. You wait there at the centre, and in time you will get a sense that one of these directions is calling to you, almost like an invisible tug on your sleeve or a current of energy drawing you down that path. However the signal comes to you, allow yourself to be called down one of these paths …

And if you choose to now, just imagine yourself walking down the path, the path that has beckoned you, chosen you for today's exploration …

And as you go down the path, just notice anything along the way, what kind of terrain it leads you to, what the weather is like, any other people that you might meet along the way …

Notice also how you feel. What emotions are with you as you go down this path?

Then, at some distance, you begin to see a dwelling of some kind. Just take whatever comes … this dwelling could be anything from a castle to a burrow, a hole in the ground.

Just allow the shape of this dwelling to show itself to you. As you arrive before the entrance of this dwelling, get a clear sense of this place. It may not be a human dwelling; it may simply be a place in nature …

But it certainly has an entrance and you wait outside this entrance, noticing its character, and eventually somebody comes from this place which you are to visit, whatever it is, however it looks, somebody comes to fetch you inside …

A person who is like the guardian of this place comes to take you through the entrance and into this place … It could be indoors, outdoors, whatever, just take whatever comes.

Walking along, if this feels appropriate now, just ask this figure, or this person, who they might be and what it is that they might be wanting to show you at this time … then wait for the response, which might come in words or in some other way. So here is a guide for you, into this terrain. Here is your chance to get to know that guide a little bit, to also see whether there is anything that you need to know at this time …

[Long pause.]

As you walk along with your guide, take note of the details. Are you inside, or outside? Notice any objects or plants or other people or animals that might be around and continue to leave open the communication lines with your guide … just leave them open …

You may want to ask the question 'Why did you call me?' and wait for the response, knowing that it may come in any form, and also it may not come immediately. If you wish to, ask to know why you were called to this terrain, this place ...

[Long pause.]

Begin now preparing for the return journey. So look around for the last time for now.

Perhaps there is something that you need to see that you missed ...

Take a last look now and, as you begin to walk back towards the entrance with your guide, think about a gift that you would like to give. Whatever you wish to give, you will find that you have it with you. You may have forgotten about it, or it may materialise as you need it. You have it ... it can be a material gift or a gift of the spirit.

Now you thank your guide for all the things that you saw, and for the dialogue and communication, and you give your gift to your guide ... and he or she in turn gives you a small gift to take with you through the doorway back into the other world. And so allow yourself now to receive this gift ...

See how you feel ... let it become clear in your imagination so that you can easily remember it, and bring it back with you if you choose to.

You are arriving now with your guide at the entranceway to this area, as you will journey on alone, back to the centre place again. You exchange farewells ... you express your gratitude, and now you leave through the entrance, and you go walking back down the path into the centre of the crossroads where you found yourself sitting, and you sit down once again at the centre of the crossroads, carrying your little gift.

Sit down, centre yourself on the ground, on the Earth, feel the sky above you and in your own time begin making the transition from this magical sacred place back into the room, into the here and now.

You may want to do so by focusing on your own weight as it presses on the chair, and becoming aware of your breathing, and then little by little begin to take in the external sounds. Become aware of your neighbours. Just gradually let yourself reorient, first through the physical senses, feeling the chair underneath supporting you, then through your ears, hearing the sounds around. Then when you are ready, open your eyes slowly. I would suggest open them halfway first, and in that twilight place, give yourself some time now to write about that experience. See if you can draw the thread of the experience out with you as you go, as you write.

[Time allowed for personal writing.]

Some Processing

For any of you who might want to share part or all of your journey with us as a group, what I would do is just put your main astrological significators on the board. I won't write up your whole chart, as we are focusing on the angles, but it may happen that most of the chart will anyway come into the symbolism of what happened for you, or the content of your journey. So we will just play it by ear. Is there anybody who would like to do that, to discuss your journey?

Audience: I got a picture I don't really understand.

Melanie: A general remark first. With guided imagery, it doesn't matter if you don't understand. It is one way of interfacing with the inner world of the psyche, which often speaks in ways that the rational mind cannot understand. It may be that in two days, two months or two years you will understand or it may be that you won't. I think that engaging in the process yourself is at least half of what does matter, because a great deal goes on in our unconscious that never does become conscious.

I don't know the quote exactly but Jung apparently said that what people forget is that the unconscious is unconscious, and always will be, because there is always more! There is no end to it. That is a great comfort, especially if you are somebody who really needs to understand things and you get a dream or a piece of imagery that you don't understand at all.

Also, in that journey, when you go into that magical other realm and find yourself sitting at the crossroads, obviously the four paths were the four angles. So you might find that whichever of the paths you were called down does indeed correspond to one of your angles.

So, can you orient us with some astrology to provide the background for your experience?

Audience: I have a Taurean Sun in the 7th and Leo at the Midheaven. Sun in Taurus, and I went up.

Melanie: So you went to the Leo Midheaven? The place of the Sun, which is in the 7th house in Taurus.

Audience: I have Saturn on one side of the Midheaven, and Pluto and Mars on the other.

Melanie: They are all in Leo?

Audience: No, Saturn is in Cancer, and the other two are in Leo.

Melanie: Can you tell us a little about the journey and what happened for you?

Audience: It starts on the path. There is a very dry white dusty road, uphill.

Melanie: May I comment as we go? Can you already see the imagery there? It is uphill – to Saturn's angle, the MC. This is an uphill struggle and it is hot and dry – this is fire – Leo Midheaven.

Audience: Across the hill was a building, like a farmhouse, but then I realise it is more modern.

Melanie: Building (Saturn), farmhouse (Cancer) … but then you realise it is more modern.

Audience: Yes. It has got great big windows that you can see right through to the back of the building and out beyond.

Melanie: You will have recently had Uranus opposing this Saturn by transit, and Neptune following along soon, almost there now. But in terms of your chart, how would you associate that? This image suggests something Uranian, or Jupiterian. There is an element of vision, transparency, space, perspective. Where does that come in? This chart has Jupiter right on the Ascendant and it aspects Saturn. So first a big building, quite spacious, more modern than you had first realised.

Audience: I have no idea what its purpose is. I don't think it is a farmhouse, it doesn't look right.

Melanie: Can you see the chart speaking? 'I had no idea what the purpose was' – 9th house Saturn. 'Thought it was a farmhouse' ... this 9th house area is naturally ruled by Jupiter which is rising. So continue with your story ...

Audience: Eventually a young man comes to the door in jeans and a T-shirt and he looks very like a young Gerry Adams.

Melanie: What's his demeanour?

Audience: It is totally neutral. He is inscrutable. He is not unpleasant, but he is completely inscrutable the whole time, throughout the whole session.

Melanie: How's that for a Mars-Pluto figure? With Mars-Pluto, we think of explosion and violence, because most of us read too many newspapers! But in fact what is even more common on an individual level is a sense of pent-up energy and intensity, where nothing is showing most of the time, but a lot goes on under the surface. How else would you describe Gerry Adams?

Audience: Threatening.

Melanie: Potentially explosive, potentially dangerous. But as you say, also inscrutable, not offensive, or alarming. That is very Plutonic actually.

Audience: He has a public face.

Melanie: Like the Midheaven is the public face. So then what happened?

Audience: Then he takes me across this hallway and there is a games room. I thought 'So what? What am I doing here?', and I sort of asked him why and he just shrugged, not unpleasantly but like it wasn't his job to tell me. His job was just to show me round. Now I see that's why he wouldn't accept my question. Then we go down some little steps, and we are tremendously high up, and there are little platforms, like tree houses.

Melanie: So you are effectively making a descent, although still high up.

Audience: Very steep. And it takes ages to get to the bottom. When we do, it is suddenly as if I'm in there. One moment I'm up above and next I'm on the ground. Lush, but not terribly tropical with a wide shallow river. Beautiful, peaceful and very green.

Melanie: Note that the Descendant is Aries, even though the Sun is Taurus. Mercury is also in Aries, so the Descendant and Mercury are both disposited by that Mars. There is something interesting about him not responding directly to your asking him to help you gain some meaning out of the process. He just shrugs and says he is basically just doing his job, which was showing you round. Remember the Midheaven is about authority and power issues. Perhaps his attitude is significant. Is he perhaps saying, 'Well, I'm not here to show you that, actually.' Or 'How could I possibly help you with that, why me?'

Audience: That's more what it was. He wasn't being unpleasant. It was more like he was showing me that it was my issue, I chose to go there.

Melanie: Reflecting on it now, how do you read that?

Audience: Well, I would like to understand what it was trying to tell me. I feel completely at sea with it.

Melanie: Perhaps continue with the story. How did you return?

Audience: We didn't have to go the same way we started, but came round the back of the property. Although we climbed down all the stairs, coming back was just going round the back. So I didn't have to struggle up all those steps, because suddenly there I was.

Melanie: There are two further things I'd like to mention. One is about the fact the MC is on the parental axis, and is usually mother. This scenario may be showing you some residue that belongs to your relationship with your mother, which may have affected your own attitude about vocation, success in the world, authority and so on. The other thing that occurs to me is that perhaps his response might itself be the teaching. In other words, perhaps his manner is implying something like 'You know the answers, don't give it away.'

Audience: Don't give authority away to someone else!

Melanie: Exactly. Midheaven questions do revolve around authority issues. If that area is very loaded, getting the balance is a large part of the work, because it is easy to either take on too much, or try and find ways to shrug off the pressure of authority on to someone else. Or to rebel or avoid.

Audience: It is like a 'Catch 22', that Pluto-Mars. The feeling is that if I come to the surface, they hold me down and if I don't, I get trodden on anyway.

Melanie: That's part of the loop. Wherever Pluto is, these 'Catch 22' experiences can occur, because there is no way through except transformation, surrender into the unknown. As Saturn is involved, I know that you can say 'Yes, but I have seen it happen to me for real, in my life, I know that this is how it really is,' and I would not doubt you for one second, but I would also say that once you have located the 'Catch 22', then you are really in the territory of transformation.

Audience: It feels foggy.

Melanie: You feel foggy?

Audience: I can't find a key to it ...

Melanie: Well, with Mars and Pluto in early Leo, you will very soon be experiencing Uranus transits opposite them. Perhaps they will provide the key you are looking for! As this transit comes from the 4th house, and Neptune is trailing behind, opposite your Saturn in the 9th house, it's perhaps not surprising that you feel a bit foggy at the moment. Neptune is making fog in the background, like a stagehand with the dry ice. Here is the theme of perspective and vision, too. Think about your house with the windows. If we include the imminent transits of Uranus in Aquarius to your Mars and Pluto, and think about Gerry Adams again, could it be that he is also embodying and demonstrating an attitude of detachment? Something which you need in order to allow these energies to move? That's the stock in trade of Uranus transits. There is something we have to detach from, something that has become too restricting. It is as if the transit is saying 'Give it up, stop it, move on, you've got to detach.' What do you make of the bit where it's clear you don't have to go back by climbing all the same stairs again, but suddenly you are there? That is a very interesting ending.

Audience: I'm beginning to see that perhaps my own struggle to understand is what sometimes gets in the way. Maybe these transits will be about trusting what I don't know I know! And something about my personal sense of authority in my life.

Melanie: Saturn in the 9th – the struggle to understand! Maybe the fog of Neptune is the accompaniment to the dissolving of your entrenched beliefs about your own knowing – it is transiting over Saturn in the 9th house. Perhaps you can learn to 'get there' without such a struggle. Trusting that the meaning will show itself, that something within you knows. Thank you for exploring that with us.

Is there anyone else who would like to describe their journey?

Audience: Yes, me. I knew there would be a crossroads – I get to a beautiful little white house.

Melanie: Can you hand me your chart please, so that I can comment on the astrology as you describe your journey.

Audience: It was far away, but there was a little lamb which I think was killed.

Melanie: I will mention a few points now, to refer this image to the astrology. Capricorn, the goat, is on the MC, and Aries is rising. 'Far away'… a few years ago, Uranus and Neptune both crossed the MC, which is at 13° Capricorn. Intense transits like that could well have felt like the strong goat becoming the sacrificial lamb, and that image also applies to the sign of Aries. So already your imagery is anchored very strongly on two of your angles. But there is something more immediate, too, if you check your transits for today. Your natal Chiron is at 23°18' of Capricorn, in the 10th house, and natal Jupiter is at 23°36' Cancer in the 4th, a very close opposition. And this morning, when we started, Mars was at 23°39' Aries, having recently crossed your Ascendant, and also having made exact squares with this axis over the last few hours. Which angle do you think you went to, as three are already implied?

Audience: I think first the IC, then I came up to the MC, which was another house. This one was made of brick, elongated, no doors. Windows without glass, very dark, and I knew that I had to enter it through the windows. Suddenly I realised that it was a spacecraft. There were no creatures or anything, and I wasn't frightened. I was touching the walls for a long time, the brick walls. They were solid. Something was guiding me. I said 'What do you want from me?' and they said 'We want to take you from here.' I said 'Who are you?' and they didn't show me. I thought, 'Well, they are like midgets.' Then I said 'Well, I have to leave now.' They said 'You can't leave.' I said 'Well, I'll fly back,' and they suddenly turned into monsters.

Melanie: And then?

Audience: The whole thing turned into black jaws. Black holes. I wasn't frightened, but I felt physically sick and like I might die. I had to fly with my back to them to return to where I was before, in the meadow of green. I gave him a little white marble and a white daisy, also for my daughter. Then they said they would give me something and touched my arm. They put on it a blue band, which would give me power. Then it felt horrible to come back.

Melanie: As I am listening to you, what seems very prominent is the energy of Uranus.

Audience: Yes, at one point during the experience, I was thinking that too.

Melanie: Let's consider the Jupiter/Uranus/Chiron again, that axis being exactly stimulated today. Even in the sign of Cancer, Jupiter-Uranus is a high-voltage combination, and can be high-voltage feelings. Uranus is the planet of electricity, shock, the unexpected, that which is strange, alien. You even got space imagery. Spacecraft, space beings, alien energy, etc. By transit, it is not that long ago since Uranus was opposite your own Uranus, and Neptune is there now. So, in other words, you have had a very strong stimulus from Uranus by transit, to your own Uranus, as well as strong energies of change moving for a long time through Capricorn, conjunct your MC, and now, quite recently, your Chiron too.

That is going back a few years, but wherever Capricorn is we don't really like change, even if we know it is for the better. All of us have had potent transits over many years through our Capricorn area, because Uranus and Neptune have been there, along with several companions at times. When Capricorn is on the Midheaven, it is really exposed and vulnerable up there, and doesn't have an easy time rolling with the changes. Capricorn tends to go into 'coping' mode and grind along, or tense up and break. So now the pressure is beginning to release from that, as the transits sequence to all your angles and planets in Capricorn is concluding.

I imagine that you may be releasing stored up stress, and also experiencing an introduction to something strange, alien and unknown. Your own Uranus is in the 4th house, with Jupiter, and this may be a reflection of changes in consciousness that you are going through, now that some of the external pressure is subsiding. All the Capricorn activity was public, exposed, but this may be bringing it back home, to the 4th house, the private place in yourself. That is where you were returning at the end of your imagery process.

Audience: I was not frightened during the imagery, but I am frightened now by what I have seen.

Melanie: Yes, I noticed how you said several times that you were not frightened. I remember thinking how brave you were! I wonder whether you are now beginning to feel the fear that you could not feel before, as you had to just keep going? Fear is one of Saturn's 'normal reactions', and the feeling and releasing of it can be a very empowering rite of passage.

Around Saturn's position, or Capricorn planets, we can sort of 'collect' fear, and sometimes it is only when the pressure starts to release and things calm down that we suddenly feel the fear. While everything is happening, you can be too scared to even feel the fear, so you don't even register it because, if you did, you wouldn't be able to cope. When you are better able to feel it, when things are easing up, this incredible fear can come up. I have noticed this time and time again. Does that make sense to you?

Audience: Yes, this does feel like something past, that I must now somehow feel.

Melanie: Also, your Saturn is in Scorpio, conjunct Venus in the 7th. If we think of Saturn as our style of defending ourselves against fear, Scorpio is a fixed sign so it doesn't get hysterical with fear. It goes first into bravery, survival instinct, and then into dread and horror, which is what you did. That is a prototype Saturn in Scorpio reaction, except it doesn't always process right through to the deep feelings of fear of annihilation, which are in the Scorpio terrain. If you can, I would suggest you take some more time this evening with this. Don't push the fear away, but you don't have to escalate it either. See if you can just sit with the fear and breathe through it.

Audience: I just want to cry.

Melanie: Are you a person who easily cries?

Audience: No, not really. I mean, I keep thinking I should be, because I have Moon in Pisces in the 12th house. But other people's suffering is easier to feel, to cry about, than mine. I try and be tough a lot of the time, for a lot of people, family and others too.

Melanie: Maybe that's what you need to do, like a releasing of energy. Crying can be the expression of many different things, and you may be experiencing a release from tension that has accumulated over a number of years. Also, remember that your Moon is very early Pisces, so Pluto is squaring it now, and that may be just what is needed to help dissolve old fears.

Audience: I never ever had that – I mean, so much imagery.

Melanie: It may have released some energy on that mental level, which then allows space for your feelings. If you look at the chart for today again, you can see that several planets are aspecting your Neptune, so no wonder your imagination was so stimulated! Today, the Moon is in Cancer, opposite Jupiter and Neptune in Capricorn, on the very axis we have been considering, plus making squares to your Neptune; and the Mars that we mentioned already. Oh, yes, the Nodal Axis has recently crossed your Ascendant/Descendant axis as well, with the transiting South Node in Aries.

Audience: It does feel like new beginnings, but I am not good at letting go of the past. My Jupiter and Uranus are not conjunct the IC, but when I was in my teens, we left our home country and came to live in England. We left everything. It was a complete and total change, language also. It was very difficult for my mother, and I became a mother too very young, although I did not want a child yet. I managed, but it was hard. Now I see she is OK I feel so relieved.

Melanie: Thank you for telling us about your experience. Anyone else?

Audience: I'm still thinking about Chiron crossing the Ascendant …

Melanie: OK ... I'll say a few things about this. Remember that Chiron will have been going through the 12th house before it crosses the Ascendant. The connection with the 'ancestral field' is already a very Chironian theme, and so when it crosses the Ascendant, light may be shed on our ancestral legacy. This is about differentiating ourselves out of the matrix of our ancestral past. People often have important insights about their 'deeper past', and this can include ancestral patterns or 'past lives'. This arises not so much as something we need to 'work on', but rather as insight about what is being released. That is often an important distinction, as it can be quite shocking sometimes to realise the degree to which we've been living out the unfulfilled hopes and dreams of our parents or ancestors, or indeed blindly repeating the same patterns.

In one way or another, Chiron crossing the Ascendant is a time of awakening and healing, and often involves the letting go of false self-images, too, which can be very relieving. Particularly if that involves 'false heroics', where we've come to believe we always have to be strong, have others depend on us, and so on. Remember that Chiron's famous wound was accidentally inflicted by Hercules, an archetypal hero. So the experience and expression of our Ascendant shifts from the more masked, ego-version of the energy to something wiser and more compassionate. We sort of 'grow up' spiritually, a little!

I see now that we are fast approaching the end of this day, and so I would like to thank you all for participating so fully, and for your questions and input too. I hope also that the continued processing of your experiences during the guided imagery will be useful.

Thank you!

Part Two: The Nodes of the Moon

This seminar was given on 24 November 1996, at Regent's College, London, as part of the Diploma programme of the Centre for Psychological Astrology. The transcript was later augmented by material from similar seminar events and classes given at various venues in the UK and elsewhere.

Introduction

We have a whole day focusing on the Nodes, and this has been a very interesting seminar to prepare. I was amazed at the number of sub-themes this material led into.[16] Predictably, as today was arriving, I had to make some decisions about how to keep us more or less confined to the practical consideration of the Nodes in the chart, and themes that have direct bearing on that! So there will be times when we will wander a little down a trail and then back off, because of the time constraint. Today, in addition to reviewing some familiar ideas about the Nodes, I hope to introduce you to some new ideas, possibilities, techniques and connections which you can explore further on your own afterwards.

As always, I would invite you all to consider your own horoscope first, with any new material, and see how it works for you. If astrology is to be a useful aid to deeper self-knowledge, it means that the techniques and perspectives which we learn are best anchored in our own understanding of how that dynamic works in our own chart, our own life. Some of you will have heard me say this before, but this is another 'DIY day'![17]

Firstly, I want to give you an idea of the material I hope to cover today. I'll begin with some astronomical descriptions, which are very important for understanding the Nodes. When you study a planet, there is a 'thing' there in the sky, with a huge body of mythology, imagery and astrological tradition woven around it – the planets are rather definite and have been well elaborated over thousands of years. But the Nodes are not solid 'things' in space and this makes a difference to what happens in your mind when you start the process of thinking about them ... you focus on the *multiple inter-relationships between things*.

So, first the astronomy, and then a review of some background material about the Sun, the Moon and the Earth, as the Nodes consist of the relationship between these three bodies. Then we will look at the symbolism of the Nodes and their meanings, and I will suggest some ways to focus your own attention when you are looking at them in charts, and also when you are using your own chart to accompany your own inner process of self-enquiry. This morning, I hope to present most of the actual information, then we'll do some group exercises and experiential work later on. I will also mention eclipses, although we would need a whole day to do justice to that topic. Here again, with eclipses, our focus will be on the practical use of the information.

Sun, Moon and Earth

So off we go on the Nodal journey. As I'm sure you know, the Nodes are an axis across the chart with a north and a south end. It's easy to remember which symbol is which, because the North Node points up, while the South Node points down. The Nodes are composed of factors that involve the relationship between the three primary bodies – the Sun, the Moon and the Earth. The Luminaries and our 'Home Planet'! The Nodes are found where the Earth's orbit around the Sun, the Ecliptic, is intersected by the Moon's orbit around the Earth. If you keep remembering that – Sun, Moon, Earth – it cues you in to what the Nodes are about as a thematic axis, although they also lead beyond that, as we shall see.

The Equinox Points

The Nodes have an interesting relationship with the equinox points, 0° Aries and 0° Libra, spring and autumn respectively, in the northern hemisphere and the reverse in the southern hemisphere. *The equinoxes are the points during the year when the Sun appears to cross the Celestial Equator. Similarly, the Moon's Nodes represent the points where the Moon crosses the Ecliptic, on its journey round the Earth.* In each case it is like the symbolic 'middle' zone is involved.

The symbolism of the seasonal turning points, where day and night are balanced, may be referenced as we consider the meaning of the Nodes in the chart. As we shall see, the motif of *dynamic balance* is an important and useful one for the Nodes.

Some Astronomy

Let's look at a simple diagram of the Nodes ...

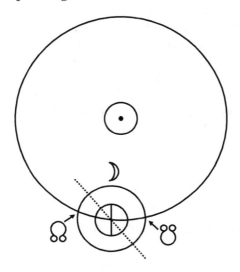

The Nodes – not to scale.

This diagram is drawn as if you are looking down on the solar system, if you can imagine that. You can see the Sun at the centre of the diagram, and the ring around it represents the orbit of the Earth around the Sun. The symbol for the Earth is the cross inside the small circle. Around the Earth, the pathway of the Moon is drawn as another circle.

The astronomy doesn't diagram out so easily, for several reasons. Firstly because the orbits of all the planets are more or less elliptical, and also because these circles actually represent planes. The plane of the Moon's orbit is tilted at about 5°, relative to the Ecliptic, so the Nodal Axis could be pointing in any direction, not only as drawn.

An ordinary New Moon occurs when the Sun and Moon are on the same side of the Earth, and an ordinary Full Moon occurs when they are opposite each other, with the Earth in-between them. Also, the Moon will be quite far from the Ecliptic, in other words, on the furthest part of its upward journey or downward journey on its orbit around the Earth.

However, depending on the time of year, and thus the tilt of the Earth relative to the Sun, an eclipse will occur when the Sun and Moon are positioned on or near the Ecliptic, so both aligned with the Nodes, which are positioned on either side of the Earth. As I mentioned, we will look at eclipses in more detail later. For now, I want to give you a simple description of what the Nodes are, to emphasise their connection with eclipses, and also to introduce the fact that even a superficial understanding of them will reveal mystery and complexity. It's like they lead us out of the ordered structure of the solar system, and our Earth-based Soli-Lunar identity, into something beyond.

True Node and Mean Node

In fact, the True Node, which is not listed in all ephemerides, wobbles to and fro, sometimes direct and sometimes retrograde in motion. You can see this clearly on a 45° graph:

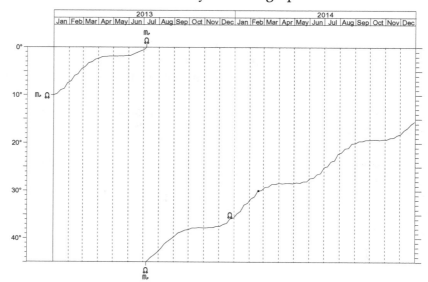

We usually think of the Nodes as always travelling retrograde, an even 3' of arc per day. But that's actually the Mean Node, or the nodal positions averaged out over a long period of time. However, the True Nodes weave about and their position can differ from the Mean Node by as much as several degrees.

I personally use the Mean Node, so that is what I will be referring to in this seminar. However, I have found it useful to check the True Node positions if the chart you are considering has the Node very near the end or the beginning of a sign, because there might be a difference. Also, if the transiting Node is about to change sign, the True Node position might change some months earlier or later. Likewise, if you consider transits or progressions to the Nodes, there will be a difference in the timing. When the Progressed Node is changing signs, the difference between True and Mean could even be measured in years, which can be very interesting! But apart from these specific situations, I mostly use the Mean Node. In charts that I am studying in great detail, I like to know where both sets of Nodes are – True and Mean – and then I can watch transits more accurately, because it sometimes broadens the range of time when the transit is active.

Audience: Is there a regular rhythm of the True Node changing direction?

Melanie: If you look in the Ephemeris, you will see that mostly it moves in one direction for about two weeks, sometimes less, sometimes more. Occasionally, it changes direction quickly, after only three or four days. I understand that the Nodes are more often retrograde when the Moon is waxing than when it is waning, but that there are a number of complexities, including the difference between the True and Mean positions of the Moon itself, which will mean that this is often not the case.[18]

More Astronomy

Remember these three – Sun, Moon and Earth – are all in motion in various different ways. That's where this 'wobbling about' comes from. In fact, the more you think about it, the more incredible it is that the solar system doesn't just fly apart! There are so many checks and counterbalances that keep the solar system as we know it intact, with all the planets orbiting around in such a way that the movements are predictable. It is truly extraordinary, and by contemplating the Nodes you get some idea of that mystery.

For example, if we were to try and show some of this on our simple diagram, then, for it to be correct, we would have to show the polar tilt of the Earth, varying according to the season, inclining more towards or away from the Sun, depending on the time of year. Also, the Earth is spinning on its axis, and the Moon is travelling round the Earth, spinning on its own axis too, in such a way that relative to the Earth it moves in a ratio of 1:1. In other words, the Moon spins in synch with the Earth, so that approximately the same face of the Moon is always seen by us on Earth. However, the Earth spins in such a way that we have seasonal variations of temperature and light throughout the year, as it orbits round the Sun. The Nodes, then, concern the relationship between those three things: the Sun, the Moon and the Earth.

Some Numbers

I'll read out some numbers to blow your mind! The scientists do periodically revise these numbers up or down, so they are only 'factoids', really, but here are the latest estimates:[19]

- The whole solar system is moving in the direction of the star Lambda Herculis at a speed of 12 miles per second (20 km per second), assuming a frame in which everything else is standing still. This is 45,000 m.p.h. or 72,000 km/hr.
- The Sun (and therefore the whole solar system with it) is moving downwards, out of the Milky Way, at the rate of 4 m.p.h. or 7 km per second. It is positioned about fifty light years above the Galactic mid-plane, which it last crossed about two million years ago.
- To complete its daily rotation on its axis, the Earth needs to rotate at a speed of 1000 m.p.h. (1600 km/hr).
- To complete its annual revolution around the Sun, the Earth needs to travel at 67,000 m.p.h (104,000 km/hr).

Nodal Wonders

Now I have a handout for you. Please take one and pass them on.[20] This is one of the trails which we will wander down a little, and then back off!

As you can see, this material comes from Robin Heath. Do read his books, of which the most well known is probably *Sun, Moon & Stonehenge*.[21] I had some very interesting conversations with Robin, and the result of one of these was a wonderful set of cartoons that he sent. I redid them as a handout for today, which I'd like to explore briefly now, so you can get an idea of how significant is the movement of the Nodal Axis through the Zodiac.

The top circle at the left is like a bird's-eye view, and a geocentric view, of the Earth. Around it is shown the circle of the year with 365 days, and the Sun going once around this circle in a year. If you focus on the North Node, in the second circle from the left, you see the Sun and the Node meet once a year. Now, the Sun moves roughly 1° per day – the actual maths is underneath there – and the Node moves in the other direction. That is obvious, as the Nodes go retrograde, backwards, while the Sun goes forwards through the Zodiac. You can see that in your diagram with the two circles. The Sun goes one way, the Nodes go the other way.

Relative to the Zodiac, then, the Sun and the Node will next meet just over 18 days before their previous meeting point. Do you see that? Furthermore, it takes 18.618 *days* for the Node to transit backwards through 1° of the Zodiac and 18.618 *years* is a Nodal year, in other words a Nodal return. As if that wasn't enough, it also takes 18.618 *months* to transit one sign of the Zodiac, all of which I find quite mind-blowing. The bottom part of the page is about the *Eclipse or Draconic Year, 18.618 days shorter than a solar year*. The rest you can read and enjoy at your leisure.

When we are considering eclipses, we sometimes forget that they are actually alignments of the Sun and Moon with the Nodal Axis. Robin's information also serves to remind us that the eclipse season occurs about 18 days earlier each year. It will mark out a specific degree area, an axis across our horoscope, when the Sun conjuncts the North Node and South Node in turn. These are the only times when eclipses can happen, and the 'eclipse seasons' occur twice each year.

Audience: What do you mean by an 'eclipse season'?

Melanie: We will cover eclipses in more detail later on, but in brief ... eclipses usually occur in pairs, one solar and one lunar, but this can vary. However, although there can be more than one eclipse of either kind, there are always two weeks between them, because eclipses occur at either the New Moon or the Full Moon. So, in practice, the 'eclipse season' lasts from a few days before the first eclipse in the sequence to a few days after the last one.

The Astrological Glyphs

If you think about the Sun and the Moon as the two 'primary lights', or 'luminaries', as they were called in traditional astrology, and combine this with the Earth, it gives you an idea of how the symbolism of the Nodal Axis is related to the theme of physical conception or incarnation, the product of the union of the two opposites, male and female, father and mother, here symbolised by the Sun and Moon.

In astrology, all our symbols are made of very simple components, like circles, dots and lines.[22] Our glyphs are like a kind of celestial alphabet. There are hieroglyphs and petroglyphs ... and we have astro-glyphs. We read them like runes, or like a language, and their shapes inform our intuition. So, the circle is an image of wholeness, the wholeness of spirit, or what hasn't yet been put into form.

It also includes what is already in form, as it encompasses 'everything'. It both contains empty space and also symbolises totality because it is a container, a round thing itself. In astrology, our symbol for the Sun is a circle with a dot in the middle, and what we are indicating is that the Sun is like the individualising spark of light, reflecting a greater wholeness which is ultimately invisible. On the physical level, on Earth, we get most of our life energy from the Sun, which is at the centre of our solar system. On the spiritual level, we can see ourselves as animated by a small flame or light which has its origins in the greater unnameable light.

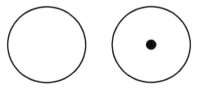

The astrological metaphor for this is that the Sun and our solar system revolve in turn around a still greater centre, the centre of our galaxy, the Milky Way. We are actually way out on one of the arms of its spiral form. I am sure you have all seen pictures of that. There are many galaxies, too, and it is also possible that the Milky Way revolves around an even greater centre, which in turn may revolve around another ... and so on into the realm of 'multiverses' rather than 'universes'! But to return to our humble Sun ... it is like the lens, or the prism, through which we see the light refracted from the greater whole in which we are actually embedded.

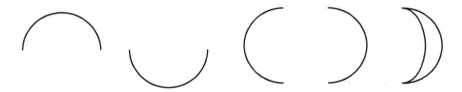

The half-circle is said to be the symbol of soul, because it symbolises duality. It has two points. It is also a line, but with a beginning and an end, unlike the circle, which has no beginning and no end – it is one unending line. Therefore the circle symbolises eternity, timelessness, or things that endure and continue forever. It goes beyond time, really. But a half-circle, a line, has a beginning, a middle and an end. So it is about temporality, and is closer to the world of form, because likewise all forms have a beginning, middle and end. They have duration in time, and dimension in space.

You can think of a half-circle as receiving, depending on which way you draw it. Upright it looks to me like an ear, or an echo, which implies listening. It can be drawn curving over, like an umbrella, a cover, or a container allowing something to pour down. Seen the other way up, it is like a containing bowl. A mixing bowl, a fruit bowl, a bowl for cereal or soup. All these images imply reception, response, giving out. A half-circle also implies exchange, whereas the circle doesn't, because there is no break in the line. It is whole in itself.

The symbol for the Earth in astrology is an upright cross within a circle. Unfortunately, this same symbol is often used for the Part of Fortune, although now you often see the cross drawn with two diagonal lines.

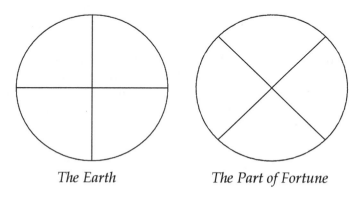

The Earth   *The Part of Fortune*

If you superimpose the Earth symbol on the symbol for the Sun, the resulting circle will still have its dot in the middle, but could also be imagined as showing the different phases of the Moon, or perhaps the tilt of the Moon depending on the latitude from which you are viewing it. So, all the symbols for the Sun and Moon are implied and contained within the symbol for the Earth or, indeed, vice versa!

Now, what about the symbol for the Nodes? As you know, it consists of one line, looped around itself, making two small circles on either end. It is like a circle cut open, and the two ends are wound back on themselves. What do you make of that?

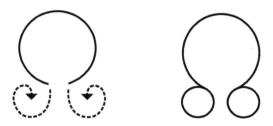

Audience: It looks a bit like the symbol for Leo.

Audience: I see it like a gateway.

Audience: Or an arch in a garden …

Melanie: Going back to our primary symbolism, if you think of the circle as the wholeness of spirit, here the circle is cut, and sort of opened out. Perhaps we could see the Nodes as symbolising the gateway to a higher consciousness which goes beyond the individual level but includes it.

Audience: The Nodes are called the Dragon's Head and Dragon's Tail, and I just saw the symbol as a dragon.

Melanie: Oh, yes, of course, I never thought of that! We will actually be exploring the image of the dragon later on. When I'm wanting to indicate the North Node to a client not familiar with astrology, I sometimes refer to it as the 'headphones icon'! First I used that analogy just because it looks like that. Then one day it dawned on me that perhaps this also had meaning, in reference to the North Node – that it is a place where we receive and act upon 'invisible instructions'! Where guidance reaches us through the airwaves, as it were!

Your Earth Sign

In Esoteric Astrology, the system of Alice Bailey, the Earth's position is included, located precisely opposite the Sun – this notion is probably borrowed from Heliocentric Astrology where of course the Sun is not shown on the chart as it depicts the sky from a sun-centred position! When we look at the Nodes, their meaning can be amplified by considering them relative to the themes of the Sun and Moon in the horoscope. I would invite you to also include this 'Earth position', as I think you will be surprised at the insights it can provide.

If you think about it, the Sun, being the source of all light, is also the main planetary body which casts shadows. A bright Moon will also create shadows, but they are rather different in quality, tending to be more diffuse and blending objects together in the somewhat shadowy night world. And, of course, the Moon's light is anyway reflected from the Sun. When the Sun shines on an object or a person, the shadow connects directly with the space behind them, or on the Earth itself. It also has a link with the psychological concept of the 'shadow', meaning that which is behind you as you face the light of conscious intention, and which you may not see or know. In some cultures, there is considerable reverence for the shadow, and it is said that to injure a man's shadow can wound or even kill him. There are folk tales of people who lose their shadows and have to go on a quest to find them again. It's like a parable of soul loss, and has a parallel in the psychological concept of the shadow, which we need for the sake of balance and wholeness. It is usually thought of as containing the more archaic layers of the psyche, which may be feared by the ego, or the more 'adapted' aspects of the personality.

In astrological terms, you can see some of this in the sign opposite your Sun, which is your 'Earth sign'. The qualities of your Earth sign can anchor, ground and support the Sun sign, in the same way that the physical shadow falls on the ground, and the psychological shadow may need to 'fall on the ground of life experience' in order to be seen.

Audience: How would you use the Earth sign in a horoscope?

Melanie: Firstly, by simply including it in your awareness. For example, remember that any transit that affects the Sun will also affect the Earth. Secondly, if you want to explore the Earth sign in your own chart, think about your relationship with the opposite sign to your Sun sign. Many people have at least one important relationship with someone of their opposite sign. It can be any kind of relationship, but it has powerful resonance and a reflecting quality, often holding up a dark mirror, or having a quality of fascination about it. Someone who we can clearly see is very different to us, and yet with whom there is a curious and subjective sense of similarity. The Nodes themselves have a great deal to do with relationships, the kind that shape your life on one level or another, and which impact strongly on you.

Earth is both central to the Moon's orbit, and also peripheral to the Sun, travelling around it. Here is another pair of opposites that is symbolised by the Nodes: the relationship between the centre and the periphery. This is another trail that we can only peek down, but suffice it to say that the whole of creation seems to show this dynamic. Think about it ... the solar system, the cellular world and the world of subatomic particles all demonstrate this.[24]

Sun, Moon and Earth – the Image

Consider again the relationship of the Sun and Earth for a moment. In Egyptian mythology, the Sun god Ra was said to travel across the sky every day in his solar barge, and then enter the underworld at night, when his warmth and light disappeared. In other mythologies too, the movement of the Sun across the sky is symbolically linked to the hero's journey. When night falls, the hero god must battle a dragon, or overcome an enemy who would seek to chain him in the underworld, thus preventing his daily resurrection at dawn and reappearance in the eastern sky. In the imagination of humanity, sunrise has a profound association of victory over dangerous and potentially death-dealing forces, the enemies of light and life, so that rebirth can safely occur.[25] The mythological version of this astronomy sees the solar hero undergoing the ordeals and trials of symbolic death, renewal, threshold struggle and rebirth into the daylight world. The Sun may go across the sky by day and then disappear, but it is always the same shape. It always looks the same, unless there is an eclipse or it is obscured by clouds. So it has come to symbolise and model the eternal, as that which may die, but is reborn, unchanged, each morning at dawn. Clouds come and clouds go, and night also comes and goes ... but the Sun remains.

We can see this image in another way, as the Sun, the primary light, being renewed by immersion in the darkness, and the light of the darkness is of course the Moon. By contrast, the shape of the Moon is always changing. In fact, if you watch the Moon regularly, you can see the difference every night. Its times of rising and setting also change quite rapidly, as do the points on the visible horizon where it appears and disappears. It is amazing ... to me it feels like it's weaving a protective net around the Earth. Hence the Moon comes to symbolise that which changes its shape, appears and disappears, and yet there is rhythm and regularity if you observe it *over time*. The constancy is revealed through time. Do you see the contrast with the Sun? The shape-shifting Moon comes to actually symbolise the world of form, where everything changes shape, including us. We start out very tiny in the womb, growing at an incredible rate; we continue growing vertically and quickly until our teenage years; eventually we may shrink or bend as we get older. All forms wax and wane, like the Moon.

The Nodes, then, signify the relationship between the Sun and the Moon as complementary opposite principles, how they seek to manifest or what they generate. That's their relationship to Earth. We can think of the Sun as 'father' or the masculine, the Moon as 'mother' or the feminine, and the Earth as the 'child'. The Nodes, being concerned with the combination of these three factors, also symbolise *that which leads us beyond the immediate mother or father image* that we have encountered through our actual parents, and which will be modified over time from experience, and through our connections with authority figures. I think this may be why the Nodes are sometimes called 'the axis of destiny', leading us beyond our origins, through the gateways of the opposites we must encounter en route, progressively refining them through an inner alchemical process, as the archetypal and spiritual levels of the masculine and feminine relate, unite and separate. The 'spiritual Earth-child' that results is perhaps the ground of being from which we arise as individuals.

The Moon

Now I'm going to review briefly the Sun and Moon in the horoscope, as understanding their symbolism is important for the Nodal Axis. Starting with the Moon, it shows where and how we blend and adapt. It is a place of response to, and reflection of, the outside world, because it is where the habits and emotional patterning of our origins are stored. So we can retreat there and sometimes we will do this instinctively. Gut responses are linked with the Moon, and they can serve to inform us and support our primary lines of defence. The theme of nourishment – of ourselves, others and our life in the world – is connected with the Moon, as are our issues around home, place and belonging. In the lunar sense, the desire to retreat also brings in our sensitivity to rhythm, and knowing when it is time to wax, or time to wane, to rest or be active. All being well, that kind of rhythmic intelligence is housed in our Moon position, astrologically, and our actual relationship with the Moon's cycle through the calendar month. It is through lunar intelligence that we know when it is time to rest, when enough is enough, or when we need more of a certain food, be it physical, emotional, mental or spiritual. If you think about it, at the basic physical level, we all need roughly the same things in order to survive: food, water, warmth, shelter, human contact. But when we consider the 'soul-needs', which help us thrive rather than just survive, it gets very interesting because we are all so different in our needs. These 'soul-needs' are signified by the Moon.

To take a very obvious example, if you have the Moon in Cancer, you are happy and contented when there is a feeling of closeness, familiarity, bondedness, continuity and intimacy. If your Moon is in Aquarius, however, there may be ambivalence about this and, although you want this intimacy, you need and feel you must also have your own space, whatever that means. For some people that means living alone, for others it means periodically taking time out from primary relationships. You have to find your own way, but this need for space is there just like any instinctive need. For Moon in Aquarius, the need for *mental freedom* is as important as the Moon in Cancer's need to collect family photographs to show the next generation.

There is an instinctive way of reacting with the Moon. On the plus side, it can be where our instincts for nourishment and security work well. However, that can be overlaid by the quality of our early relationship with our mother. The Moon refers to our experience of our mother, and thus reveals the whole nexus of patterning around our expectations of other people, nourishment and intimacy. It also shows ourselves as a mother. Whether or not you have children, the Moon will show how you engage this instinct, or how it engages you. How you give and receive nourishment on various levels, including to yourself. How we 'self-mother' and look after ourselves.

For example, Moon in Aries is what I call the 'animal mother'. I don't know if you have seen films of a lioness playing with her cubs? She will be lying there quietly, and the cubs seem to have plenty of freedom and space to play about, but if one of them gets out of line or goes towards danger, she will pounce and whack them back to safety. Mothers with Moon in Aries have very strong fighting instincts, protective on behalf of the young, the vulnerable, the innocent. They will fight tooth and claw to ensure the well-being of their cubs, their children, their creative projects, whatever they are nurturing.

I want to say something about 'self-mothering' too, which is also signified by the Moon. We may find that our capacity to provide for ourselves, both physically and also at the level of soul, is influenced by the background patterns of our relationship with mother, and indeed there is a great deal of healing that can occur in this way ... You had a question?

Audience: Our experience of our mother and the way we are going to express our mothering, the continuity of the line – how can it change?

Melanie: The recognition of our experience is the first step in being able to go beyond it. For example, let's say you feel you are a certain way because your mother did or did not do X, Y and Z. While on one level that may be absolutely true, it is never the whole picture. Here is a true Moon in Aries story. This person was nervous about other people showing their anger, and actually did a lot of placating of others – the Moon was opposite Neptune in this case. Her mother was someone who showed her feelings passionately, often by getting angry first, which left my client, as a child, feeling very jangled and insecure, because she experienced her mother as a very aggressive woman. Much later she began to realise that this was not aggression like in a personal attack, but often her mother was aggressively protective on her behalf, and generally over-emotional. Her mother would show anxiety and concern by getting quite vociferous or explosive, leaving her feeling frightened and wounded. She gradually realised that her mother did not intend to be aggressive, but was reacting out of her own habitual reactions, which may have had a long history. She also had strong protective instincts, good intentions and volatile passions. Initially, however, all this fire had left my client more identified with her own Neptune, rather than her Moon. Later in her life, with her own children, she was forced to grow out of this identification, and had to learn sensitive ways of expressing this Moon in Aries. One of the things she did was to run a playgroup, where the Aries dynamism and qualities of initiative did very well, and the sensitivity and imagination of the Neptune also found a positive outlet.

Recognition of what is happening is the first step in being able to move beyond it, but the means is through letting go, not through trying to force change. Remember that from a Moon point of view there may be resistance to going beyond what is known, because the Moon looks for continuity and security, so what is familiar exerts a strong pull. The Moon in the sky goes through its changes, disappears, but it always comes back. That is a wonderful metaphor for the development of the internal image of a 'good enough' mother – she may change, she may go away, but she always comes back. Doesn't that also remind you of when you think you have left something behind, it seems to disappear, then it turns up again like a bad penny? Of course it is never quite the same. However, the more you try to change something, from the Moon point of view, the more it stays the same.

Audience: Some people react to the way they were mothered by doing something different.

Melanie: Yes, indeed. And sometimes you can tell that from the chart. I am thinking of examples here ... one woman with Pluto exactly on the MC, and lots of fixed squares to it, has dedicated herself to just that, and seems to be doing very well. Another has Chiron in the 10th house, squaring the Moon in Taurus, and had a very difficult time with her mother. However, the Moon is in a mutual reception with her Venus in Cancer, and she found the inner resources to go very far beyond this when she had her own children. It is interesting that you often find that both the negative inheritance and the positive outcome are symbolised by the same thing. In my first example, the expression of Pluto on the MC was transformed from an experience of huge oppression and negativity from her own mother, to a commitment – that's very 10th house – to transforming this. The intensity of Pluto was dedicated to her own inner process, and not wanting to simply repeat patterns. For example, when her first daughter was reaching puberty, having already had years of analysis before, this woman went back into therapy to help her separate and rework the memories of the difficulties she had experienced at that time.

Also, her Moon was in Aquarius, on the IC, and you can see this shift from the difficult aspects of her origins to the more positive expression of that Moon. Her own mother had been experienced as oppressive, controlling and also alternating between being quite cold and rejecting – that's the Moon in Aquarius – and being moody, negative and sometimes volcanic – that's the Pluto in Leo. She also experienced her father as distant, although kindly, and she longed to reach him. With awareness of her own similar tendencies, she was able to find a different expression of this opposition. Her Moon in Aquarius loves and uses astrology to help her understand and work with herself, and also her children's charts. She also became rather focal in a background way in her children's school, as many parents would come and speak to her about their concerns. This is very Aquarian – being involved with the group, the network, the social system. Her style of mothering was indeed very spacious, and through her own inner work she had developed a high level of trust in her children's growth and integrity, and had learned not to be over-solicitous and interfering in her anxiety to get it right.

Trust versus mistrust is shown by the Moon, and it is also where we are like everybody else, where we touch the common humanity in ourselves and in others. It rules the digestion, and so it also shows our style of processing experience. This is useful to understand, because if you don't process experience, you can get emotionally or mentally constipated, like if you don't digest food you get physically ill. Some brief examples … with Moon in Gemini, you may need to pick up the phone or meet up with a friend and talk, to make an experience real and absorb it by reflecting upon it, but also to have the input of somebody else, to have a dialogue, or write in your journal. Without at least one of those possibilities, insecurity breeds. Moon in Scorpio may brood in solitude, or make sure that everybody else knows there is an emotional issue going on, but will not necessarily speak about it. In this case, someone attempting to draw them out prematurely will not only create insecurity, but may get to feel the Scorpion's sting, too. Moon in Virgo may tend to get manically busy with all kinds of practical things. Any of these done with awareness can be a good way of giving yourself the time and the space to allow the processing to occur by itself. We don't consciously digest food – the body will do it for us, unless we interfere!

The Sun

Now let's consider the Sun. The Sun in the chart reflects a fundamental creative urge to be oneself. But what does that really mean? Because we are a culture very oriented around doing, when we use words like 'individuate' and 'purpose', mostly we mean something you have to do, a task, a mission, like 'What I am supposed to be doing? How can I fulfil my life purpose?', meaning 'What is my task?' However, this is only half the picture. I think the Sun is as much about *being* as it is about doing. Both the Sun and the Moon have their being and doing sides, but it is perhaps more obvious with the Moon, giving and receiving nourishment, waxing and waning. The Sun is usually considered to be yang – active, positive, dynamic, masculine. To round out the picture, and include the inner and spiritual levels, I think you have to extend your definition to include the 'being' quality that is perhaps like a radiance or invisible sense of inner vitality. This also has dynamism, actually, but it is not about action.

When you are 'on beam' – there's a nice solar phrase – life is purposeful and you feel vital and centred, almost regardless of what's going on. If you are in a muddle and things aren't the way you want, that may impinge on you but, at the core, it's all right. Even in the midst of emotional turbulence or external difficulties, there is an inner radiance you can turn towards. This contrasts strongly with the state of feeling 'en-darkened', when externally everything looks fine, and yet somehow your inner light is eclipsed. Do you know what I am talking about? With the former, there is still that sense of pulsation, of life force, and this is what it feels like to be simply in touch with the Sun, the centre inside yourself.

Now when we translate this state into 'doing something', we have the more active side – purpose and self-expression. If you have the Sun in Libra, you seek to fulfil your sense of direction and purpose through the aesthetic, through relationship, through ideals involving justice, harmony and balance. You know the picture. But the actual quality is as important as what we do with it, and I think that's the part that we often leave out. After all, the Sun just shines. Here on Earth we do all sorts of things with that light, but the Sun is symbolic of a still and radiant core centre, as well as the active flames leaping forth from its surface.

I would like to refer to the work of Rudhyar here, as we will look at his chart later. He writes in a wonderfully poetic manner about the Sun, and talks about the various layers of the physical Sun relating to different dimensions of being. Here we go ... this is entitled 'The Song of Light'.[26]

> *The heart of the Sun is the unknown deity, the photosphere, his robe of glory. Light is the effulgence of this glory, it is the song of the celestial hosts, conveying to the outer world the inner reality of the One, who is the beginning, the middle and the end of all there is in the solar system. The supreme integrator, the all-encompassing and compassionate one. Light is the compassionate gesture of God towards matter, the flow of love which ever redeems the residue of the past. Light is the call to life.*

I find that just exquisite. You can see, I think, how the notion of being, at the fiery core, is like the power source sending all the convection currents which create these pyrotechnics on the outside, the corolla. The flames flaring off the surface of the Sun may be like the fire that seeks to manifest in action, expression or doing. You can't really 'do your Sun sign to order' in the sense of complying with something, following orders or trying to get acceptance or approval. That does not help your Sun to shine, as it is a more Saturnian thing, to do with achievement or duty. The Sun just shines. It just is, it radiates, and doing flows from that.

So the Sun is a source of vitality, where we also seek to develop and express the creative principle. If the Sun is underdeveloped, we see it shining in others and we don't like it because we want to shine too. Then we envy it, and want to destroy it, eclipse it or undermine it. That is the shadow side. The shadow side of the Sun has to do with very uncomfortable feelings of envy and also narcissism. Narcissism is the state when we have to be the centre of the universe, with everything related to our own reality, and it can stem from a lack of early mirroring. If you are in this state, everyone else must be the Moon so you can be the Sun, so you reduce others to the condition of only existing to reflect your glory. This can range from the gross and obvious, to very subtle states, where we are convinced that our own emotional reality and interpretation of events is the absolute truth of the matter, and we edit out everything else.

Envy occurs when you stand only in the eclipse, or in the shadow of the light, of what you desire. Initially, we might be in the shadow of our mother or father or both, but in an envious state we are always in a condition of feeling scarcity, lack, want and emptiness, without sufficient sense of substance.

Audience: What about jealousy? Is it the same?

Melanie: Although the dictionary definitions blur the difference somewhat, a useful way of differentiating the feeling states is to consider that envy occurs between two people, and jealousy between three people, or 'objects'. In other words, if I am jealous, I fear that someone will take away something I have – something I value and even identify with. But it is *something I fear losing or feel insecure about*. Another woman might steal my boyfriend, or a rival might outdo me professionally, taking away my position in centre stage. Jealousy usually involves sex or power, and it sort of relates to feeling possessive. These jealous feelings may prompt us to try and oust or undermine the third party, the one 'responsible' for our painful feelings.

However, envy is a feeling stemming from a lack, real or imagined. Someone has something, or indeed *is* something, that we do not have, or cannot be. It has the additional charge of wanting to destroy the envied object and incorporate it, devour it, so that it will be ours forever. Wanting what we don't have, or *imagine we don't have*. With murderous jealousy, we want to get rid of the offending person. However, with envy we are in a double bind – we can't do that because at a deeper level the envied person represents some precious aspect of ourselves, projected. This person has or is what we desperately want. Melanie Klein writes a lot about this, describing how envy is based in the feeling of primary separation from mother, and the complex feelings of emptiness, need and dependence that a baby has towards her. There is also the paradox that we envy what we desire most. If something gives us pleasure, in its absence we may feel envy towards it, and 'destroy' it in our minds. This can poison our connections with others if it is completely unconscious. Many a good relationship, project or possibility has foundered under this feeling, especially if it is unrecognised. Both envy and jealousy have to do with loss, or fear of loss. However, the deepest level of envy is about the loss of self, which is projected out.

Sun themes are about identity and the feeling of having the right to exist, to just be, without having to prove it all the time. The Moon is more about security, nourishment and issues on the feeling and emotional level, and to do with bonding and merging in relationship. The Sun is about mirroring, affirmation and appreciation of difference. In daylight, the edges and differences between objects is obvious, but by night, or moonlight, things blur and blend and lose their definition, appearing more unified.

Audience: Is there such a thing as an 'underdeveloped Sun'?

Melanie: Thank you for asking that … I think it's more about our *awareness* of our Sun being underdeveloped. To be in touch with the Sun is a subtle thing, to do with feeling a simple sense of our being, our existence, and allowing that to shine. It's not necessarily about being centre stage, being brilliant and shiny and spectacular. If you received enough affirmation of being 'central', particularly from your relationship with your father, then your radiance was affirmed, and it is then easier to get in touch with that yourself. You can almost forget it, take it for granted, like mostly we take for granted the miracle that the Sun will shine every day.

Audience: Why is this kind of affirmation to do with father?

Melanie: I think for the simple reason that, whether you are male or female, you spend the first nine months of your life inside mother's body. So father is in a better position to affirm your separateness and individuality, and in this sense he is always 'other'. In indigenous societies, boys nearing puberty will go through elaborate initiation rituals which remove them firmly from the sphere of the mother, and introduce them to the world of men.

Audience: In astrological terms, how can you assess the condition of the Sun?

Melanie: Traditionally, the Sun is said to be in detriment in Aquarius, and it falls in Libra, so let's look at domicile first.

If the Sun is crowded by aspects from other planets, especially from Jupiter outwards, then it can signal difficulties. The outer planets blur the boundary of the personal, and bring in elements of the collective, or what is larger than personal. That can bring creativity, inspiration and power, but it is not necessarily conducive to the development of any sense of personal inner light. To take another obvious example, if the Sun is in a hard aspect to Saturn, then it may feel chronically eclipsed, having to prove its own worth through achievement and activity designed to compensate for this feeling, trying to fulfil the deeper need.

Audience: Which is what?

Melanie: To be in touch with our own inner light. To feel that simple radiance. In the words of Ram Dass, it is like 'Doing your being'.

Rulerships

I discovered something very interesting about the rulerships of the various planets and signs linked with the symbolism of the Nodes. They concern the relationship between the Sun, Moon and Earth, as we have seen, with the additional reference of the two equinox points, ruled by Aries and Libra respectively. In traditional astrology, Jupiter was said to rule the North Node and Saturn the

South. So if we use traditional rulerships, look at this pattern of connections ...

Planet	Dignity	Exaltation	Detriment	Fall
Sun	Leo	Aries	Aquarius	Libra
Moon	Cancer	Taurus	Capricorn	Scorpio
Earth	Sagittarius (esoteric ruler)			
Rulers of signs mentioned above				
	Sun	Mars	Saturn	Venus
	Moon	Venus	Saturn	Mars
	Jupiter			

See the Mars-Venus cross-connection? And also the Jupiter-Saturn connection? I find this quite lovely, because it is another way of describing the linking and balancing of opposites, the alchemical process implied by the Nodes. The result of these various unions is symbolised by the Earth. The Nodes, then, *show what stimulates the invisible work of the soul, and where and how it seeks to manifest in form.* In this sense it is indeed 'the axis of destiny'.

The Nodes

You are probably aware that some astrology books give the impression that, in order to evolve, one has to move from the South Node to the North Node, or that the South Node is the past and the North Node the future. I hope that the preparatory material on the Sun, Moon and Earth will have served to begin broadening this definition a little.

Some Reframing

First of all, I am not questioning the assumption that what we are here to do is evolve – I will leave that to the philosophers! – but I am certainly questioning the assumptions about what this might be implying, because unfortunately the idea of 'evolving' can easily become linked with a rather exclusively solar, masculine view, with left-brain dominance and 'progress-ism'. If we unwittingly view the Nodes from inside those cultural distortions, we become part of the problem, rather than part of the solution, which I believe may lie more in the idea of a fluid and dynamic balancing of opposites, an exchange between them, and of inclusion rather than exclusion.

Thinking again of what the Nodes consist of, although they represent the inter-relationship between the Sun, Moon and Earth, they are also *not* these bodies, but are rather like gaps, holes, points in space which I think of as windows into another kind of space/time. In physics, there is this idea of 'wormholes', which in my rudimentary understanding would seem to represent the interface, entry or exchange point between parallel universes. Perhaps the Nodes are like the wormholes of the chart, leading us into incarnation, and also leading us beyond the forms that we identify ourselves with, pointing the way into another dimension of consciousness.

These are some of the reasons why I think that the straightforward linearity of 'from and to', or 'past and future' or 'good and bad', is not the whole story. Moreover, you will find that it doesn't work too well in the actual life stories represented by charts – life rarely consists of things which go in straight lines! To use that framework too simplistically can be to impose a static view of something which I believe to be far more interesting and subtle, as I think you will see if you take the time to focus deeply on your own Nodes. I will be suggesting some ways of considering the Nodes, not exclusively based on the traditional linear view.

'There be Dragons ...'

As I pointed out before, when you study the planets you can draw on a huge body of tradition, mythology and associated images. When it comes to the Nodes, however, the main image seems to be the dragon, or serpent, which crops up in many diverse mythologies, some of which are specifically linked with cosmological themes. The traditional Latin names for the Nodes are Caput and Cauda Draconis, the head and tail of the dragon, North and South, respectively. These names may have come from the myth of the ancient Babylonian god Marduk, the equivalent of Jupiter, who was said to have created a great dragon which carried six of the signs of the Zodiac on his back, and six on his belly, like a great uroborous coiled around the Earth. His head and tail cut through the Ecliptic, at the Nodes.

In Vedic astrology, the Nodes are called Rahu-Ketu, the Chayya Graha or 'shadow planets', and are considered to be very powerful, as they can blot out the light of the luminaries, the Sun and Moon. So they specifically reference them as the *eclipse axis*, and are said to be like the thread of karma which ties us to attachments such as Desire, Passion, Anger, Intoxication, Greed and Jealousy. The path of awakening cultivates sufficient non-attachment to these instinctive states so that we are gradually freed. The Nodal Axis references this process, which is also envisioned as the arising of the serpent energy of the Kundalini. We can think of the Nodal Axis as a kind of spine, an axis of orientation in our incarnation, as borne out by the astronomy. And as this is cleared of 'shadows', it helps our lights to shine – our Sun and Moon.

Rahu is the name of the North Node, and Ketu the South Node, and there are many stories about them, but one of my favourites is the one told by Komilla Sutton in her book *The Lunar Nodes, Crisis and Redemption*. This one features a Naga, or demon, called Vasuki, ruler of the nether regions of the Earth. The Nagas in Hindu mythology are snake-like creatures, with great wisdom and knowledge, but also demons, nonetheless. A marvellous ambivalence.

So 'once upon a time', there was a war between the gods and demons for control of the Universe. This battle centred on the ocean, which was being churned to find the precious Amrita, the nectar of immortality. Vasuki had helped the gods by literally becoming the rope tied around the spiritual mountain of Mandara, and being pulled to and fro as the ocean was churned. So the 'ocean' of desires which leads us astray is churned up by the interaction of the opposites …

Once the Amrita had been found, however, the gods wanted to keep it for themselves, being convinced that the demons would use it for the wrong purpose. Vasuki, being a demon, was naturally focused on personal glorification and materialistic happiness rather than universal good, and he secretly drank the Amrita. Then the Sun and Moon, having noticed this deception, complained to Lord Vishnu, the creator of the Universe, who became very angry. He threw the Sudarshan Chakra at Vasuki and cut him in half.

This weapon, the Sudarshan Chakra, is a spinning disc with one hundred and eight serrated edges ... it was given to Vishnu by Lord Shiva, pleased with his devotions. The disc is not thrown, physically, but sent with willpower, and is capable of defeating any number of demons. However, because Vasuki had drunk the nectar of immortality, he could not be completely destroyed. He remained in the skies as a permanent reminder to the other planets, or gods, of the darker side of life which must be confronted in the pursuit of immortality.[27]

Pamela Crane points out the significance of the serpent in Christian mythology, as connected with the Nodes. The North Node is a point of unity, linked with the spring equinox, or Aries point, as we have already seen, and the South Node is linked with duality at the vernal equinox, or Libra point. Eve draws Adam into the world of duality, relationship and further incarnation, by listening to the serpent. Later, Eve having given birth to Mary, God enters mankind through her, thus bringing the Christ out of Adam. Here I would understand Eve and Mary to be representing two different facets of the cosmic feminine principle. So by listening to the serpent, we move further into duality and the world of form, and by listening to God, we are reconnected with unity.[28]

Here is a rather nice picture of an uroborous, accompanied by a long poem of which I shall read the opening couple of lines, which also describe what is in the picture.[29]

> *Time is a Fading-flower, that's found*
> *Within Eternity's wide round.*

Around the edge some Greek writing refers to the 'timeless' and the 'timely'.

Time *is a* Fading-flowre, *that's found*
Within Eternities *wide* round.

In English folklore, dragons were associated with infertility and failing crops, and so they needed to be slayed in order to ensure fertility and protect the continuity of the clan. In Celtic mythology, Herne the Hunter is very much connected with dragons, and he was sometimes accompanied by a 'Criocephalus', or ram-headed serpent. This same strange creature is also found as the god Amma, the four-coloured rainbow, in the mythology of the Dogon people in Africa, who are known to have had a very elaborate star lore, especially involving the star Sirius.[30] In Chinese mythology, dragons are a highly developed symbol, with very different and individual characteristics attributed to them. They can be linked with power and good fortune, as well as having dominion over various aspects of life. In Buddhism, dragon-like beings are said to guard the four cardinal directions.

I have another 'once upon a time' story, this one from the Chinese culture, kindly given to me by Rod Chang. The Chinese people believe that eclipses are caused by a monster swallowing the Sun and Moon. This monster is called Tiangou – 'Tian' means 'sky' and 'gou' means 'dog'. According to ancient legend, Tiangou is a mythical sky creature like a dog or fox, whose link with eclipses is also found in the story of the Moon Festival and Ch'ang O, the Moon goddess.

One upon a time, there were ten suns in the sky and they began to cause drought, and the Earth was burning up. So the great archer Hou Yi shot down nine of these suns, leaving only one, and thus the problem was solved. After this heroic deed, the people made him Emperor, but in time Hou Yi became greedy and cruel. Wanting also to become immortal, he obtained the elixir of immortality from the Great Queen of the West. However, his wife Ch'ang O was concerned about her husband's cruelty and didn't want the people to suffer any longer under his rule, so she decided to prevent Hou Yi from becoming immortal. She swallowed the elixir, and this made her fly to the Moon. However, Hou Yi's hunting dog also swallowed some, chased her and swallowed the Moon.

The gods then had to ask the hunting dog to return the Moon, and in return the dog became the Guardian of the Sky-Gate, the Sky-Dog Tiangou. The Chinese people believe that gods, stars and spirits alike come to Earth to incarnate and become mortal via this Sky-Gate. But the fierce Sky-Dog guarding this gate made them afraid to come, and no babies were born for a while. But Zhang-Xian, the 'God of Zhang' or the 'God of Chang', was able to shoot the Sky-Dog and drive him away from the Sky-Gate. He is an archer – the meaning of 'Zhang' or 'Chang' is 'open bow' – so he enabled the Sun and Moon to return into incarnation, and also the gods, stars and spirits could become human. In this way, Zhang-Xian also became a God of Giving Birth.

As a generalisation, in Eastern cultures, the dragon image seems to be significantly more integrated, and seen as a valuable part of life, while the 'dragon-slaying' motif seems to dominate in the West, at least the Christianised West. We even have the nickname 'dragon' for a woman who is irascible or perhaps merely standing up for herself and not backing down from conflict! This must be significant, I feel. Perhaps it reflects what I was referring to earlier – the unbalanced emphasis on solar principles, without a corresponding value being given to the lunar side of life and the inner psyche. It is this distortion I personally feel we need to avoid in our interpretation of the Nodal Axis.

Here is a quote which I think sums up beautifully the potential of the Nodes as a developmental axis of consciousness. Perhaps significantly, it comes from the Sufi perspective, a tradition with its roots in the Middle East – thus between East and West. It also refers to the eclipse season, when the Sun meets the Nodes.

> *Entering the gateway in the journey to God brings one into a dichotomous situation. One has embarked upon the Way; but one's psyche has been opened to all the perils that the journey offers. These perils are often described in traditional myths as the demons or the dragon ... In astronomy, the Dragon relates to the Nodes, two diametrically opposed points of intersection between the paths of the Moon and the Sun ... To the mystic, the Dragon symbolises the place of encounter between the Sun and Moon within. The dragon can either devour the Moon, seen symbolically as the mystic's spiritual heart, or it can serve as the place or container of conception. By entering the Dragon when the Sun is at the Nodes, the Moon or heart conceives. Thus, in full consciousness of the perils, one must enter the Dragon in order to await the eclipse in its cosmic womb.*[31]

The North Node

First, let's talk about the North Node. We can see symbolised at the North Node the mythic meeting of the hero and the dragon. The solar hero goes out on a quest, where he must find something that has been lost, win a prize or contest, or perhaps free a heroine who is imprisoned or in trouble. Needless to say, he will encounter various ordeals on the way. The North Node, then, with the trails that lead off it, will describe something of the nature of this quest. Like if your life was an opera, or a fairy story, it shows the purpose, the main plot, the heroic undertaking. We, the audience, however, know that wherever there is a hero, there is a dragon not far behind! Solar heroes constellate dragons, and vice versa. We are talking about the Sun and Moon here, as well as North and South Nodes, in case you hadn't spotted it.

In the fulfilment of this journey, if you stray too far from your own origins, instincts, appropriate cycles of nourishment and rest, and all these good lunar and South Node things, the dragon will come roaring forth. Trying to be exclusively shiny and solar will attract the dragon – from inside yourself, from dreams, from the environment, another person, through one means or another, it will inevitably come. It may come as symptoms within the mind, as emotional distress, or through the body and material life, when things go wrong and you are pulled back into the past, down into depression, or you simply land with a bump from a flight of fancy.

At the North Node, then, is represented a potential solar hero who also runs the risk of getting swallowed up by the dragon, which somehow has to be faced down. There is a great paradox here. You can't always just kill the dragon outright, because it might multiply, like in the story of Hercules and the Hydra. Something else may need to happen. If the dragon is an image of the terrible and devouring aspect of the lunar feminine, she may also need to be honoured and courted until we are allowed to see her other side, that of the feminine soul quality which can invisibly nourish, support and inspire the hero in his time of need. However, some dragons do simply need to be killed! In other words, discrimination is needed at the North Node, and the hero's weapon is preferably the sword of insight, balance and justice, rather than a club or mace swung with the desire to forge ahead regardless of the consequences. See the Libra/Aries symbolism?

In this sense, the North Node does feel like 'where we are going'. With the qualifications I mentioned, it does indeed show where we are meant to go beyond our own past. The imbalance would mean thinking the purpose of life is *only* about this, or lacking discrimination, as I described. Then you will fall foul of the lunar realm, and find yourself fighting dragons for a living! The North Node is where we break new ground. There we may have to engage with something for which we do not feel naturally very well equipped. It takes effort, work and application of intention and will. North Node activity does not just come automatically, even if you have favourable aspects to your Nodes. It's where you are ploughing new ground, or at your own leading edge, to mix metaphors!

Now in traditional astrology, the South Node was considered to be ruled by Saturn and the North by Jupiter, which in a way would seem to contradict what I am saying. However, I think the Jupiter dimension of the North Node shows itself when you really apply energy to the area of life symbolised there, by house and sign. Then the returns can be quite significant, like compound interest. If we think of the hero's journey again, at the North Node you are also likely to attract assistance, like the helpful animals in folktales, or kind people who accompany you on your journey, or a fortunate turn of events which occurs at just the right moment. The nature of this help can be sometimes be seen by examining the ruler of the North Node, and its general condition in the chart, by house, sign and aspect.

Audience: What if you have Pluto conjunct the North Node?

Melanie: Well, sometimes it's a case of 'with friends like that who needs enemies'! Joking aside, having difficult aspects to the North Node might mean that your most useful lessons and productive opportunities come disguised as obstacles, difficulties or problems. Dealing with them is what helps to generate the energy of forward momentum. It also means that being on good terms with your South Node becomes even more important. Also, if you think of the *qualitative* dimension, the Nodal Axis is as much about the development of character, soul and inner qualities. The 'hero's journey' is a parable, a metaphor of an inner process, and how far that takes external shape and form will depend on the particular individual's life.

Audience: Could Jupiter also be a significator for the hero as well as the Sun?

Melanie: Not quite. When you are looking at the Sun in the sky, you are always looking towards the centre of the solar system. I find that so poetic. It is actually the most inner of all the planets, although we tend to forget that. The hero's journey, whatever its outward form, consists of the journey to meet that inner spiritual Sun, within ourselves. By contrast, looking up at Jupiter, we are looking outwards. Jupiter is in the social realm. So it is not the hero per se. It is almost like the hero's journey needs both individual effort, but also the blessings of the gods, which is the province of Jupiter. Jupiter can be the grace, the recognition that although you may be on a solo journey, you also cannot do it alone. You need help from other people, and also from the world of the spirit, or the unconscious, however you understand miraculous intervention.

Audience: How come you are looking outwards? I don't get it.

Melanie: Well, simply, the Sun is the centre of the solar system, and the orbit of Jupiter is further out than the orbit of the Earth. Also, when Jupiter is on the same side of the Earth as the Sun, the inner side, it is not visible, as it will be above the horizon during daylight hours. We can only look at the stars from within the shadow cast by the Earth, like a tiny window through which we contemplate the cosmic immensity beyond our busy life in the daylight world.

Audience: Is Jupiter the tribe of the hero?

Melanie: Yes and no ... nice question! At the end of the hero's journey, he or she will need to, want to, socialise what has been learned or discovered. This is not necessarily a mission to convert others to the truth of your experience – that is perhaps Jupiter's style. However, the return of the hero does include the dilemma of how to be in the world and honour the inner radiance. In that sense, I would go along with your idea that there is a resonance with Jupiter as well. The question is how to expand your participation in society, in the world, in such a way that it is congruent with your own faith and beliefs, including your belief in your own deeper self. Remember the Nodes are the relationship between the Sun, Moon and Earth, so something does seek to be incarnated.

Audience: Might Jupiter be the edge of what your capacities are?

Melanie: Of your possibility and potential, yes, definitely. Jupiter is also your sense of hope, faith and vision. After all, if the object of the hero's quest is to go fetch a golden ring from the bottom of a well, he must have some vision of possibility, some sense of hope and faith in a positive outcome, or the dragons will simply have him for breakfast! Also, the quest isn't over until he gets down there, gets the ring and takes it back to the princess. Then the consequences of that act are a further stage of the journey. Perhaps he marries her, which brings the story into the social realm, and that will usually be where the fairy tale ends! That's all North Node symbolism – where the fairy tale ends and real life begins, with the manifestation of something in the world.

The South Node

Now, moving on to the South Node ... this is about heritage, a legacy, what you bring in with you. That can sometimes be specifically ancestral, but for some people it is even more individualised, like an aptitude or gift for which there is no precedent in the family. If the metaphor of reincarnation is meaningful to you, then at the South Node you may find echoes of what your soul brought here to work with. These ancient issues and pressures can support or impede the expression of potential, and thus become very much part of the journey.

Audience: Could you clarify that? I mean, are you equating potential with the North Node, and what impede or supports it with the South Node?

Melanie: Not entirely. It can work either way. The South Node can also indicate potential, but it's inherited in one way or another – it's what you have brought with you. Often it cannot be released in the form in which it came to you. It has to be reworked, updated, upgraded, at the North Node, by engaging consciously with those qualities or re-working gifts. Bringing something out of the past and into the present. Sometimes the South Node indicates specific ancestral themes, or past life connections, that make it difficult for you to manifest what you might seek to express at the North Node end. By the same token, it can mean the support, the positive side of heritage and ancestry that actually assists you. Either way, it is about what you brought with you. For example, if you are innately musical, becoming a musician able to play an instrument doesn't happen by magic. It requires time and effort, and if you stay enchanted by the image of your own potential, which would be the South Node, you will not manifest anything with it, and then you cannot satisfy that creative possibility.

Reincarnation

Some people connect the South Node with past lives. I think if you engage that perspective, you need to include the entire Nodal Axis, in fact the whole chart. After all, the Nodes lead into the *timeless* dimension. If you are doing a reading for someone and they ask about this theme, it is a good idea to ask them what *they* think. In other words, explore the information from within *their* perspective and their particular philosophy. If you refer to the South Node as a heritage, or similar words, and use the basic astrological language, your client can inwardly connect the information to the appropriate levels of his or her inner experience, and to whatever cosmology makes sense to him or her. If someone tells you a specific memory or scenario, engaging with that information in such a way that it helps energy to move may be more useful than worrying about where it comes from, or whether it is 'really' a past life memory.

Belief in reincarnation, like any concept, including psychological or astrological theory, can trap us in rigid patterns of thinking, and so become an escape from the present. However, our language about time is often not sufficiently flexible to embrace the subtleties of this area, and if we then lapse into inappropriate mechanical thinking or get too linear with it, we may enter the realm of illusion and speculation. Needless to say, this doesn't promote clarity or inner freedom.

Time is not only linear – there are many kinds of time. Sometimes people ask about past lives as a way of pushing causality into another dimension, and to collude with this by 'fixing' information in this way can mean further disempowering your client. However, it would be naive, indeed narcissistic, to think that this life here is all that is happening at any one moment. There are more things in heaven and earth than we know about, to misquote Shakespeare! As astrologers, I believe we can best serve our clients by being open-minded enough to really listen to them, not imposing our own metaphysics, but endeavouring to find ways of conveying information from the chart that leave room for the client to take it in their own way.

Balance

So the gifts and possibilities that exist at the South Node tend to need some anchoring or reworking to make them a viable, useful and productive part of that person's worldly life in the present. Here, the qualities of the North Node are needed. I think you can see where we are moving with this. I am going to take the position that the Nodal dance is one of balance, but not of stasis. It is not 'You've got to get your South Node working, and North Node working, and then you'll live happily ever after.' It is about a dynamic process of continual balancing, then becoming unbalanced, and needing to rebalance.

If you think about it, the Moon crosses both ends of the transiting Nodal Axis, North and South, once a month. Likewise, the Sun crosses both ends once a year, and this will define the annual eclipse seasons, as I mentioned earlier. In addition to that, the Nodal Axis itself works its way slowly backwards through the Zodiac, clockwise round the chart every 18.618 years. It goes click, click, click, backwards through the chart, balancing, rebalancing and stimulating each planet in turn with either the North Node or the South Node.

As well, we are constantly getting transits, both quick and slow, crossing our own Nodal Axis. We will look in more detail at this later, but I wanted to introduce this picture of the multiple stimuli from the connections between the transiting Nodal Axis and the planets, and also the natal Nodal Axis receiving those impulses. I think all of this helps us to expand our thinking beyond a straight line drawn across the chart!

Relationships and Fate

The Nodal Axis is where what we are on the inside becomes distilled on the outside and therefore it can feel like Fate. In fact, Marc Edmund Jones calls it 'The Axis of Fate'. As we have seen, the Nodal Axis is the meeting of the solar and lunar principles, involving the Earth as well. It is where something is meant to happen, to be part of our life, and also influence our world view. If we stretch our definition, the Nodes involve not only our incarnate life, but also other levels of existence, some known to us and others not. Thus they have a great deal to do with important relationships, allegiances, alliances, with both individuals and groups. I would also emphasise the dimension of inner relationship with the Nodes, where they symbolise the path that leads to the *conjunctio*, or sacred marriage of opposites within, united in harmony and producing the divine child from the ground of our being.

Nodal relationships can be of any kind – a lover, life partner, friend, co-worker, colleague, rival, enemy, parent, brother, sister, mentor, guru – and they can be dead or alive. The precise form of the relationship is not stated in the axis itself. Nodal relationships can even be with somebody you will never meet, because maybe they died centuries ago – a composer whose music you are deeply inspired by, or the story of a particular explorer by whom you feel completely and mysteriously entranced, and through whom you learn all kinds of things about yourself. The hallmark of a Nodal relationship is that when in connection with the other person, you somehow feel more *yourself*, more aligned, more whole. In astrology the opposition, the aspect of 180°, is the aspect of awareness – often gained through a process of conflict, oscillation or indeed encountering one's opposite through others.

Nodal relationships, allegiances with groups or individuals, touch you right to the core. Even though I had observed this to be true, at first I didn't understand why the Nodes were so connected with group alliances, institutions and the like. Then I realised that a group is a lunar organism, like a womb or a tribe. So to some extent, our attitude and way of being in relationship is indicated by the Nodal Axis. It is like a seesaw. Our attitudes and style of merging at the South Node, and separating at the North Node, can be shown, as well as the activities, qualities and conditions which prompt that oscillation. Very often, when there are transits occurring by hard aspect to your Nodal Axis, or indeed when the transiting Nodal Axis is stimulating one of your natal planets, you will encounter a person or situation that somehow embodies your own opposite, what you need to encompass for the sake of your own wholeness. In that way, Nodal relationships are always challenging, for they lead us beyond what we have become identified with, or confront us with our own unresolved past. We will continue with the theme of relationships later, when we consider ways of exploring the Nodes in the chart.

Dane Rudhyar's Perspective

Continuing to explore the Nodes, I'd like to include a perspective which comes from Dane Rudhyar.[32] He uses the very biological imagery of metabolism, with ingestion and intake at the North Node and elimination, release or illumination at the South. If we add our image of the dragon, it is like the North Node shows what needs to be taken in and digested, or indeed where one can feel devoured, and the South Node contains what one needs to eliminate, transform or release. At the North Node, he talks about chewing and eating, implying effort, and also mentions the providential help of Jupiter. Here we build the personality, bringing new material into life for metabolising and assimilating. We bite into life at the North Node, and must assimilate experience, and make the effort to adjust to existence.

At the South Node, a certain automatism is implied. It symbolises that which is no longer needed, comes automatically and therefore may lead to self-undoing. Here again, in order to avoid the 'from-to' fallacy, we can think of this as a natural cyclic process. Then there will be times when the South Node shows that which can become poisonous if it is held onto, as it is decaying and archaic and must be released. This is the negative implication of the South Node. It can be where we take things for granted, where things come easily, and so we can be controlled by this, relying inappropriately on it, and then we stagnate. Perhaps this is the Saturn connection, where we can become stuck, imprisoned, by the apparent ease, or what seems 'natural'.

The South Node, then, can be our line of least resistance, where we require the least amount of exertion to do something, and where we keep repeating experiences and indulgences. By contrast, the North Node is more about effort and the application of intention and will. Rudhyar basically says that the positive focus of conscious existence should be established at the North Node. At the South Node, he says one doesn't really build personality or life stories, because it is the place of release, not development as such. However, what one holds or who one is at the South Node can be 'developed' by consecrating it to a larger ideal, thus releasing it into life, which will also require the agency of the North Node. Here is another perspective that makes nonsense of the idea that one end is 'good' and the other 'bad', because very creative things can also be released via the South Node. Just to round off Rudhyar's ideas here, he talks about a planet conjunct the Nodes being like a focus of consciousness, a lens which concentrates energy in a very powerful and even compulsive way. Someone has a question ...?

Audience: Release can be a positive thing ... not as in 'Bye, bye, let go', but can it be a release to actually work with something?

Melanie: Yes. It can be either or both. If we consider Rudhyar's analogy of digestion, release is where we eliminate as waste what has been digested and assimilated, as we don't need it any more. In fact, to hold on would poison the organism. That's one kind of release. The other is to release the fruits of something out into life, which is also a South Node function. The North Node is where the hard work must be done, the testing of our will, endurance and perseverance. Sometimes that is precisely inspired or supported by the nature of what is being released.

I hope this has served to develop the notion that the oscillation, the dynamic balancing between the two ends of the Nodal Axis, may be something of a key here. To be focused on one end or the other means to be out of balance, and to try and freeze the elusive sense of balance as it appears would be to stop living.

Snakes and Ladders

Last night I was talking about the Nodes with a friend and she said 'Oh, it is like snakes and ladders – the North Node is the ladder and the South Node is the snake.' So if your life was a board game, if you land on a ladder, you must then do a North Node climb and you make effort, you want to progress. On the way, however, you throw the dice again and land on a snake! Down you go, down to the bottom of the ladder, 'Return to Go and get fined £200' or whatever![33] This is a lovely image for the dynamic balancing process of the Nodes, and also of the backwards and forwards wobble of the True Node through the Zodiac, 'snaking' its way along, weaving to and fro. These subtle oscillations also serve as a reminder of the dynamic moving quality of Nodal experience.

The Nodal High Wire Act

Of course the Nodes tend to raise the whole question of fate and destiny, and I have a definition here, from Antero Alli, which I really like. He says 'Fate is whatever happens to us which remains unknown until it happens.'[34] The implication also being that if you reflect and dig, you might be able to discover the why or the how, but Fate is what *happens* to us that remains unknown until it happens. Then he defines destiny as 'How we chose to approach our Fate, with a vision of purpose.' A tragedy will occur and one person will begin painting themselves into a corner labelled 'Victim'. Another will put up a sign saying 'I am not going to let this defeat me', and therein lies the difference.

Antero Alli also describes how the Nodes can instruct us on where and how we get off track, and he uses the image of a tightrope. The Nodes, being points in space, are like the high wire slung between the Sun, Moon and Earth, and the Nodes in the chart are perhaps an image of us carrying the balancing pole, walking that high wire, with space all around! He talks about the Nodes showing where we can decode instructions for our pathway of progress by seeing, via the North Node, how the inertia and habits of the past impede our growth – that's the South Node. Balancing, as well as moving, between the opposites is perhaps the Nodal journey.

He uses the word 'resistances' for the South Node, and 'excitements' for the North Node. This is very interesting, and it works in practice. He talks about the North Node as a vortex of novelty, and a place where we get shocked out of what he calls our 'familiarity trance'. In other words, running on automatic, staying with the known rhythm, is the South Node end, the Moon/Venus/Saturn end, and what shocks us out of that is a North Node experience – the Sun/Mars/Jupiter end. So it is a critical challenge point, and a gateway to the future self. On the other hand, if you are always

171 The Nodes of the Moon

biased towards the North Node, you become an 'excitement junkie' or an 'adrenalin addict', compulsively pushing against your own resistance all the time. The rest of the chart might even support that. If you are biased in the other direction, towards the South Node, always pulling back from making the leap, taking the risk, you may become bogged down in resistance and inertia.

However, he also talks about the South Node as a safety net which is woven from what is given. I really like that image, as it goes beyond the one-sided idea that the South Node is 'bad', or we must leave it entirely behind. He says it is where we have 'karmic homework', where there are loose ends to be tied up. I guess, though, if you stay too long, you might get tied up yourself! For example, if your South Node safety net is full of holes, you are going to fall through into the stagnation and toxins. Perhaps a good safety net is precisely made from all kinds of loose knots which have been secured, mending the holes and making the net sound. In real life terms, this will mean completion, finishing unfinished business on various levels, including parental patterning, and even ancestral business, or past life material. Getting entangled in this net will mean inertia and regression, certainly.

Antero Alli also says that the 'net' of the South Node is the place where we receive 'what is owed to us'. That does assume that life or the Universe might owe us something. If you believe that might be so, then the South Node is the place where you might receive it. I would certainly concur with this, but within a framework of reciprocity rather than 'debt'. Certainly if you just look at the image, it is like a bucket or a container which receives rain or perhaps blessings from above. He talks about it as 'where we must learn to get out of our own way.'

Audience: Is that the North Node?

Melanie: No, the South. Or, come to think of it, perhaps both! Remember the theme of release? For that to happen, we must get out of our own way. Even with the North Node, you can't put effort and commitment into something which you are busy denying is even there in the first place. Being the receiver at the South Node means you can consecrate your potential and do something with it at the North Node. But if you are in denial, saying 'No, no, I don't have that, that's not me,' then the energy gets stuck and you can't do anything with it.

He talks about the North Node as where we update our lives into present time experience. In that sense, the South Node is where we can easily rest on our laurels or bask in past glory – that could even be the glory of our ancestors. But the North Node is where we come into present time and start consciously determining our future, so there is an interesting timeline implied here, providing you don't take it too rigidly.

Exploring the Nodes in the Chart

As we focus on ways of exploring the Nodes in the chart, I will show you several charts, some of well known people, and also one case study which I'll be referring to several times, illustrating different avenues of exploration.

When you come to explore the Nodes in a chart, first of all note the position of the Sun and the Moon and the Earth. Then consider the house and sign placement of each Node, and the aspects to it. If you keep your orbs small, differences in either end will show up. For example, if a planet is trine one end, it is not necessarily sextile the other. A trine is a big aspect where you can allow 7° or 8° of orb, but a sextile is only a tiny aspect, 60°, so my 'default' orb for the sextile is about 4° maximum. I know some people use quite big orbs for it, but I tend to shrink orbs down according to how many degrees the aspect covers. However you fine-tune your preparation, though, be willing to extend this when you are actually reading a chart, according to what makes sense from what the person tells you of their life. Obviously, a square will always involve both ends of the Nodal Axis, as will the other hard aspects like the sesquiquadrate and semi-square, providing you keep the orbs small.

The Trail of Dispositorship

Following the trail of dispositorship is fun, and will reveal some significant links. If you take the Nodal Axis and note the ruling planet of either end, then consider the ruling planet of the sign in which it is placed, and so on, you will gain an enhanced understanding of the meaning of each end, as well as discovering planetary themes which set the Nodal Axis resonating, so to speak. Let's look at Dane Rudhyar's chart as an example of this.

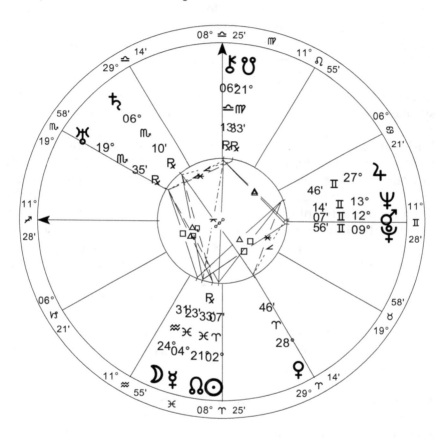

Dane Rudhyar
23 March 1895; 00:20:40 UT +0:00; Paris, France

I am aware that there are several different rectifications of Rudhyar's time in circulation, but fortunately all the ones I have seen have the North Node in Pisces in the 3rd house, South Node in Virgo in the 9th. With the North Node in Pisces, we look to Neptune and we find it in Gemini in the 7th house. Gemini is ruled by Mercury, which we find in Pisces. So in Rudhyar's case, there is a mutual reception between Mercury and Neptune which rules the North Node. When we consider the South Node, we see it is in Virgo, also ruled by Mercury, and just look at this – following the trail from either end, we arrive at the same mutual reception of Mercury and Neptune. As that axis lies across the 3rd and 9th houses, to me that describes the essence of his destiny and what he offered. He was an accomplished musician before he was an astrologer, as well as being an accomplished artist, a visionary and an extraordinary speaker who also left behind a huge body of written work.

Rudhyar could be thought of as the 'father' of contemporary psychological astrology, in that he was one of the very first people to embrace the concepts and framework of modern psychology, and link them into the interpretation process. He was active in the first part of the twentieth century with this, right up until his death in 1985, also building on the work of people before him like Alan Leo and Charles Carter. He was really the one to bring humanistic concepts and the person-centred orientation to the horoscope. This was Rudhyar's gift to astrology, in addition to his visionary and poetic turn of phrase, like we heard in his material on the Sun.

I've just realised that I'm assuming you have all read some Rudhyar, and that this probably dates me! There was a time when it seemed everyone was reading his work.

Audience: Can you recommend a title of his?

Melanie: Yes, all of them! It was reading *The Pulse of Life* that sparked my commitment to astrology, even though I'd already been interested in it for some years. I then worked my way through everything he wrote. I suppose *The Astrology of Personality* might be thought of as his *magnum opus*, and *The Sun is Also a Star* is another of my favourites. Anyone with a Mercury-Neptune aspect will probably appreciate his writing immediately, but it is not to everyone's taste. Do also visit the website www.khaldea.com, where a lot of his material is archived.

Let's refer again to his chart. Note the 3rd house North Node, signifying all the conceptualising that he did, communicating, writing and speaking out of the inspiration that came to him. It is in Pisces, ruled by Neptune in Gemini, which is also widely square the Nodal Axis, and symbolises his versatility, and the sheer volume of his output of writing, music and paintings. The South Node, in Virgo in the 9th house, symbolises the meticulous dedication to making productive his various gifts, and there is also the Teacher, the Philosopher, the Wise Man, and the Traveller. Although born in France, he made his home in the United States, and was steeped in many spiritual traditions and influences, Eastern and Western. A central theme in his writing is the idea that our times are crucial to the seeding of new ideas and beliefs which will regenerate society in the future – all 9th house themes. The holistic view with which he approached the chart can also be seen as reflected in his Pisces North Node. The South Node in Virgo in the 9th synthesised an enormous breadth of detailed understanding into an approach which is inclusive and holistic, but based in sound technique and understanding – Virgo in the 9th.

Audience: Will both ends always reduce to one theme like this?

Melanie: Unfortunately not! If the chart has an overall dispositor, then that will also rule both ends of the Nodes. Sometimes, you get a different picture if you use traditional rulers. Let me give you an example. This person has North Node in Aquarius, South in Leo. Taking the traditional rulers first, this means that the North is ruled by Saturn, which is in Libra. Venus is in Leo, Sun in Virgo, Mercury in Libra. Here it reduces to this loop of Venus, Mercury and the Sun. If you follow the South end, it is the same, it enters the same loop.

However, if you take the new rulers, in this case you get a very interesting difference between the two. Uranus will rule the North end, and it is found in mutual reception with the Moon in Aquarius. So the two ends come out quite different. This person teaches speech and drama, and also performs. Stories from different cultures around the world are a passion – the Sun and Mercury are in the 9th house, Venus in the 8th. These planets also suggest refinement and artistry. This person is much concerned with philosophy and the spiritual life, and the Aquarius/Leo Nodes are also expressed in his link with a specific philosophical system which involves community life. This Nodal high wire act is based on the dilemma of being solo and being part of a group, whether leading groups or performing, and also the ambivalence about belonging. And note, the two ends don't necessarily match. The Moon/Uranus link on the North Node end has driven this person into more detachment than is comfortable at times, in contrast with the very personal quality of the Venus/ Mercury/ Sun loop. If we compare the two different stories told at the North Node end, Saturn is demanding a considered, responsible and balanced engagement in relationships, with groups and individual people, while Uranus demands freedom, detachment and understanding. Needless to say, they don't always go together.

Helpers and Hinderers

Returning to our metaphor of the hero's journey, you can think of the ruling planets of either end as helpers or hinderers, and that trail of dispositorship will show you where they live, what part of the forest they emerge from. In the case of Rudhyar, with Neptune in Gemini in the 7th, he obviously read and absorbed a great deal of other people's writing, as well as turning it into his own unique understanding.

Aspects to the Nodes can also be thought of in this way. Let's take another example, and look at both the dispositors and the aspects. I've chosen one rather similar, by way of comparing and contrasting. Here is the horoscope of astrologer Jim Lewis, founder of AstroCartography, with his Nodes in the same houses, but opposite signs, to Dane Rudhyar.

In addition to Neptune ruling one end of the Nodes, it also aspects both ends, like in Rudhyar's chart, but here it is actually conjunct the North Node in the 3rd house. There is a strong similarity, as here is another man of great vision who left as a legacy for astrologers an enormous body of work. However, the difference is that Jim Lewis will mainly be remembered by astrologers for the *technique* of AstroCartography, while Rudhyar is mainly remembered for his

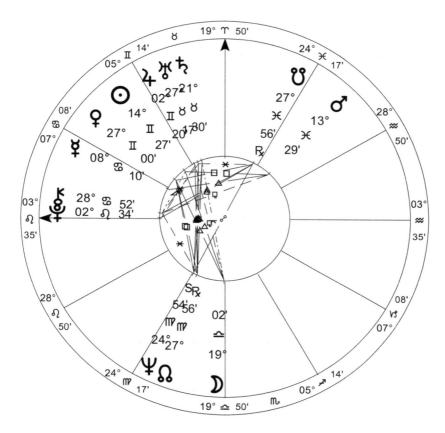

Jim Lewis
5 June 1941; 09.30 EDT; New York, New York

visionary quality. Technique is a Virgo matter, Jim's North Node, while vision is more the province of Rudhyar's North Node in the 9th house in Pisces. Interestingly, they both have Jupiter in Gemini, and in each case it aspects the North Node; there are also three or more Gemini planets in each chart, and both Mercurys are in watery signs.

Jim Lewis' vision was the understanding of man's physical location on Earth as participating in and reflecting the larger cosmic situation of our life. AstroCartography is a way of mapping the horoscope on the surface of the Earth to show those particular resonances. It would not have been possible to work out something as complex as this without a very powerful vision supporting it – this is the South Node in Pisces in the 9th house of vision. I can imagine Jim sort of above the Earth, seeing the way that an individual's life pattern literally wraps itself around the Earth to incarnate. Jim was in the process of organising further his huge body of ideas when he died, and the work was carried on after his death by Kenneth Irving, Erin Sullivan and others.[35] Friends were involved helping him complete his life's work, and note that he has Uranus in Taurus in the 10th, and Venus is in Gemini in the 11th, the house of friendship. They are both in the exact same degree as the Nodal Axis.

Let's follow the trail of dispositorship. The North Node is ruled by Mercury, which is in the 12th house in Cancer. Its ruler, the Moon, is in Libra; Venus is in Gemini and Mercury in Cancer, ruled by the Moon. So there we get a loop, and we get to the very same loop when we follow the other end. Neptune rules the South Node, but it is in Virgo, and Mercury takes us into the same loop.

Audience: What happens if the loop nearly covers the whole chart?

Melanie: This could happen. Like with anything in astrology, when you boggle out with too much dispersed information, it becomes meaningless. When you experiment with this trail of dispositorship, it will sometimes lead to a blind alley or a maze! Then stay with something more focused, like what planets aspect the Nodes, and their sign and house, etc. In astrology, when you try different techniques and perspectives to help you manage and order the volume of information you can draw from the chart, don't be afraid to abandon something if it seems to go nowhere.

Audience: Wouldn't the fact it goes nowhere be significant?

Melanie: Yes, it could be. Interesting thought. Charts that have an overall dispositor, or a small loop which encompasses everything, often indicate highly focused lives that can also be compulsive or one-sided. Perhaps a chart where the trail of dispositors never forms any definite pattern might indicate a feeling in the person that their life goes round in circles with no goal. However, I would hesitate to draw hard and fast conclusions on the basis of information alone. You can explore this kind of thing in dialogue with a client, however, by asking a 'clean' question – one not designed to prove your astrological theory!

Let's consider again the loop in Jim's chart. Firstly, the loop encompasses his Moon in Libra exactly on the IC, which beautifully symbolises his interest in the process of people relocating! The IC is about roots, home, where you live or where you come from. The vision, with AstroCartography, is that by understanding the cosmic and geographical resonances of a particular place, you might be better able to choose a location to increase your quality of life and personal well-being. Or, indeed, to understand more clearly why you are living where you are. This Moon is disposited in turn by Venus in Gemini in the 11th house, in the exact Nodal degree. Friends were indeed like family to Jim, and he valued highly his friendships. Venus, along with the Sun and Jupiter in Gemini, is disposited by Mercury in Cancer in the 12th house. This is a symbol of his feeling self, and his involvement with the underprivileged and less fortunate in the community. It is perhaps not so well known about Jim that he was a revolutionary spirit in all sorts of ways – Uranus in the Nodal degree – and was involved in political issues that were controversial and mostly quite hidden. He had a strong sense of social consciousness and was involved with minority rights groups, prison work and so on – there's Mercury in the 12th house. Like Rudhyar, then, what we know of Jim Lewis' work in the astrology field represents only a small part of his life's work.

Audience: Isn't there something about Fate and Nodal degrees? Where does that come from?

Melanie: In Horary astrology it is said that any planet found in the Nodal degree has a 'fated' quality about it. It represents something which is out of your hands, which must unfold as it will, but it will significantly affect the outcome of the matter at hand. In a natal chart, I think it is a bit similar. You can see very precise examples of that in Jim Lewis' chart, in his involvements with friends, ideas, groups and matters of social concern. The Venus in Gemini in the 11th is also expressed by his moving between different circles of people. Does anyone in the room have this?

Audience: Do you mean in the exact same degree, not, say, conjunct or trine within a few degrees?

Melanie: No, it must be in the exact same degree. Jim's Chiron, for example, is only 56' separating from an exact sextile with his North Node, but this does not count as a Nodal degree.

Audience: I have Pluto in the 9th house in the last degree of Leo, and Mars in the last of Pisces, and my North Node is in the last degree of Libra in the 12th house. The crunch came for me when I had to face a choice between having a child and taking a place at university. That was when Uranus was approaching the square to my Nodes. I chose university, but I was tormented the whole time, and kept on sabotaging myself. It did feel like a sacrifice, and I am still mourning it, really. I know I made the choice, but it also felt like it was the only one I could have made. I can see rationally that is not true, but that's how it felt.

Melanie: Perhaps by the time Neptune squares that Nodal Axis you will feel more at peace within yourself about your choice.

The Balance Points

Something else that is illustrated in Jim's chart is the importance of the degree axis that squares the Nodes. I call these the 'balance points'. As we have seen, one of these is occupied by Venus in his chart. Linking this with the image of the 'high wire act', I think that we can see any natal or indeed transiting planet like the balancing pole carried by the person walking the high wire! In other words, anything that occupies the T-square points to the Nodes can facilitate balance. Jim's Venus in Gemini worked by bridging and accepting differences, Gemini being the opposites that don't necessarily synthesise. They are different and they need to stay that way, but the gap can be bridged by artful manoeuvring.

Audience: The balancing point in Gemini in the 11th house is also about creating mental patterns within a framework. You can make earthy patterns, or patterns out of chaos, but you can always make patterns.

Melanie: Yes! Jim reflected the celestial patterns on to the surface of the Earth.

These 'balance points' are called 'the bendings' in traditional astrology. This evocative word is also a nautical term and, for some time, I thought it referred to the turning arc of a ship. Unfortunately, though, I learned from the Internet that this wasn't true! Such a fabulous image, so a great pity! It is indeed a nautical term, but it refers to a hitch or a knot. There is much discussion about what 'the bendings' signify in traditional astrology, where Horary charts are the ones most commonly worked with. It is considered as an obstruction, a hindrance. Or a 'turning point'. However, in natal astrology, what seems clearly demonstrated is that if a planet is 'on the bendings', squaring the Nodal Axis, its significance is greatly increased, and the manifestation of this energy becomes central to the person's life story. As usual, the closer the orb, the more likely it is to manifest in external events. But as the square is fundamentally an aspect of 'happening', where something wants to manifest, the pressure and the dynamism can be considerable. So whether a planet on 'the bendings' helps or hinders the person's destiny needs to be carefully assessed. We'd need to look at which planet it is, and its general condition in the horoscope. And if we think of the Nodal Axis as representing a dynamic process, rather than a straight line, it is likely to be both, at different times.

Planets Conjunct the Nodal Axis

There is a sense of imperative with a planet on either end of the Nodal Axis, and, inevitably, the question of orbs will come up. Obviously the smaller the orb, the more precise the meaning. But the question is really like that question 'How long is a piece of string?' Thematically, a planet that is as much as 12° away from one of the Nodes could still be considered conjunct, but you have to assess it in terms of the overall picture, and listen to information from your client. Referring again to Jim's chart, he has Neptune conjunct the North Node, in the 3rd, perhaps reflecting the struggle Jim had to publish another work, entitled *Peter Pan in Midlife*. This wish, although sacrificed while Jim was alive, was fulfilled after his death. It also reflects his humanitarian involvements with the underprivileged. Also, at the time of his death, transiting Chiron was at 24° 49′ Virgo, moving retrograde, after stationing a few weeks earlier on Jim's NE/NO midpoint.

A planet on the South Node end, using the image of release, can be released in the sense of wastage, something that is done to death, wasted, like being consumed. Or it can signal a very powerful release of creative output and energy which occurs at specific moments in life, like when that planet is receiving transits. Rudhyar's image of consecration seems to really make sense here, in that this planet will probably operate in a larger-than-life way, and will need to be consecrated, dedicated to the greater whole. While it may show a very strong aptitude or gift that you brought in, it may present as a dragon that takes quite a bit of subduing, as it may show the negative side strongly and need considerable work to transform it. A planet on the North Node end will have a strong imperative to be manifested in some way, and thus the source of great pressure, potentially of a creative variety. On either end, a planet conjunct the Nodes is usually obvious in someone's life pattern, both inwardly and also outwardly.

The Nodal Journey

I want to mention the transiting Nodes. I got intrigued by this, because the axis itself goes backwards, retrograding through the chart at the rate of 1° every 18.618 days. Now a planet transiting in its retrograde phase has the implication of something more intuitive, more right brain. It moves into the inward arc of activity of the psyche, activating our inner being, and the retrograde phase is about processing experience and clearing debris. It occurred to me that the whole Nodal Axis by transit must have that implication – like an axis of integration that moves around quietly in the other direction to the way the planets move, overall, apart from when they too are retrograde. It made me think of the snake, or the dragon, moving invisibly in the underworld, an axis of consciousness working in the background of our life experience, as it goes slowly round and round, reviewing, processing and digesting our entire chart, our entire life experience, in terms of its opposites, assimilating and releasing, and perhaps yielding a harvest accordingly. I also got very inspired thinking about worms, which refine the texture of the soil as they wriggle through it, and deposit nutrients as the soil passes through their body ... if the horoscope is the soil of our life, then perhaps the Nodal Axis is like the worm!

So I set to work exploring the actual sequence, first on my own chart, and then on the charts of family, friends and selected clients, and I was amazed and delighted at what I discovered. I simply followed the transiting Node, noting only conjunctions and oppositions, for simplicity. I did four complete cycles for my own chart, giving a long overview. Let's follow it through on a chart as an example.

Obviously, what I wanted to see was whether there was any meaning in the sequence, and I believe there is. Let's put this Nodal theme under the microscope. What I did was to list down one side of a piece of paper all the planets in the order in which they receive contacts from the transiting Nodal Axis. I limited the aspects to the conjunction and opposition. If you use an A4 sheet sideways, and rule the lines you need, it does very well, and on one page you can do your whole life up to about the age of seventy-two.

For example, in this chart, the South Node will first contact the retrograde Mercury, then Venus, then Chiron, the Sun, the MC/IC, then Neptune. The next contact is the North Node conjunct the Moon, then the Nodes square their own axis. After that there is again the South Node conjunct in turn Saturn, Mars, Pluto, Uranus, the Descendant/Ascendant, the North Node, IC/MC, Moon, the Ascendant/Descendant, and lastly Jupiter. Then there is a Nodal return. To make it easy, take a pencil and lay it across the chart, and turn it slowly clockwise, noting the sequence of planets touched by either end.

On this chart, immediately you will see that in the first half of the Nodal cycle, up to just over nine years old, all the Nodal contacts except for the Moon are from the transiting South Node. Then, of course, in the second half of the cycle, up to the Nodal return at 18.618 years old, it will be the other way around. This is indeed significant in the life of this person, as we shall see. If you explore several Nodal cycles in your own chart, of course the sequence will be the same in each first half, and then a mirror image in the second half. If you then write the dates of all those contacts, you can see

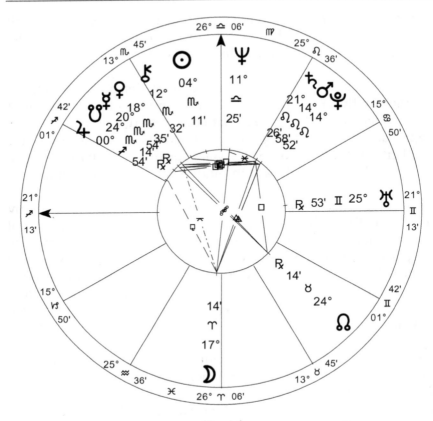

'Rosie'
28 October 1947; 12.10 BST; Solihull, England

where they will repeat, and I assure you some interesting themes will emerge. Also, this cycle is absolutely regular, more so than any transiting planetary cycle, so everyone gets the Nodes aspecting themselves at almost exactly the same age. Roughly every four years and eight months, the transiting Nodes make a hard aspect to their own axis.

If this is a metaphor of the hero's journey, because the Nodes are going backwards, this is perhaps the hero's subconscious which is depicted, that which lies underneath, and perhaps counter to the conscious intention, providing support or sabotage, depending on one's state of inner balance, and the particular lessons of one's life journey. As the journey starts, what is the first thing that you meet?

Is it a foe? Is it a helper? What's the first task? The first obstacle? Are you mainly travelling alone or with others? On the handout that I will give you later, you will see that I have suggested you write yourself a story in the style of a folk tale, 'Once upon a time ...', taking the planets in this order. The purpose of this is to see if there is a dominant metaphor in your life as to how your journey unfolds. In NLP terminology, this could be similar to the idea of a 'meta-programme', like an umbrella structure under which everything else in your life happens, or doesn't happen. Becoming conscious of that meta-programme can be very empowering.

Considering the sequence in my own chart revealed something I immediately recognised. The first contact is the South Node to a 12th house Neptune in Libra, the only cardinal planet, then to Saturn in Leo. This reflected why things seem so chaotic at the beginning of any new stage of my life, sort of without strategy, and why I don't feel particularly motivated to start new things, or to break new ground in any North Node sense, unless and until I get some kind of Neptunian inspiration, which I have to wait for, but then I have to take time to sort fact from fiction. This will come usually from solitude, or a dream, like the 12th house. If this was my heroine's journey, it goes something like this ... just as I set out, a thick fog descends, a real pea-souper, and confusion reigns. I'm lost, scared and definitely feeling sorry for myself. Then, after what seems like a very long time, out of the fog there comes a wizened little figure, who turns out to be a Wise Old Man. He is a helper who has arrived – this is Saturn in Leo, who comes next but, in transit timing, more than two years later. Perhaps he simply says 'Wait five minutes and the fog will clear'. He has experience, a sense of timing and a wry sense of humour, as you would expect from Saturn. He might also show me how to encourage this fog to enter a bottle, like the genie, and if I am careful it will shine with beautiful colours through the glass. I think you can get the idea!

Audience: Do you mean that every time the Node transits your Neptune you stay in a fog for two years?

Melanie: Sort of ... but doing this sequence 'fairy tale style' will draw out the metaphor in the sequence, and take it into the timeless, where it can stretch or shrink. The subjective sense of endless fog is there, but the actual timing varies according to the situation, and of course there are other transits too.

Audience: It seems this could be an interesting way of doing a life review for yourself, or a framework to use also for a client.

Melanie: Yes, exactly. In many spiritual traditions, and also in psychotherapy, the process of reviewing one's life from the beginning onwards is an important aspect of inner purification. It is not just a morbid preoccupation but a powerful way of assisting the emergence of the true self, releasing it from the obscure chains of past situations that still hold an emotional charge that may be unprocessed. It is about coming into the present more fully. Contemplating this Nodal sequence, when you log all the dates and life events that happened with these Nodal contacts, I think you will be amazed. The fairy tale is fun to do, and can reveal the structure of the metaphor of your journey, but logging the dates on which contacts occurred will also give you plenty of life experience to chew over. The transiting Nodes are like a spotlight going round the chart, highlighting the condition of the planet they touch, and bringing things into awareness.

The transiting North Node, when contacting a planet, seems to highlight possibilities and excitements, and evoke a sense of forward motion. With the transiting South Node, you might be called upon to clean up your act, eliminate what is no longer useful. You might be shown the degenerate state of a particular area of life, as symbolised by the planet house and sign, and you might have resistance to seeing that. I also think of the transiting axis as a mirror, one of those two-sided mirrors. The North Node shows you the future potential of whatever it is, or where something is heading, and the South Node can show you the past, how things have been. Then there is pressure to release something, or embrace it in order to rework it. Of course, there's no exact formula, and both ends are always involved. The transiting North Node might say 'This is how it could be. This is where you might want to try and move. But in order for that to happen you need to complete this or that.' In other words, it also refers to the South Node. Remember the Jupiter-Saturn rulership of the Nodes? I once heard Liz Greene use a wonderful image for the relationship of Jupiter and Saturn, to do with getting a donkey to move. Jupiter is like the carrot in front of the donkey's nose, and Saturn is the stick that beats it from behind!

Nodal Squares

Let's focus on the Nodes as they aspect their own natal axis, by square, opposition and conjunction. These points often concern relationship themes, with individuals or groups. The transiting Nodal Axis will reach the 'balance points' – the square to itself – just over four and a half years into the cycle. That's a time of balancing, and therefore sometimes of crisis, but of potential integration. All being well, you get some help balancing on your tightrope. For example, in my case, the transiting Nodal Axis makes its square across the 3rd and 9th houses, and the last four times this happened I have been immersed in a particular teaching, or studying with a teacher. There was both an element of intense personal relationship, and also a philosophy, a psychological or spiritual path that was very challenging, but also integrative, and accompanying a deep sense of inner well-being.

Nodal Half- and Full Returns

The Nodal half-return, at just over nine years into the cycle, and the Nodal return, every 18.618 years, both seem to have the quality of a turning point. With the half-return, the theme of laying the past to rest, or finishing unfinished business, or resolving dormant conflicts, often dominates. Often we are shown a cul-de-sac ahead, if we have been acting on a compulsion that will inevitably keep us stuck in the past. Hard decisions may have to be made, and yet it may feel like there is no choice. We are also called upon to release the residue of whatever was not fulfilled in the first half of the cycle, what cannot manifest further. This can be a really wobbly time, and you might even fall off your tightrope. That's when the strength of your South Node safety net will be tried and tested. Your relationship with the past, your lunar self, your sense of soul nourishment is in focus in some way. Do you feel devoured, or are you devouring the fruit of the first part of the cycle? You may have a significant meeting or encounter with someone who personifies, or evokes within you, whatever needs to be integrated and balanced. Something may try to draw you back into the past, and you have to deal with that pressure. Like the proverbial donkey, you may be offered the carrot and subjected to the stick at the same time!

During the Nodal half-return, when the transiting North Node reaches the conjunction with the South Node, if your life has biased towards the North Node, and you have been firing very strongly on that solar cylinder, your body may rebel with symptoms, or you might fall in love with somebody and be plunged into a very emotional, sensual and physical dimension. Family relationships may need attention. Transits involving the Nodes tend to personify very easily, maybe because they are fundamentally about relationship. These significant encounters are not always with new people entering your life. An old friend could step into a new role, or a relationship could change. You may suddenly realise that you have been colluding with a friend's tendency to self-pity, and think 'I don't want to hear that same old story again.' Whatever the circumstance, you can expect important personal contacts to occur during these Nodal points. However, if your life is biased towards the South Node, work may be needed to release yourself from entanglements, sometimes not even recognised before.

The Nodal return is a time of new beginnings, which will start you on a trail which culminates at the next half-return, just over nine years later. There is often a surge of energy towards the future, which may be preceded by a few months of psychological or physical 'house-cleaning', like preparation for a birth. Forward momentum can be strong, and the appearance of helpers, fortunate synchronicity and meetings with significant people are likely. If you were the donkey, this is the time to watch the carrot carefully, as it might come close enough for you to take a big bite. If you are too busy worrying about the stick behind at this time, you might miss out! There is often a vulnerable feeling too, with a strong sense of impulse, and the exhilaration of facing a new cycle, an unknown future. This turning to the future may also mean loss, leavings and separation, for the urge to streamline our life and follow our destiny is strong at this time.

Audience: What about the Nodes to the angles?

Melanie: They do highlight the meaning of the particular angle very clearly, and the emphasis on that area of life experience will be strong. Also, it will signal the time when the transiting Node is changing house. That is very interesting to track as well. If we think of the houses as fields of experience, when the Nodes are transiting a particular axis, the 'worm' enters and tills the soil!

Transits to the Nodes

Now let's consider transits to the Nodal Axis. Taking an overview, one thing that is useful to check is which end of the Nodal Axis, if any, receives outer planet transits in the person's lifetime, or whether the balance points receive the most intense stimuli. Since the mid 1960s, with the Uranus-Pluto conjunction in Virgo, all the outer planets have concentrated their activity in the signs from Virgo through to Aquarius, and eventually Pisces. That will mean that some people have quite a sequence of conjunctions to one end or the other of the Nodal Axis, and others to one of the balance points. The chart we explored for the Nodal sequence is an example, where all the outer planets have already made conjunctions with the South Node during this person's life.

Transits from the outer planets to the Nodes will last several years, during which time the quality of the transiting planet is very prominent. It can also be interesting to note when the faster moving planets connect with your Nodes. Because Mercury and Venus stay quite close to the Sun, there can be times during the year when they all cluster together around a New Moon, and if an outer planet is also involved, this will mean an acceleration of energy into the dominant themes of your life. When transits occur to the North Node end, you are challenged strongly. Your evasions, inertia and resistance may be discovered, your self-deceptions pierced, and you may feel at times as if you are on a roller-coaster, with no sense of where you are going, or how to get off! These periods of life are when a quantum leap is possible, and you can make big changes in your life. Indeed, they may come about anyway, and your task will be adjusting to them.

When transits occur to the South Node there is an emphasis on the themes I have already described. Using our image of the safety net, these transits can be like the fishermen who, when unable to go out and fish, stay at home and mend their nets. This means dealing with unfinished business, clearing the past, letting go of ties, a vague sense of preparing for the future, waiting for the tides to be in your favour again. All being well, this results in enormous impetus later on, at the North Node end.

As we are always dealing with a polarity, transits to one end of the Nodal Axis may show more obviously in things that are seemingly related to the other end, like a ricochet. Also, we may be forced to compensate. For example, if you have a long sequence of transits over the South Node, where you feel pulled back to the past, or there is an impetus to revisit your own unfinished business, you might have to also engage the North Node very strongly to maintain a sense of balance. That's another dynamic that can occur between the two ends. The work may also be about coming down from the buzz of North Node activity, into some rest.

Audience: Which are more important – transits to the Nodes, or aspects made by the movement of the transiting Nodal Axis?

Melanie: They serve different purposes. The Nodal cycle itself, as we have seen, can give you a useful overview of significant themes in a chart and, if you explore it fully, it can take in a long period of time, as the Nodes are moving consistently round and round the chart during your whole life. However, transits to the Nodes will define shorter periods of time, as even a slow one like Pluto will eventually move away. Unless you live past eighty-four years old, the Uranus return, none of the outer planets get all the way round the chart. In practice, then, it is useful to consider both. For example, if you are seeing a client near their Nodal return, check back to note the date of the previous half-return, and full return, and also the most relevant transits of those periods. An entire cycle is ending and beginning, and that can make a useful framework within which to lay further information about other current transits.

Audience: So one is a cycle and the other one isn't?

Melanie: They are both cycles, really. No transit is an isolated event, but is part of a cycle, even if that began before you were born. Each planet's position at any point in time can be defined in terms of numerous different cycles, depending on which is the most relevant to the purpose at hand.

Audience: I have a particular week in the year where something important usually has happened. It is the first week of April. I am making sense of what you say because I have got Jupiter on 11° Aries right squaring my Nodes.

Melanie: So every year the Sun triggers that degree.

Audience: Yes, and I have just realised that certain experiences in childhood connect with that week, like the birth of my brother. Also, when the Sun was opposite that point I met my ex-husband. I left my country on April 6th for the first time in my life, and before that I ran away from my mother's house, the same first week of April.

Melanie: What are you going to do next year?

Audience: I don't know!

Melanie: The obvious connection here is with Jupiter and the Nodal degree, which may have become additionally sensitised through early events in your life.[36] When you have what I would call a 'deciding moment' in your life – which could be a traumatic experience – where a thread of continuity is broken or cut, or important unconscious decisions are made. In order to mend that, you may have to do some going back, some reweaving or letting go.

An Example Chart

I'd like to look further at the chart we used to illustrate the Nodal sequence, and explore this person's Nodes in more detail. Here is the chart again:

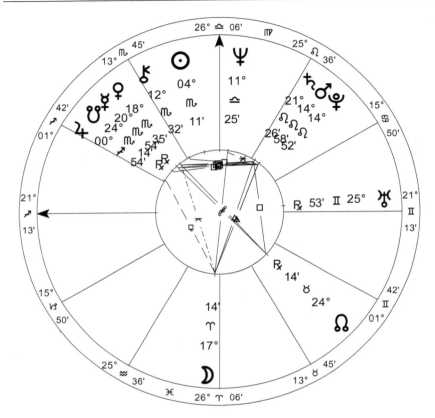

This person, who I'm calling 'Rosie', has the North Node in Taurus in the 5ᵗʰ house, and the South in Scorpio in the 11ᵗʰ house. As we might expect, being a multiple Scorpio, her life journey has been one of enormous intensity and certainly during the last Nodal cycle she has been preoccupied with a personal journey of transformation. Rosie has been in therapy, made enormous changes in her life, and has anchored herself deeply in commitment to her inner journey. Not that she didn't do that before but, being a Scorpio, she lived this South Node connection more in terms of emotional engagement, becoming involved in very intense and sometimes complicated relationships, also with her family and work colleagues. She has worked in various co-operatives, very much an 11ᵗʰ house theme, which has also expressed itself through her strong political ideals, and become involved in quite high profile political activism, almost by happenstance. Being the South Node, she did not deliberately set out to become a revolutionary. Also, this Scorpio South Node has seen conjunctions from all the outer planets, and Rosie's heroic task has been how to get those energies working for her, rather than against her.

When we listed the order of Nodal contacts, do you remember that it began with the South Node conjunct Mercury, and the only North Node conjunction in the first half of the cycle was to the Moon? A big feature of this person's life is that she is one of twins. It was a very difficult birth, and her twin was born first. Such was the struggle that Rosie's arm was broken during the birth, and a few months after the birth it was discovered that her twin was epileptic. You can see that symbolised in the sequence – the South Node first contacts Mercury, who rules the arms and also siblings. Note that this Mercury also disposits the 7th house Uranus in Gemini which, apart from Neptune, is the only air planet. Like something misfiring. The twin was born before her, and has that Scorpio cluster in the 12th house. So Rosie was the twin who did all the coping.

Look at the Moon in the 3rd in Aries. Up to about ten years old, this was the only conjunction made by the Nodal Axis, and this symbolises both the sibling – 3rd house – and the fact that the whole family experienced enormous disruption and chaos caused by her twin's severe fits, and the high level of distressing emotion in the family. Rosie largely played the role of active mediator and peacekeeper, trying to help her mother deal with her twin, and trying to connect with her father, who was out at work, and often had no idea of what had gone on in the home during the day. Remember my description of the Moon in Aries as 'animal mother'? Rosie began that role very early.

Mercury begins the sequence, and Jupiter in Sagittarius ends it. This has shown itself through Rosie's ability to draw meaning from her life experience, going into the thick of things, and at the end there is a fortunate release of some kind, a lucky break. Something shifts or a new perspective dawns. This is a very Plutonic chart, but the metaphor of the overall journey leads from darkness and tumult into hope, faith and meaning, which in her case is congruent with having Sagittarius rising. Rosie also writes a personal journal, something which has helped her find her way in her inner world, and has become a further expression of Mercury in Scorpio conjunct the South Node.

Note also that this North Node in Taurus is the only earth point in the chart – there are neither planets nor angles in earth. This does place a great emphasis upon it, and in a while I will tell you how this has expressed itself in her life. First, let's look at the trail of dispositors. Venus rules the North Node, and Mars the South, and note also that her Nodal rulers, Mars and Venus, rule the IC and MC respectively. Venus is in Scorpio, ruled by Pluto in Leo and, with her Sun being in Scorpio, there is a mutual reception. Mars is in Leo, ruling the South Node, therefore also connecting with the same mutual reception. In this case, whether we use old or new rulers, the picture is the same. Finding ways to give shape and form to, and express her connection with, Plutonic transformation processes has been an important life theme, and still is. The Sun is in the 10th house, of profession, career and place in the world. What do you think this person might do?

Audience: She works with children?

Melanie: Not exclusively.

Audience: I see kids, not working in the actual home with them.

Melanie: No, although that's what she did in her childhood home, in a way. She was caretaking from a very early age because of the situation with her twin.

Audience: A psychotherapist?

Melanie: She has had in-depth psychotherapy but she is not a psychotherapist. Good guess, though!

Audience: Does she create on a physical level?

Melanie: Keep going …

Audience: Using the environment …

Melanie: Yes! At this person's first Nodal return, she was leaving school, and trained as an architect. She eventually became very successful, and also managed to do work which aligned with her strong ideals. For example, she was custom-designing spaces for people with disabilities. Her mother was killed unexpectedly in a car accident in 1982, when transiting Pluto was conjunct her own MC, within 30' of arc, conjunct transiting Saturn, in Libra. That day, transiting Nodes also reached the same degree in which there had been a lunar eclipse a few weeks earlier, and they were also applying to square Rosie's natal Moon, 2°5' from exact.

By the time of Rosie's second Nodal return, she had realised that the motivation for doing architecture was to get approval from her father. Obviously he was a major source of support for her during her childhood, because her mother was often so preoccupied with the epileptic twin. Or perhaps it would be more accurate to say that she held out hope of a kind of support from him that was not really forthcoming, so she felt she had to earn it. This is reflected in the mutual reception of Sun and Pluto, which was strongly highlighted at the time of her Nodal return, because by then Pluto was conjunct her Sun, ushering in a very long period of Pluto transits, currently just finishing with Pluto conjunct her Jupiter. So by becoming an architect she was hoping to please her father, and 'pleasing society' by doing something respected, and making a contribution through it. Also, remember when there is no earth in a chart, Saturn becomes even more important. At this stage, the second Nodal return, she wanted to change her work situation, so joined a co-operative – South Node in the 11th – and that made quite a difference. She also began therapy around this Nodal return, and making this move required an enormous step of overcoming a certain prejudice against therapy which was held within her own network of friends. Note South Node in the 11th house, of friends and ideals. It is the Aquarius house, of belief systems too, which can include prejudice.

When Pluto was conjunct her Chiron in Scorpio, she was in therapy, and the work focused around the honouring of many hurt feelings from her childhood. Grieving the sudden loss of her mother took her far back in her life, even to birth, and exposed much pain. She began to discover the angry, out of control 'epileptic' twin within herself. As her own needs were often pushed aside in favour of the twin who had dominated the family through her unfortunate illness, all the hurt and indignation poured forth under this transit, as she released the need to placate and mediate, a role in which she was still expert. Interestingly, transiting Chiron was also in Gemini at the time she was healing her relationship with the inner twin, her own other half. This also had the effect of making important adjustments in her relationship with her actual twin, and releasing the feeling of somehow being responsible for her misfortune.

When her Pluto square occurred, it also involved the square to Mars, ruler of the South Node, and its next contact was to Venus, ruler of the North Node. An idea occurred, an impulse began gestating, which took further shape as Pluto crossed her Venus. By the time Pluto was conjunct her South Node she had given up her job, rented her flat, and she was in Africa, working on a co-operative housing project, physically making bricks out in the sunshine. During the previous years, preparing for this change, she also qualified in massage and various holistic physical therapies. Once in Africa, she also met and worked with traditional healers, while living a very earthy lifestyle, literally making bricks and houses with village people.

She has deeply engaged this earthy Taurus North Node for the sake of her own balance, and the rewards indeed have been considerable. Working with those qualities has given her enough sense of substance herself to better deal with some of the emotional complexities within her family.

The Sabian Symbols

Do you all know what the Sabian symbols are? No? OK. In astrology, there are several different sets of symbols relating to each degree of the Zodiac. My own favourite is Dane Rudhyar's interpretation of the symbols which were channelled by the clairvoyant Elsie Wheeler, and originally noted by Marc Edmund Jones.[37] It is a very inspiring book, and a very useful springboard for one's imagination and intuition.

The two symbols for the North and South Nodes are often very interesting, and can provide images which sum up the axis very neatly. Let's consider the same chart. The North Node symbol is 'A vast public park'. Here's some of the interpretation ... 'the cultivation of natural energies for collective use and recreation.' Remember she was an architect, focused around community-based projects. 'Positive and impressive results of man's collective endeavour to life in peace. The public park is designed and kept for the enjoyment of all the people of the city. It is a symbol of collective enjoyment.'[38] That is very interesting, considering her work in a co-operative architectural venture, and then again in Africa working within the community, building bricks and houses.

One of her balance points is at 25° Leo, which is the cusp of the 9th house ... transformation through long-distance travel. Note it is near her Saturn in the 8th house and its symbol is ... 'A large camel seen crossing a vast and forbidding desert ... self-sufficiency in the face of a long and exhausting adventure ... the organism sustaining itself independently ... self-reliance and self-sufficiency.'[39] That has been an important motif. Being a very watery chart, Rosie won her freedom not by cutting off from any of the difficult relationships, including that of her twin, but by hanging in there with great tenacity.

The other balance point is even more amazing. This is 25° Aquarius, in the 3rd house. 'A butterfly with the right wing more perfectly formed.' Remember I told you she was born one of twins, and with one arm broken! The interpretation here is 'The capacity to develop aspects of the conscious mind ahead of normal.'[40] Rosie has no personal planets in air, but she does have Uranus in Gemini and Neptune in Libra. Perhaps by way of compensation, she got a degree in architecture. She was very intelligent, but by her own admission was 'flying by the seat of her pants' intellectually. I guess this is a good description of 'transpersonal air'!

Audience: I'm confused, it is 24° 14', not 25° degrees ...

Melanie: When you reckon the degrees for the Sabian symbols, the convention is that you round them up to the next degree. So 24° plus any number of minutes, even 01', is the 25th degree. If you remember that 00° 00' up to 00° 59' Aries is the first degree of the Zodiac sequence, it makes sense.

Synastry

From everything we have explored, it should be obvious how important the Nodes are in synastry, given that they are about relationship, inner and outer. When the Nodal Axis is activated by transits, or indeed the transiting axis is stimulating a planet, important encounters with others are likely. One of the most powerful links between two charts occurs when the Nodal Axis of one person lines up along one of the angles of another. This is likely to be a link of great intensity, whether comfortable or not, and one which resonates deeply, over a long period. It is like your life is joined to that person's life, whether you like it or not. Even if the relationship founders and ends, the impact of it will last. This is a connection frequently found in the charts of couples, and I've seen quite a number where the connection existed both ways round. People with Node-Angle conjunctions often find it difficult to separate, almost as if their lives were meant to flow together in some way that may or may not be congruent with more superficial levels of compatibility.

For example, if a person's North Node conjuncts your MC, you can expect this to be an association that may concern your professional life. Your ambition will be stimulated, as you are assisted and supported. However, the North Node person might also want to take over! It also means that their South Node will conjunct your IC, and so you may find that the intimate personal level of this kind of contact becomes fraught with residue from the past. If it were the other way round, the presence of this person would stimulate your desire for security, comfort and familial intimacy; they might even feel strangely familiar from the first time you meet. With their South Node on your MC, however, you might find that they also want you to take authority, make the decisions, or perhaps they ride on the back of your professional success. You always need to consider both ends of the axis, and as the MC/IC is also the parental axis, those themes are almost sure to surface too. With the other angles, the Ascendant/Descendant, the emphasis is on issues of identity, and your style of relating. If the Nodal Axes of the two people are in square to each other, there can be a feeling of literally being 'at cross-purposes'. One wants more than the other can give, or there is no easy agreement on what form suits the relationship. Because the axes will also contact each other's balance points, however, inter-chart Nodal squares can be very valuable, too, accelerating the process of psychological maturing for both people.

When the North Node in one chart contacts a planet in another chart, if we think of our image of the dragon, it can seem to devour that planet, to eat it up and digest it. If it is your planet involved, you might have to work to get it back, metaphorically speaking! Paradoxically, this may mean a strengthening and improving of the functioning of this planet for you, as the Nodal contact from the other person lends you energy. However, if this is unconscious, and this is a planet whose qualities you have not integrated, you could end up feeling bereft of it. An example of this was a woman whose partner's North Node was conjunct her Mercury, and he was always the talkative one when they were together, although friends reported that he was not always this way. In tandem with this, my client found herself not very verbal, slow in her thinking, and confused because this was quite out of character for her! If someone has their North Node on your Venus, you might feel suddenly self-conscious, notice your imperfections or, positively, you feel appreciated, or feel compelled to go and buy a new outfit. Extra awareness is focused on that planet, and if your connection with it is good, you will immediately benefit. If not, difficulties will be highlighted, and this in turn can ultimately be of benefit as we process fears and negative patterns.

On the other hand, South Node contacts have the effect of releasing energy. If my South Node conjuncts someone's planet, they may be stimulated to release a lot of energy from it, which could be very creative, or also a bit chaotic. Conversely, my own South Node issues of past, inertia and resistance might be highlighted, and I will find myself sliding down the snake in the game of snakes and ladders. Regressing, re-enacting past patterns. I think you get the picture.

Audience: What if it's Chiron and the Node between charts?

Melanie: The Chiron themes may be strongly activated, putting one in touch with deep wounds, and also the inner resource of healing, broadening one's perspective, and so on. I believe it was Jung who said something like we don't really cure our neuroses, but we can outgrow them. A Node/Chiron contact in a relationship often signals an opportunity to do just that. Outgrowing a particular area of suffering may include an uncomfortable exploration of the 'secondary gains' we have established from it, which may initially evoke resistance, and lead us to feel that the relationship is wounding us, because of the challenge to grow. The Chiron person may function as a teacher or mentor, but that doesn't mean an easy ride!

Audience: Could you say more about someone's South Node conjunct another person's planet? I mean, how the planet person feels?

Melanie: Obviously it will depend on what planet it is. But if a significant area of your chart is highlighted by somebody's South Node, then you can be the recipient of quite a lot of their past stuff that is energised by the connection. Let's use Mercury again … there you are innocently talking away and that's interpreted or misunderstood through the filter of how the other person used to argue with their brother, for example, or they felt they could not get a word in edgeways in their family. An actual example of the Moon conjunct another person's South Node was that the Node person's resistance to nourishing and being nourished were such that the Moon person risked misinterpretation every time she made a gesture of caring or support. The Node person thought that they were being taken over, manipulated or undermined. The past patterns of both people were subtly involved, as they will inevitably be in any relationship, but they were highlighted. On the other hand, the positive version is that the person's planet can also be the witness to something creative which is actually released. That word, 'release', at the South Node can mean the discharge of toxins, or release of creative output.

Audience: One example, how is it when the South Node of someone is on the North Node of another person? Are the transits to do with balance?

Melanie: Yes, the transiting Nodal cycle is about balance, and reaches the half-return just over nine years into the cycle. This means that the Nodal situation you describe will occur between people who are about nine years apart in age, or about twenty-seven or forty-five years. These are interesting gaps, because the two people will also have rather different patterns from the outer planets forming the collective backdrop of their charts; they are informed by different visions, understandings and preoccupations. Also remember that any opposition, any half-cycle, carries the element of awareness and consciousness often gained through conflict or certainly appreciation of difference. If this is enshrined in the synastry through the Nodal contact, this can be a very dynamic connection, bringing the perception of difference, and ideally the wish to understand and encompass new perspectives and ways of being. Major misunderstandings and so-called incompatibilities between people are often very clearly reflected by the Nodal Axis. After all, if this is the high wire act of your life, and you find someone's Nodal themes too jarring, you will feel like you are about to fall off!

Also, this person with their Nodes the other way round to your own will reactivate areas of your past experience that occurred on previous Nodal half- or full returns. That theme of release and clearing out at the South Node, and challenge at the North, will be an important part of the relationship. Memories, history and inertia at each person's South Node will be stirred and shaken by the other's North Node, so you can see how fruitful a combination this could be. On the other hand, it can feel like each person is going in a totally different direction with their life, and sometimes this causes conflict and eventual separation.

The Draconic Chart

Audience: Have you found Draconic astrology useful?

Melanie: This is another trail which we will go a little way down, and then back off! The person to read on this subject is Pamela Crane,[41] but I will try to give you a résumé of my limited understanding of it. Firstly, to calculate a Draconic chart, you make the North Node

0° 00′ Aries, and you recalculate the whole chart and the angles in relation to that. Let's take a really easy example. If your natal North Node was 5° 00′ Aries, and you replace it with the Draconic North Node, which is always 0° 00′ Aries, that is 5° 00′ degrees backwards. So you then subtract 5° precisely from the position of everything else. You will then have your Draconic chart. Luckily, many computer programs now calculate this chart for you!

Bearing in mind that this is a chart set using the Nodes as 0° 00′ Aries, the beginning of beginnings, the primary impulse, then we could perhaps see it reflecting the impulse behind our life, behind this incarnation. In that way it often supports the natal Tropical chart – that's the normal Zodiac – feeds it, nourishes it and underpins it. Qualities reflected in the Draconic chart are like a pool of resources that we can draw on, the quintessence of who and what we have been up to now. Given the symbolism of the Nodes themselves – the interaction between the Sun, Moon and Earth – this chart might be seen as our cosmic inheritance at a subtle level.

I will leave the metaphysics up to you, but here is a 'smorgasbord' of different perspectives. In psychological terms, you could say that the Draconic chart shows a transpersonal level of the parental *imagos*, your spiritual parents, as it were. In the work of Rudolph Steiner, it is said that our subtle body is actually woven from the etheric substance of the planets, so we could perhaps extend this to consider the Nodal Axis carrying this information. The word 'astral' refers to the stars, from the Latin word *astrum*, and it is no accident that the *astral body* has this name. This is the layer of the subtle body which deals with emotion, not strictly personal, but linked with what we might call the collective unconscious. Also, from radio-astronomy, we know that the same actual chemical elements that live in our bodies are also found in far-flung regions of deep space. You may favour a karmic interpretation, and take the view that the Draconic chart shows our past life heritage impinging on this life, for good or ill. However, if you prefer to stay with the astronomical symbolism and allow the chart itself to speak, I think you will still find some very interesting and useful insights will surface.

The relationship between the Draconic and natal charts is also very interesting, because sometimes there is an obviously supportive link, or themes emerge which complement or balance the natal chart. There can also be conflicts thrown up, and this too is significant, almost as if the person has to work very hard to get the different levels of being aligned with each other, or they suffer from a feeling of lack of inner resources, or they keep getting in their own way, and often feel out of kilter with themselves and others. Of course, in the Draconic chart all the aspect patterns will remain the same, and planets will be in the same houses, but the signs will change. That means that in charts that have a very strong emphasis of one kind or another, it is particularly interesting, because that will shift. A fixed grand cross might come out as a mutable cross. A stellium in Cancer might end up in Aquarius, or a multiple Capricorn person might turn into someone with a stellium in Draconic Pisces! I have found it especially revealing to consider points of conjunction between the two, as these seem to connect different levels of being, and are certainly powerful when activated by transits.

What is so interesting is that if you do Draconic charts for people you know well, you can immediately see how they 'fit'! I would invite you try out your own, because it's almost guaranteed that you will strongly relate to it. Considering it as a resource, like a well of being to draw on, has made sense to me. You see, the Tropical Zodiac, the one we normally use in the West, is reckoned from co-ordinates that begin the sequence at 0° 00′ Aries, or the time when the Sun crosses the Celestial Equator, moving north. Thus there is a solar, even Martian, initial impulse to the Zodiac, the hero's journey through the great 'circle of animals'. Hence its psychological accuracy as a mirror of development for the individual, charting the unfoldment of our becoming.

The Draconic Zodiac also involves the 0° 00′ Aries point, but in a different way, showing the Moon's Nodes aligning with it. So the Draconic Zodiac, being reckoned from something that concerns the inter-relationship of the Sun, Moon and Earth, may well show the prior summation of our own wholeness, and how it invisibly underpins the patterns in the Tropical natal chart. The seed of our unfoldment is clearly depicted within the Tropical Zodiac, but perhaps the Draconic shows the ground of being from which it grows, like a plant, towards the solar light symbolised by the Tropical Zodiac.

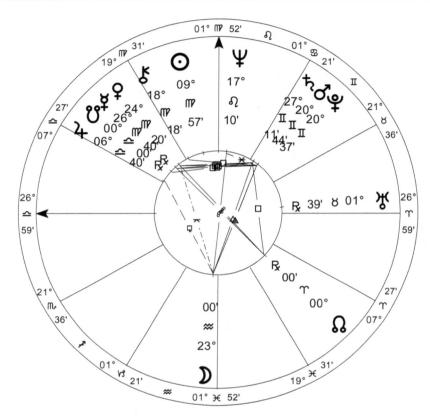

Let me whet your appetite with an example of a Draconic chart.

Here is Rosie's Draconic chart, and look at all that earth! Three of the Virgo planets actually trine the Tropical North Node in Taurus, which if you remember is the only earth point in the entire chart. Some people with no earth planets really show it, because they are ungrounded, unanchored, and need to draw a lot from their friends, or to import that energy through a job or a profession. It may be hard for them to make their way in the world and, although they may try so hard they over-compensate and appear very successful or get rich and make a lot of money, if you sense their energy, you can tell the strain. It's not easy and natural. But Rosie's life pattern, and indeed her energy, and latterly, the physical skills she has learned in the healing arts, all add up to a picture somewhat different than usual. Sometimes a strong Saturn will compensate for a lack of earth but, in Rosie's case, her Saturn is in detriment, and flanked by Pluto and Mars. It does square the Nodal Axis, and so is important, but certainly does not show her sense of ease at the physical level. This Saturn does symbolise very well the intensity and depth of relationship that she has explored within herself, with partners and members of her family, and the tumult of her childhood. That Draconic Virgo emphasis is reflected in her work as an architect – dealing with detail, facts, doing precise drawings – and now also in her work as a healer.

In Rosie's case, there is considerable congruency between the two, so there is a harmonious and productive interchange, a lot of sextiles. Note that the Draconic Ascendant is 26° Libra, which means that the recent solar eclipse (12 October 1996, chart below) was a few degrees behind it, in the 12th house, and she is currently considering returning from Africa.

Audience: Wouldn't you use Draconic transits to the Draconic chart?

Melanie: I think you can use either, or both. Several computer programmes, including Solar Fire, will do a listing of Draconic transits to the Draconic chart. These are very interesting and, in my rather limited experience, show things unfolding invisibly, under the surface, but that are definite inner movements of energy or unfolding of fated situations. Possibly Tropical transits to the Draconic, like in this example, might show something more externally defined. I'm not sure.

Audience: I'm confused – what do you mean by a Draconic transit?

Melanie: Well, consider the chart for today as an example. The North Node is about 5° Libra, which is 175° away from 0° 00' Aries. You can see that the Sun-Pluto conjunction in Sagittarius in the 11th house of today's chart is just short of sextile to this North Node, which will mean that the Sun-Pluto conjunction will be at the end of Taurus in the Draconic chart.

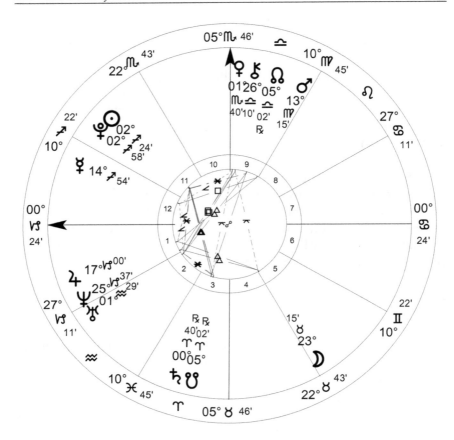

Seminar
24 November 1996; 10.00 GMT; London, England

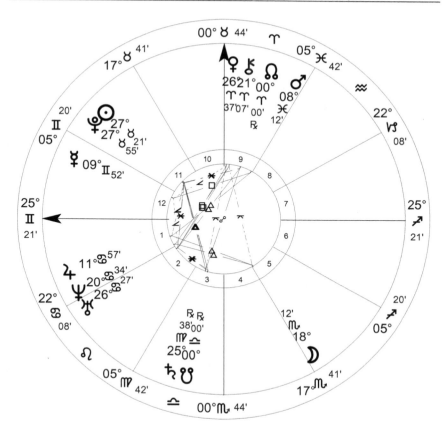

Seminar - DRACONIC
24 November 1996; 10.00 GMT; London, England

The Huber Method Moon Node Chart

There's one more Nodal chart which I want to mention – here's another trail that we will only peek down. Here is Rosie's chart done as a Huber Method Moon Node horoscope. I'm not sure it is fair to simply add this as an extra technique or perspective, because the Huber method is really a whole system in itself, and probably we should interpret the whole chart as embedded fully in that system. However, as Mercury retrograde in the 8th house rules both ends of my own Nodes, perhaps that will allow me to beg, borrow and steal for today's seminar. In case you hadn't noticed, I've done a fair bit of that already!

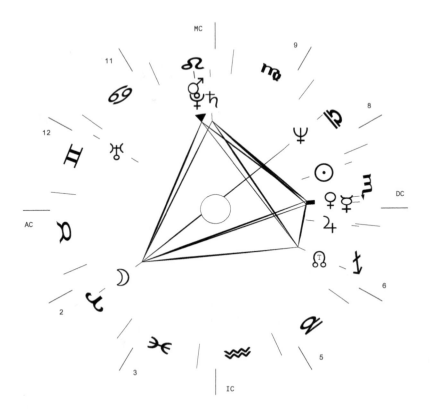

Like the Draconic, this Moon Node chart should also be used alongside the Tropical natal chart.[42] Here, as you can see, the North Node is used as the Ascendant, and its usual degree become the Nodes, so they are switched around. If you want to do one of these for yourself, take your North Node, put it at the Ascendant, then make a set of equal houses right the way round, but with the *Zodiac going clockwise*, and don't forget to add the Node, using the Ascendant degree. Otherwise, all the degrees and minutes of the planets stay exactly the same. So what you get is like a mirror image, like the chart inside out. Do you see that?

In the interpretation of the Moon's Node chart within the Huber system, the framework of reincarnation is used, and this chart is seen in terms of what they call 'reincarnation archetypes'. This chart, then, is seen as a repository of images that may serve as an access point for deep memory, from the collective unconscious, where deeply engrained themes are encapsulated in these archetypal images. These also have individual karmic resonance, as well as reflecting shadow aspects of the psychological dimension. For example, if you spent a life in a monastery, yearning for connection with the Divine, that structure will imprint very strongly, and may act like an undertow, a deep current of unfulfilment which may interfere with your happiness in this life. Certain people also identify strongly with other cultures, other historical periods, and these archetypal themes will then be relevant in terms of this life. If you consider this perspective, it is important not to judge and attribute blame, because releasing subtle feelings of misplaced guilt is important in clearing these imprints. Louise Huber connects the Moon Node chart specifically with the astral body, which we mentioned earlier.[43]

Rosie's Moon Node chart is interesting, because the 7th house is emphasised. This is called 'the house of encounter' in Moon Node charts, and we know from Rosie's life that this has indeed been a major theme. Within this framework, we could speculate that her relationship with her twin might have a history longer than this life, and that she has been working to release and resolve particular resonances from this deep past. There have been other intense partnerships too in her life that could fall into this category. The Leo stellium comes out in the 10th house, the place of mother, authority and the drive to scale the heights. This is called 'the individuality axis' in Moon Node astrology. Again we see that clearly in Rosie's life. Remember it was the loss of her mother that actually triggered off the beginning of a very inward and intense transformational process. Although not the eldest in age, she has assumed the role of the elder in the family. Her father is now old and frail, and there have been many complex situations involving her twin to deal with, and through her relationships within her own family, and also her professional work, she has been progressively rediscovering her own sense of authority in life, and standing apart from situations that she knows she must separate from.

Nodal Polarities

That's enough input from me for a while! In this next session you will have some time to focus on your own Nodes. I have made a handout for you,[44] which is really intended to facilitate your own exploration after the seminar, as to go through it systematically would take quite a long time. However, it might also be useful now, to give you clues and leads. We will divide up into groups according to the six polarities by sign, which means that your whole Nodal Axis is under consideration. Explore this axis in any way you wish, but try and use some of the basic features that we discussed – dispositors, aspects and the like. Check transits too if you have time. See how your own experience compares with that of others, and also what distinguishing features highlight the difference. You may have a chance to compare notes with someone who has their Nodal Axis the opposite way round to yourself, and so understand your own more deeply. Afterwards, we will take some time go through this all together, so we can all benefit from each other's work. Finally, you might look for an image, either together or singly, of your axis ... something that encapsulates all the meanings you have discovered. This may be a way of engaging your intuition, which often summarises what you have been exploring.

[Time allowed for the exercise.]

The Aries/Libra Polarity

Melanie: OK ... we need to reconvene as a whole group now, and take some time to go over what you discovered. Let's go systematically, and start with Aries/Libra, which looks like quite a big group. What did you discover?

Audience: We seemed to be alternating between agreement and disagreement, and there was quite a bit of difficulty in getting going, because we wanted to include everyone's input about how to do it!

Melanie: Was there a difference between those with North Node in Aries and those with it in Libra?

Audience: Yes, it was really interesting. Mostly, the ones with North Node in Aries were actually the ones listening and mediating and trying to include everyone, and then getting frustrated because we were not getting on with it!

Audience: Those of us with North Node in Libra wanted to just do it!

Melanie: So you were mostly expressing South Node attitudes. That makes me think of the safety net image we were talking about, and the fact that the South Node is like the line of least resistance, what we can fall back on.

Audience: Once we got going, and decided how to do it, the North Node in Aries people tended to be more definite, direct and wanting to speak about their experience.

Audience: We did find that the sign and house placements of Mars and Venus made a difference as to how the balance was experienced. I have Mars in Sagittarius, and I spoke first, and got impatient. I was wanting us all to explore as much as possible of the handout, then report back, but not everyone agreed with that, because they thought it was too much to do in the time we had!

Audience: She got the vision, but it wasn't possible!

Melanie: Can you see the time-honoured theme Aries/Libra there of me/you/us? And action/reflection? With this axis, the balance between self-assertion and consideration of others' ways is a theme, as is the desire to find balance without having individual impulses crushed. Did you come up with an image?

Audience: Not really, except that of weighing scales being upset, but we did not feel that did justice to the positive side of Aries.

Melanie: You wanted justice! This is also an interesting axis, because of the large number of transits that have occurred in Capricorn, which is one of the balance points for this axis. So each of you will have had Uranus, and possibly Neptune also, making a square to your Nodes – balance or bust!

Audience: When I realised this, it shed some light on a very intense period of my life, when I was feeling very torn in a relationship situation. It was like a see-saw, and I did not really consider the transits to the Nodes, but this makes sense of the overall process.

Melanie: Today the North Node is about 5° Libra. Is anyone having a Nodal return?

Audience: My North Node is 20° 23' Aries, so I had a half-return in February this year. I had not noticed that until today. But it makes sense of some things. I have the Sun in Pisces, trine Moon in Cancer, but my North Node has Mars and Saturn conjunct in Aries. I always try to avoid conflict but, during this time, I was forced into a situation of having to stand my ground.

Melanie: What enabled you to do so?

Audience: I'm not sure.

Melanie: What about your South Node resources? Where is your Venus?

Audience: In Aquarius, tightly conjunct Mercury in Aquarius and quincunx Pluto in Virgo. They are all within less than a degree.

Melanie: If you think of the South Node like a safety net, or something innate, brought in with you, what does that suggest?

Audience: Well, I guess I had to clarify my principles and think things through. I usually flow with what others want. My North Node, Mars and Saturn are in the 4th house, and in my family there was a lot of harshness, judgement and arguing, and so forth. I said I never wanted to be like that. But I found out that I had sort of cut myself off at the roots, with no ground. And I had to find it, quick!

Melanie: There is the North Node activity of upgrading, updating something. Although you had experience of negative Mars-Saturn, and were determined not to be like that, you were challenged to find the positive expression of it. Was it in a work situation? I'm thinking of the South Node being in the 10th house.

Audience: The actual situation, yes. But the changes I went through also had repercussions in my family. The image of standing my ground applied equally to both in the end.

Melanie: You will soon have your Saturn return, too, and this is an interesting prelude, because Saturn does consolidate gains made previously.

The Taurus/Scorpio Polarity

Melanie: What about the Taurus/Scorpio group?

Audience: We seemed to concentrate on the theme of resources, and the feeling of having or not having. We only had one person with North Node in Scorpio, and she said she felt a great resistance to things getting too complicated, although they inevitably did, emotionally. She tried to simplify her life all the time, loved nature and sensual things, but had difficulty with her sexuality because she felt wary of the emotional complexity that it led her into. The people with North Node in Taurus seemed to almost court intensity, however, and had to learn to appreciate simple things and earthy values. One person said she had to learn to value her productivity at work, in other words the money in the bank, as much as her appetite for high-risk emotional situations!

Melanie: You seem to have only one spokesperson? Did you decide it that way, or did it just happen?

Audience: Most of us are hiding in Scorpio, and the rest are being lazy in Taurus!

Melanie: And the spokesperson ...?

Audience: Well, I have Mars in Aries, trine Venus in Sagittarius, trine Moon in Leo. It's not quite a Grand Trine, as there are about 13° between Venus and the Moon.

Melanie: Where is your Jupiter?

Audience: Early Libra, so actually Jupiter and Venus are in mutual reception, ruling my North Node in Taurus. I enjoy taking initiative, but it wasn't always like this. Saturn is also conjunct my Venus, and although I have all this fire, I used to feel quite timid really, sometimes, sort of afraid of putting my foot in it, or letting the side down. I think it changed a lot recently, when Pluto went over my South Node. I started to really own my Mars.

Audience: We spent quite a bit of time comparing notes about this transit. It was pretty difficult for most of us. It was interesting, as those who had gone through this some years ago were able to look back and report – like there is life after Pluto conjunct the South Node!

Melanie: Yes! All of you will have had this transit, a period of very deep readjustments, when you may have sometimes felt like you were losing everything.

Audience: I did lose everything, at least everything material. My husband's business went bankrupt, and we had to re-mortgage our home, which we eventually lost also. It was terrifying. Those Taurus/Scorpio themes of resources – it was very literal. I had not developed a career myself, because we never had to rely on what money I brought in. I guess I did not have much motivation, or maybe I was lazy ... sometimes lazy, sometimes driven! I never would have believed it could happen.

Melanie: Did anything positive come out of this time?

Audience: Yes, I learned about letting go, I guess, and I saw how loss opens space for gain, and I also got my own career together. That was interesting – for a while I was the breadwinner, and I had to learn about sharing when I was the one with more money coming in! It all felt very chaotic emotionally, and I was like a spiteful teenager sometimes, and then full of self-pity. It was a real initiation, and the surfacing of some deep feeling I always had, of somehow being hard done by. Not a victim, but just that life owed me something I wasn't getting. I learned about giving, I think, too.

Melanie: All of you will have Uranus squaring your Nodes, then Neptune, at some point over the next years …

Audience: I have already had that, as mine are only the 2nd degree.

Melanie: You still have one more exact aspect, very soon. What happened so far?

Audience: It was a time of breaking away from things. Not like the Pluto, which I had about twelve years ago. That was slow, and a lot about death. But the Uranus was exciting. I moved house, left a lot of the past behind, made new friends, and it all seemed quite fast. I'm still catching up with myself, I think. I got aware of how long it used to take me to change, and it feels very freeing at the moment.

Melanie: Thank you. If you are done, let's move on to the Gemini/Sagittarius group.

The Gemini/Sagittarius Polarity

Audience: There were only two of us, both with North Node in Sagittarius, and we talked a lot about the handout, and had lots of ideas. It was hard to focus, but we enjoyed it anyway! I have Mars in Gemini conjunct the South Node, in the 11th house, and I have no problem talking, and I especially like groups, discussion groups, study groups, all kinds. My North Node is in a Grand Trine with Pluto in Leo, and Venus in Aries, which is in the 9th house. So the Nodes sort of cut the triangle, like making a kite. The emphasis seems to fall on the 5th house, the North Node, but Jupiter is in the 12th house, so although my friends are mainly aware of this extroverted side, I can also be quite a hermit. And Mercury, ruling the South Node is in the 10th house, and my introverted side is also quite 'bookish'. Mercury doesn't have any very close major aspects to it, but I guess it's strong, being in Gemini too.

Melanie: What about the other Sagittarius North Node? Did you find similarities?

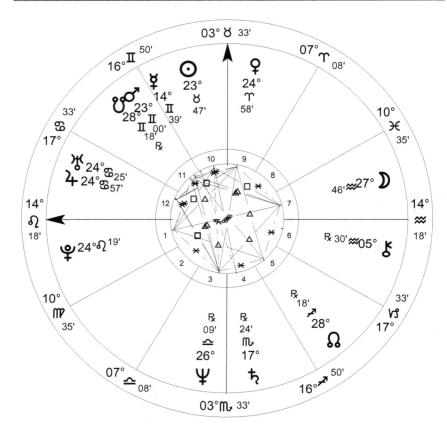

Audience: Yes, and also lots of difference. My South Node is in the 7th house, and I enjoy sharing ideas, but more on a one-to-one basis, more intimate. I have a very full 9th house, and also Saturn in the 12th widely conjunct my North Node, which is in the 1st house. Sometimes I hold myself back a lot, and sometimes I leap forward.

Melanie: Where is your Jupiter?

Audience: It's in the 9th, in Virgo, with Mercury and Pluto on either side, each about 9° away. I do feel intensely concerned with things spiritual, ethical. The search for meaning. That is very real to me. Pluto is conjunct my Sun up there, in Leo. I can remember as a child, so many things did not make sense. They still don't, sometimes! But I was always asking things, impossible things, about life and what it was all about.

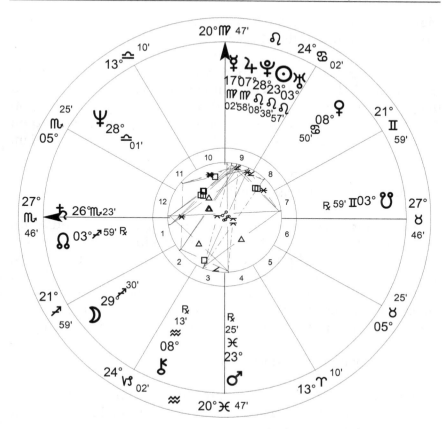

Melanie: So you have a Jupiter-Saturn theme connected with your Nodes. Jupiter rules, but Saturn is conjunct.

Audience: I always wanted to do something with religion. I mean, join the Church or something. When I was little, I wanted to be a nun, but as I grew older, I realised that would not do for me! If there were different possibilities, I would have taken religious orders, I think.

Melanie: So what have you done with your spiritual vocation?

Audience: I think my task has been to temper it, let go and internalise some of this fervour. That's how I understand the Saturn in the 12th, which is very closely conjunct the Ascendant.

Melanie: Pluto almost reached the conjunction with your North Node last month, and then backed off.

Audience: Yes. So far, I am experiencing a sense of relief, as it was crossing my Saturn and Ascendant in Scorpio for some years, and that was quite something. I felt as if I was slowly exploding on the inside. I was very depressed for quite a long time, and had no connection with what it was about. I went into analysis, Jungian, and that was really important.

Melanie: How was it important?

Audience: Firstly, it was about my feelings. I had a lot of bottled up feeling, and I can see now that this was blocking access to my own sense of meaning and purpose. I have two angular water planets, Saturn conjunct the Ascendant, and Mars in Pisces conjunct the IC. Then Venus is in Cancer in the 8th. Somehow the water sank, went underground, underneath other struggles in my life. And I suppose I felt like it was dragging me down into it. It was like drowning.

Melanie: When did you start your analysis?

Audience: In 1992, after my Chiron opposition. It crossed my Uranus, and I went quite manic. Then I crashed, and knew I needed to take the process seriously.

Melanie: Can you see the Yod here? Chiron is on the point, and Jupiter and Venus, sextile each other, form the two quincunxes with it. Note also that Jupiter is only 7° 58′ of Virgo, so it not only squares the Nodal Axis, but will also be squared by Pluto over the next couple of years. You were also in analysis over your Nodal Return, which was the following year.

Audience: I did not notice that. I was so focused on Pluto crossing Saturn and the Ascendant! But it was such a time of ending various cycles of experience, and also beliefs. I never understood how powerful beliefs were until this time. My philosophy is all-important to me, or I have no motivation. I am still sorting things out on that level, but I think I have more trust now that meaning will come by itself, and I don't have to figure it all out. Knowing Pluto is now in Sagittarius and I am not alone in this is also helpful. I mean, it is a collective process too.

Melanie: That's a very congruent expression of North Node in Sagittarius in the 1st house, and Jupiter in Virgo in the 9th squaring the Nodes. Thank you.

The Cancer/Capricorn Polarity

Melanie: What about the Cancer/Capricorn group?

Audience: We were swapping notes on what happened during the Uranus-Neptune conjunction, because most of us had it either conjunct one or other Node, or involving a planet close by. All of us seem to have at least one planet, sometimes several, conjunct the Capricorn end. The theme of security was very strong, and came up in different ways. Most us experienced a loss of ties with the past, some through work, some through family. But it was also a time of creative change for most of us. Getting free of expectations, and of deeply entrenched affiliations, ambitions, and so forth.

Melanie: Let's try and differentiate the two ends. Firstly, let's hear from those of you who have the North Node in Cancer …

Audience: One of us had the Sun, and one the Moon very near the Nodes. Does that mean that we were both born on eclipses?

Melanie: No, not unless you were born at either New or Full Moon. However, with the Sun very near the Nodes, you know that you were born within the eclipse season. We will be talking more about that in the next session. Is your Moon behind or ahead of your Sun?

Audience: The Moon is in Virgo, so there must have been a New Moon not long after I was born.

Melanie: And that would have been an eclipse. It would be useful to check that precise degree, as it is probably a sensitive point in your chart which resonates strongly to transits. Estimating roughly, it must have been at about 23° Capricorn, about ten days later. This means it would have been crossed by the Uranus-Neptune conjunction.

Audience: That is also my Mars degree, and my Mars is natally in the 10th house. This does relate to my mother ... I think it must have been around this time, she began haemorrhaging after my birth which, apart from being rather slow, seemed to have gone OK. She was rushed to hospital, and I was left with her mother. Apparently, I refused the breast after that. I have Jupiter in Aries exactly square the Nodes, in the 12th house. I've always understood this as something invisible which has sustained me inside, because I know I tend to make things difficult for myself. I have several Capricorn planets on the MC and conjunct the South Node.

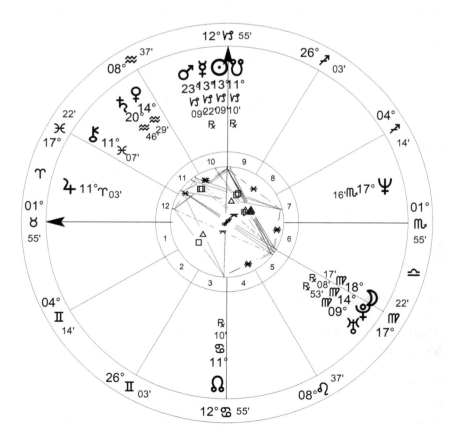

Melanie: How does the North Node in Cancer feature in this for you?

Audience: I have always thought it was about learning how to be kinder to myself, more nourishing, and more in touch with my own needs. I have often denied that, and tried to do what was expected of me. I guess that's the Capricorn. I also had to deal with a lot of jealousy from my brother.

Melanie: Note that Mercury actually rules this 3ʳᵈ house, both of which are also connected with siblings, and you were born just before an inferior (or interior) conjunction with the Sun and Mercury, in other words with Mercury going retrograde. I guess this early separation sowed the seeds of some quite strong beliefs about yourself and life.

Audience: I think I blamed my brother a lot. He was always much more confident than me, and I felt sort of eclipsed by him. Funny, I always used that word! He used to do this thing where he would just stand in front of me and look at me when I was doing my homework, or something, and I would get absolutely furious. He thought it was a funny game, but I would get incredibly upset. I felt judged, ridiculed, although he never said much. It was awful.

Melanie: The first eclipse in your life corresponded with a rupture in your relationship with your mother, and so with the South Node in Capricorn, those very Saturnian expectations of life are what comes naturally for you. You don't expect things to be easy, and you have good sterling qualities like endurance, discipline and persistence to fall back on. However, when it's time to be watery, vulnerable and feeling, on the Cancer side, you may have difficulty opening up to your needs, unless you have tested a situation over time.

Audience: Yes. Both of us who have these Nodes agreed that we often make heavy weather out of our feelings, because we expect rejection.

Melanie: What about those of you who have North Node in Capricorn? What is the difference here? There are quite a few of you.

Audience: The common theme seemed to be around the need to structure things, and how that's hard, sometimes, because there's a desire to stay in the comfort zone, in the shell, like the crab. We also get 'crabby' if too much responsibility is heaped on us, which does tend to happen. It's something about getting this balance right.

Melanie: How many of you have Uranus in Cancer? Most of you. And how many have it conjunct the South Node? Again, most of you! That can certainly be crabby, because the panoramic perspective of Uranus is very uncomfortable with the in-turning, intimate, feeling side of Cancer. Uranus in Cancer can also have high ideals about what feeling intimacy should look like and be like, and becomes very crabby if others don't live up to this! High expectations about others' ability to nourish you, and contempt if they don't.

Audience: My partner once told me that he thought I study astrology and other things, like psychology or whatever, in order to be able to tell him how he should be! I was horrified.

Melanie: In late 1953 and most of 1954, there was a very potent T-square involving the transiting Nodes and Chiron in Capricorn, opposite Uranus in Cancer, and both squared by Neptune in Libra. How many of you are in that group? Two of you. This 'soul group' was born on the waning square of the Uranus-Neptune cycle which had just ended, and seems to be looking intensely for new ways to be in relationship with others. Cancer and Libra are ruled by the Moon and Venus, and it's as if this group have an extra sensitivity to transactions between people, and desperately want to be able to do things differently to how they perceive the rest of society behaving. The North Node and Chiron in Capricorn often symbolise a deep desire to put into form something which expresses new principles, new ideals. And yet, often these people seem to find themselves working sort of 'under cover' in places which appear very conventional, or respectable in the eyes of the status quo, and feeling their idealism has to be hidden. Can you relate to this? I see you both nodding.

With Chiron in Capricorn conjunct the North Node there is often a quality of mentorship, support and promotion offered to others, but the capacity to structure activity, time and resources for oneself may be lacking, so the feeling of personal creative fulfilment becomes connected with work for the company, the system, something larger than oneself. With the Neptune connection, there is often the need to sacrifice our unrealistic expectations of others, and the Capricorn North Node is also about learning to work within limitation and restriction, in a positive way. And also the theme of not taking things too personally, which is the Cancer South Node! For some in this group, this T-square involving the Nodes is a background theme, unless stimulated by a transit. For others, if there are personal planets involved, it can be a central theme, and one is very much in tune with larger issues affecting the collective.

Audience: I feel a sense of calling, but I don't know what it is.

Melanie: Which way round are your Nodes?

Audience: I'm in the other group, with Cancer on the North Node.

Melanie: The question that comes to mind is connected with the traditional rulership of Saturn over the South Node, and Jupiter over the North. Is it a calling, or is it a pressure of shoulds and oughts murmuring in the background?

Audience: That's exactly the problem – I think it is both!

Melanie: That's a good sign! Joking aside, remember the Nodal theme of the balancing act? Sometimes Capricorn makes us very literally-minded. It is the sign of building structures, and it is ruled by Saturn. It is dense and material in its manner and orientation. I wonder if the South Node in Capricorn could be a tendency to make things too literal? Like the famous story in the Bible, about Peter, who was told by Jesus 'Thou art Peter, and upon this rock I will build my church.'[45] Peter thought he was supposed to go out and literally build a church made of rock and stones, but eventually realised that this statement was a metaphor of the inner 'church of rock', the church of faith in one's heart. Positively, South Node in Capricorn has a realistic perspective that is like a safety net, but negatively, it sometimes sees things too literally, and doesn't allow the soulful nuance that can be so strong in the sign of Cancer.

The Leo/Aquarius Polarity

Melanie: Can we hear something from the Leo/Aquarius group?

Audience: Several of us have Pluto conjunct the Leo end, although with some it is North, and others South. There seemed to be a pattern of major early loss influencing the shape of our lives. When we checked the transits of the Nodes themselves it was interesting, because sometimes the loss occurred while someone was in the womb, before they were born, or even conceived, and at other times it happened afterwards. But the age seemed to correspond with whether the transiting Node was applying to Pluto or separating from it. For all of us, though, it was like we'd lived different lives in this life. Major endings and beginnings, radical changes of scene.

Melanie: Was this chosen or enforced?

Audience: It seems it could be either. Obviously, the early changes occurred with no conscious willing of them, but sometimes the later ones did too. There was a sense of following a path that was often dark, where you were subject to things outside your control.

Melanie: So did you get a sense of Pluto as helper or hinderer?

Audience: At first, it seems like one is being hindered. With hindsight, though, sometimes you can see you have actually been helped.

Melanie: It reminds me of that apocryphal story about the man in ancient China whose son was given a fine horse. All the villagers congratulated the father on the good fortune of his son, but the man remained impassive and simply said, 'You never know'. Sometime later, the son had an accident while riding the horse and he was hurt, so could not help his father in the fields. All the villagers commiserated, but again the man simply said, 'You never know'. Then a feud broke out between two villages, and the army came to recruit soldiers to fight. Because the son was injured, he did not have to go, and his life was saved. The villagers again congratulated the man on his good fortune, and the man simply said, 'You never know'. The story goes on, through several more twists and turns of apparent disaster which turn out to be blessings in disguise, and in each episode we have the sober reflection of the father, the man who did not presume to judge Fate one way or the other, and thus remained accepting and detached. A profound teaching.

Audience: The theme of individual and group was clear, with all of us, in different ways. There was a struggle to get the balance. How to participate without crushing our need to be the star, or taking over all the time – that was Leo North Node. The Aquarius North Node was about how to work consciously towards engagement with a group or set of ideals, by dedicating oneself, or offering talents.

Melanie: Soon Uranus will conjunct the Aquarius end, followed by Neptune, so you have some years of powerful transits coming up.

Audience: Mine has already started, as my North Node is 2° 47' Aquarius, and Uranus crossed it twice already. It's in the 12th house, so it doesn't seem very clear to me, except that I've been dreaming a lot. I'm noticing more action on the other end, perhaps because my Venus is in Leo, and very close to the South Node. Now I think about it, I can see the situation … at work, there is a woman who I am very jealous of, and she gets a lot of attention from some of the men in the office. I try and tell myself it doesn't matter, that co-operation is more important, but I get really churned up.

Melanie: Can you see the Leo/Aquarius polarity there? Ideals and 'shoulds' in contrast to what you feel …

Audience: It's interesting. Apart from a semi-sextile with Mercury in Virgo, this Venus really doesn't have any other major aspects. I've always wondered about it.

Melanie: Which house does it rule?

Audience: The 3rd house.

Melanie: That relates to siblings, amongst other things. Does this situation in any way echo a previous situation, with a brother or sister?

Audience: Indirectly, yes, I guess. I was actually an only child, and I used to fantasise a lot when I was little, wishing I had a brother or sister. I most wanted a sister. I have Moon in Gemini in the 4th house, conjunct Jupiter, and it's trine the Saturn-Neptune conjunction which is in my 8th house. My mother actually had two or three miscarriages after I was born, and I can remember her trying to explain to me what had happened, why she was ill. I must have been about eleven years old, so this must have been the last miscarriage. Anyway, it upset me a lot. I've always thought about the Moon-Jupiter in Gemini as the potential siblings which did not come, and why was I meant to be alone.

Melanie: And the Venus connection?

Audience: Apparently, I found it hard to share with other kids. I guess I just wasn't used to it. I mean, if I knew I was the star, or the best, or in the centre of attention, I could be sweet and generous and charming, but if not, I would get tetchy and irritable. This is all hindsight, though. I sort of lost this 'prima donna' quality somewhere down the line. I have the Sun in Virgo, and I downplayed myself quite a bit, I think, and got self-critical. All this has been coming back to me just over the last year.

Melanie: As Uranus was moving to conjunct the Node. In Aquarius, prompting a change of perspective, taking a different view.

Audience: Yes, that is exactly what's happening. The most important thing is that I don't have to edit myself out all the time.

Melanie: Thank you. Do any of you other individuals from this group want to say anything? I'm not sure how to address you — as a unit, or as separate people!

Audience: I have Uranus conjunct one end, and Chiron the other, although they are in the next signs, Virgo and Pisces. Can you say something about that? I get confused, as there are so many themes to think of.

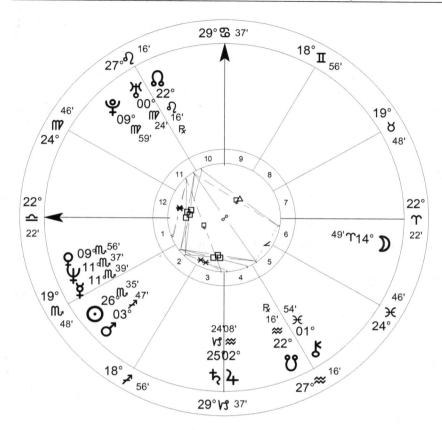

Melanie: Yes. Firstly, some general remarks about the Chiron-Uranus opposition. Then the Virgo/Pisces theme will lead us on to our last group. Between 1951 and 1989 there were about forty exact oppositions of Chiron and Uranus, through different signs. They were within range of the opposition for most of the time, and so this defines a rather large generational 'soul group'. 'Change or bust' is one of the phrases that describes this energy. Positively, this aspect denotes a willingness to embrace change, to take risks, be provocative, and to make quantum leaps in understanding, innovation and new ways of doing and being. Negatively, it can be about change, rebellion and so-called 'progress' just for the sake of it, like scratching an itch, without regard to the consequences. Sort of being propelled along. There have been ghastly mistakes made in medical science that began by being celebrated as a 'breakthrough'. Various drugs, like thalidomide and others, far from being agents of healing, have turned out to cause terrible human suffering. This is perhaps the Chiron connection. The wounding aspects of the compulsion for change. Alternatively, Chiron-Uranus can be about the healing potential contained in the quantum leap of consciousness. If people have this opposition prominent in the chart, they are often actively involved in trying to 'change the system' in some way, or raising consciousness about a particular issue.

Audience: This is absolutely true for me. My North Node is in the 10th house, with Uranus in the 11th. And Pluto is now squaring the Uranus-Chiron. It's also conjunct my Mars, in early Sagittarius, and I feel so angry about the state of the world that I could burst sometimes. I just don't know what to do. I feel passionately, but if people question me about my beliefs and all that, I don't know what to say. I just feel things. I have been getting so exasperated that I am looking into spending some years doing volunteer work in conservation, or wildlife work, or something.

Melanie: You also have Uranus by transit conjunct your Jupiter, and next February, in 1997, you will have just had your Jupiter return when Uranus will conjunct Jupiter at about 5° Aquarius. Also, it crossed your IC recently, and will be followed by Neptune, starting next year also. From this point of view, a twelve-year Jupiter cycle is in its closing stages, and the end of a Jupiter cycle is quite commonly accompanied by a temporary loss of meaning, sense of momentum towards the future, and so on. This Jupiter return will be a very interesting one, because it occurs just as Uranus enters Aquarius, and is the prelude for some quite powerful transits of Uranus, squaring your Scorpio planets, starting with Venus, which is the ruler of your Ascendant. So some turbulence and change in the area of values is on the way, and that could have far-reaching consequences, being involved with your Ascendant. It may also be that your innate idealism, as symbolised by the South Node in Aquarius, will play a more obvious role in terms of your identity. I mean, you are probably someone who identifies yourself in terms of what you feel. You said something a bit like that. This Jupiter is your only air planet, and then there is also the South Node, so I wonder whether part of your struggle at present is to formulate and thus differentiate your own ideals from the collective? You could be very affected by the beliefs and perspectives of others, because you react with strong feelings to ideas.

Audience: Yes. I have been wanting to just walk out of my life, because it doesn't line up with my own deepest principles, but the problem is I don't know how to explain what those are, so I don't know how to change things!

Melanie: Perhaps you do not need to explain them, but rather to feel them and formulate them. And with these transits forthcoming, you will perhaps find out.

The Virgo/Pisces Polarity

Melanie: This leads us to the last group – last but not least. This last material may be relevant also to your Nodes, as even though they are actually in Leo/Aquarius, the Virgo/Pisces theme is attached.

Audience: All of us except one work in the healing professions, and we all had this theme of control and chaos, somehow.

Melanie: Was it different, depending on whether the North Node was in Virgo or in Pisces?

Audience: I think that the Virgo North Node people need to learn about application of their talents to work, and also structuring their thinking and discriminating. But the Pisces North Node people need to learn more about letting go, relaxing and allowing things to take their course.

Melanie: Would you all agree with this?

Audience: Yes. She has Virgo South Node, and is good at being definite and defining things!

Audience: I sometimes get confused about which is right in a situation, or I get sort of out of synch, then I can't concentrate at work, and can't relax at home! My Nodes are backwards by house – I mean, I have North Node in Pisces in the 6th, and South in Virgo in the 12th.

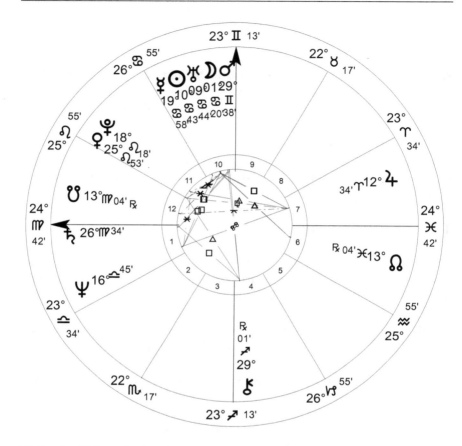

Melanie: What about their rulers, Neptune and Mercury?

Audience: I have Neptune in Libra square Mercury in Cancer.

Melanie: Is there any way that these two symbolise some kind of balancing activity which you do for yourself? The 6th/12th axis is about service and self-purification, amongst other things. How do you serve yourself and honour your own spiritual needs?

Audience: That's a good question! I have Moon, Uranus, Sun and Mercury all conjunct in Cancer in the 10th house, and Saturn rising in Virgo. After I raised a family, I trained as a therapist, and I feel 'mothered out' sometimes.

Melanie: Then what do you do?

Audience: I write. I guess that is the Mercury/Neptune! I keep journals, but I also write inspirational material, like poetry, fantasy stuff. And I love to read poetry too, but I have to be alone to do it. Perhaps that's the Virgo South Node in the 12th.

Melanie: That Mercury also disposits your Saturn in Virgo, your only earth, and also Mars in Gemini, your only air planet, apart from Neptune in Libra, which is more like mist than air! So this implies that Mercurial activities are both grounding and mentally empowering. That adds an interesting emphasis on to this South Node – 'undoing' yourself in a deliberate and structured way. That Saturn could certainly keep your nose to the proverbial grindstone!

Audience: Yes, it's like if I plan how and when I will let myself off the hook, it works. But I can't just be spontaneous. Except I know in my work I do have a spontaneous flow of feeling, and that's important to me. I trained as a therapist when Pluto was completing that Grand Trine with the North Node and the Sun.

Melanie: You were also born on the dark of the Moon. I always think of the crab of Cancer needing to be safe in its shell during this time, to brood, ruminate, and allow the tides of soul and being to flow inwardly, to re-establish that precious sense of inner connection and nourishment. As a multiple Cancerian, with such a 10th house emphasis, I would think this is very important, as your energy is so outwardly directed into caretaking. Getting 'crabby' might be the result if you get out of balance with this! There is a wonderful book called *Finding Our Way Through the Dark* by Demetra George which you might enjoy reading, as it explores in great depth this theme of 'the dark of the Moon'.[46]

And that leads us on to our final theme …

Eclipses

Now I'm going to briefly consider eclipses, trying to take a practical view of their meaning. As you know, the recording of eclipses has an extremely long history, and eclipses were one of the very first predictive tools of the ancient astrologers who used something called the 'Saros cycle', another trail we will follow only a very short way.

The Saros Cycle

In a nutshell, the Saros cycle describes families of eclipses, and although in theory they help with the fine-tuning of interpreting eclipses, for routine consideration of eclipses in the consulting situation, you can do without it. The Saros cycle is the recurrence of an eclipse in terms of its visibility. A cycle begins when there is a partial eclipse, visible at either the North or South Poles, and works its way up or down the Earth until, by the time it reaches the Equator, astrologically the eclipse is very close to the Nodal degree. At the extreme ends of the cycle, the eclipse can occur as much as 18° wide of the Nodes, on either side.

This movement of the visible eclipse path on the surface of the Earth winds from one pole to the other, and resembles the snake or the dragon, with its head and tail at the North and South Poles. I was thrilled to see this image. The two eclipses in any year do not necessarily belong to the same Saros cycle, and the area of visibility will not recur immediately. Also, there are many cycles all going on simultaneously. One Saros cycle is 1280 years long, and the overall quality is defined by the astrology of the first eclipse in the cycle, the one nearest to one of the poles. Let's look at the different kinds of individual eclipses now.

Lunar Eclipses

There are basically three kinds of eclipses, the first one being a *lunar eclipse*, which can only occur at a Full Moon, when the Moon and the

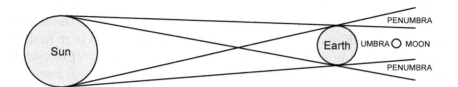

Sun are on opposite sides of the Earth and the Earth's shadow falls on the Moon and blocks it out, either partially or completely. As we go through this material on eclipses, just as an intuitive possibility, see what happens if you think this way: Sun is future, Moon is past, Earth is present. So here we have the past, the Moon, temporarily blotted out by the present.

The Annular Solar Eclipse

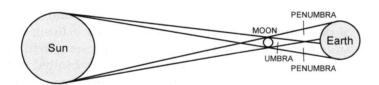

The second kind is called an *annular solar eclipse,* one of two kinds of solar eclipse. Both kinds can only occur at a New Moon, when the Sun and Moon are on the same side of the Earth. The difference between these two is simply that an annular eclipse occurs when the Moon is quite far away from the Earth, and all you need to remember is that an annular eclipse can never be total, but will appear as a partial eclipse.

The Total Solar Eclipse

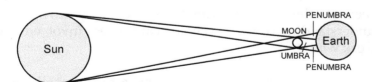

A *total solar eclipse* occurs when the Moon is closer to the Earth and so there is a narrow zone, the *umbra*, where the shadow of the Moon is precisely falling on the Earth, which means that anywhere in that middle zone it is a total eclipse, while anywhere within the wider band it will appear as partial, within what is called the *penumbra*, which means 'almost the shadow', where it is not so dense. Hence, a partial eclipse can occur when the Moon is near or far away from the Earth, but a total eclipse can only occur when the Moon is relatively close. It is extraordinary how the size of the Moon exactly covers the Sun. If it were further away, this could not happen, as the Sun would show round the edges. We do see the corolla, the flames coming out of the Sun, but the disc is precisely covered by the Moon.

Using the Information

Returning to the interpretation and use of this material, and using that analogy of past, present and future, with a lunar eclipse, the Moon, the past, is temporarily blotted out by the present. With a solar eclipse, either one, the future, Sun, is temporarily blotted out by the past and it is registered in the present, because we are on the Earth. I hope those links will start to help you make use of the eclipse seasons, and to clarify what you might experience around eclipses.

Eclipses have a mostly malefic reputation in the collective unconscious. Even people who do not approve of astrology know that, historically, bad things are said to happen at eclipses, and every time there is an eclipse season, as astrologers we are likely to get clients who are worried about the eclipse, or whose lives reflect its themes, even if they are not aware of it. A mere mention of the word will usually evoke a fearful reaction from a client, so it's important to try and dispel those negative thought forms, but without being 'Pollyanna'. This can often be done by conveying a deeper understanding of the psychological process involved and how to work with it.

When you consider eclipse points as transits to the natal chart, keep your orbs narrow, 5° maximum for the Sun and Moon and

4° for other points, and only use conjunctions and oppositions at first. Squares may also be important if they also activate midpoint sets but, on the whole, stay primarily with conjunctions and also consider oppositions. Remember that because the eclipse season occurs 18.618 days earlier each year, and that there are two each year, you may get a run of eclipses contacting a natal planet. Even if there are no exact aspects, the same axis of the chart will be activated twice a year.

This image about past, present and future can be useful. Taking the solar eclipse first, the eclipsing of your own future by the past is only 'malefic' if you have no way of working with the issues that may be presented. In fact, a solar eclipse is often an ending – something finishes, stops – and it might be exactly the thing that has been stuck for a very long time. The full stop is finally put at the end of the sentence. When I first used that phrase with a client, I realised there was a pun there – 'sentence' is also a term in jail, and in this case it was metaphorically, if not literally, appropriate. 'Adjust or bust' is another phrase I have for the solar eclipse! Every ending frees up energy for new beginnings, if you can adjust, but it is true that the mood of the ending is often dominant around the eclipse. If you try and ride over that, dragons do come – remember the quote I read about the inner process of the eclipse?[47]

An eclipse highlights an area in the chart. Something goes under the microscope, and it may be a dark vision, like a dark spotlight, until you enter deeply that area. The two eclipse seasons are very auspicious times for inner work on the psychological and spiritual levels. However, if somebody has just had an eclipse on their Sun, it may be premature to speak about future potential. Being with the dark, and the feeling of being eclipsed, and working with the past that may precipitate into that darkness is often more appropriate. That needs to be dignified and honoured if one is to move through into a new beginning. Often a solar eclipse will manifest events, challenges or situations in the outside world, just as the Sun is the luminary that involves us in the busy daylight world. Something ends, which of course may trigger off past feelings, or require an inner journey of rumination and reflection to come to terms with it, but often the trigger is outside. The physical Sun is eclipsed, but that may mean an opportunity to experience the nakedness of being, stripped of role and identifications.

By contrast, a lunar eclipse more often heralds something stirring up directly on the emotional level, which may then precipitate into events or interpersonal experiences. And of course eclipses always go in pairs. If we think of the Moon as where our dependency issues are lodged, where we have attachments and habits, and where we are most emotionally identified and self-invested, then, at a lunar eclipse, all that is put temporarily on hold by the shadow of the Earth. The past is eclipsed by the present as the shadow of the Earth obscures the Moon. Going beyond the negative image of the lunar eclipse that has come down to us through the centuries, with all kinds of catastrophic expectations, we could maybe reframe it as a window in time, wherein we are standing in the present on Earth and the past is eclipsed. The physical Moon is eclipsed, but we have a chance to experience the lunar consciousness or soul quality, prophetic and poetic in nature. And if we can see past the dark vision, sometimes we can see the hidden seed of our own future with those eyes.

I would invite any of you who are intrigued by this to try it out. Next time there is a Full Moon that is eclipsed, spend some time with it, consciously. It is a very powerful time to attune with the cosmos, especially if you need or intend to work with issues involving endings, separations, changes of state or stage of life. When the Moon is eclipsing it is a very good time for meditative work, for ritual, for ceremony, that in some way marks your coming into the present, that's the Earth, and honouring the unseen future – that's the Sun, whose reflected light is blocked out. The Sun at night, remember, is under the Earth, like the luminous seed in the ground of being. That's where the unknown future lies, in that darkness. The timing is fairly precise, as the Moon moves quickly, and a partial lunar eclipse may only last a short time, although the entire process of a total lunar eclipse will last overall for several hours. However, the general mood of an eclipse will last a couple of days.

Audience: What about if the eclipse is not visible?

Melanie: This experience is most clear when the eclipse is visible, but even if it is not, during the eclipse season in general, and particularly around the time of a lunar or solar eclipse, you will be able to access your inner world in a healing and useful way if you choose to.

Audience: You said that eclipses go in pairs ... is this always true?

Melanie: Actually, no. There can be anywhere from one to four solar and/or lunar eclipses in any given year, but two of each is about the average. You cannot have a lunar eclipse without a solar eclipse accompanying it, but you can have a solar eclipse without a lunar eclipse.

Audience: How do you reckon an eclipse season?

Melanie: There are two eclipse seasons every year, when the Sun conjuncts the North and South Nodes in turn, and they will obviously be about six months apart. If you check your ephemeris to see when this happens, then count eighteen days back and eighteen days forward from that date, you have got your eclipse season, in other words this is the range within which the solar and/or lunar eclipses will occur. So there are two months each year which are like the pathway of the eclipses, an axis across the Zodiac, and therefore across your chart, which shifts slowly backwards. Thus, every year, one pair of houses and signs will be emphasised during those two periods. Whether or not the eclipse makes aspects to anything in your chart, you can still use this time productively on the inner levels. If you are aware of these periods of time, you will notice lots of things happening to people – emotions and actions precipitate, situations end, crises may indeed happen. During the eclipse seasons, it pays dividends to prepare for and be congruent with the cosmos, in terms of the kind of activities you plan for yourself. Take them as an opportunity for inner work and you will find them beneficial. Lose yourself in distractions, and you may attract dragons!

Melanie: Here are charts of the two most recent eclipses, so you can get a sense of where and how they might have stimulated your charts.

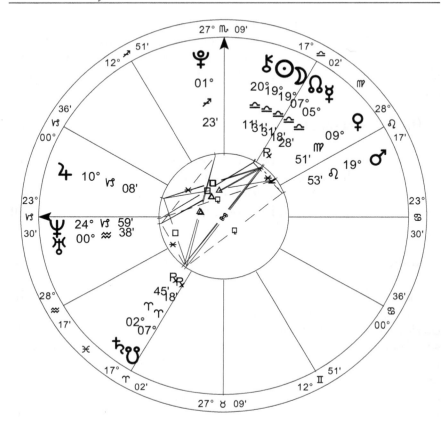

Solar Eclipse
12 October 1996; 15.14 BST; London, England

Audience: The solar eclipse was with Chiron, and it was on my Sun. I felt really empowered.

Melanie: There's an example of how positive these times can actually be.

Audience: Something has finished in my life and I am very strong about what I want to do and who I want to be.

Melanie: With an eclipse on the Sun, the themes of destiny and purpose are often presented. An important choice is offered, in the wake of an ending. The light is shone on something.

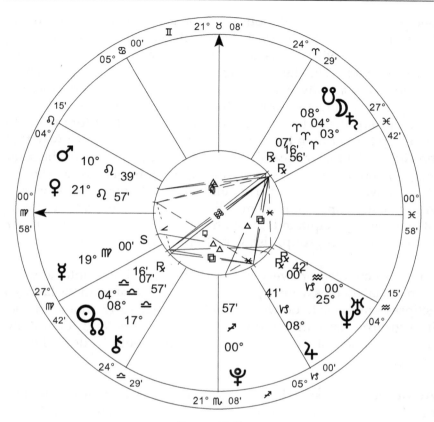

Lunar Eclipse
27 September 1996; 3.51 BST; London, England

This last solar eclipse was at 20° Libra, and I recently saw a client who has the Saturn/Neptune conjunction in Libra in her 1st house, with Neptune itself at 20° Libra. This is not an easy conjunction, and in the 1st house there is often an unsureness of boundary and identity, and quite a bit of amorphous fear. For her, that had reached such a pitch several years ago – as Uranus and Neptune squared it – that she uprooted from London, where she had always lived, and went to a very remote area, literally in the middle of nowhere. Let me add the trail of dispositorship here ... Neptune and Saturn in Libra are ruled by Venus, which is in Virgo in the 12th ruled by Mercury in Leo, also in the 12th, and the Sun is in Leo also in the 12th, with her South Node. Taking the old rulers, this 12th house Sun disposits both ends of the Nodes.

She embraced fully a 12th house experience of retreat, isolation and time for inner spiritual work. In fact, on the very day of the preceding lunar eclipse, which was actually conjunct her Ascendant, the decision that maybe she would move back to London was brewing, but she didn't really want to, so she joined a short-term therapy group specifically to work with the dilemmas raised. However, in the group there developed a boundary issue that forced her to stand up for her own territory, her rights and so on, in a way that precipitated a major breakthrough for her. By the time of the solar eclipse, about two weeks later, and right on her Neptune, she felt that she was no longer a hermit and was ready to rejoin the world. An amazing expression of an eclipse on Neptune, and the theme of endings, precipitated through some very unpleasant things happening in the group, also very Neptunian.

She was actually born very near an eclipse, and also note how her own Nodal themes were expressed in the events around the last two eclipses – an issue to do with boundaries, that's a 12th house theme, in a group, that's the North Node in Aquarius, and identifying herself as a hermit – that's Sun conjunct the South Node in the 12th house.

Audience: Does being born near an eclipse mean that you will be more sensitive to the energies of the eclipse season each year?

Melanie: Yes, it often does, although I wouldn't want to be formulaic about it. A good thing to experiment with, by tracking the Moon's cycle and tuning in during the Eclipse seasons.

Audience: It's like a seed is put in as the Moon eclipses the Sun …

Melanie: Yes, I have a feeling that it is the solar eclipse that does the seeding, when something is conceived. After all, the Sun is shining on the dark side of the Moon, that we don't see, so none of its light can be reflected to us, but the dark side of the Moon is illuminated. And maybe the lunar eclipse is like the planting of the seed, or the implantation of the embryo, as the shadow of the Earth covers the reflected light.

Audience: What if they occur in the wrong order?

Melanie: As we are talking of processes to do with soul growth, I don't think there is a 'wrong order' that affects the validity of the metaphor. Physically speaking, you cannot implant before you have been conceived, but in the journey of the soul, you can certainly be compelled to do something, take an action, make a connection, before you have a clear conception of what it's about. Note the pun there – we 'conceive' when we become pregnant, and we also speak of 'conceiving' an idea or a new understanding. However, it is interesting to consider the fact that the Sun and Moon are indeed two bodies which we know for certain do actually physically influence our life on Earth. Perhaps the physical and energetic effects of the occlusion of one by the other is more directly significant than we yet know, on our biochemistry, for example.

Let's look at the last pair in more detail. The lunar eclipse was in early Aries, conjunct Saturn, and the Sun in Libra was conjunct one of the new centaurs, Pholus, so the whole eclipse was coloured with the symbolism of Saturn and Pholus. It also preceded the solar eclipse, and I noticed with that sequence that this process of clearing the past reached epic proportions. With Pholus, a central image is the opening of the sacred jar of wine, and chaos breaking out.[48] During this eclipse season, Mercury was involved, so the lid was coming off verbally. I kept hearing stories about people who had said the unthinkable, or who had finally let the cat out of the bag, or who had betrayed somebody or been betrayed without realising it, or said the truth for the first time, sometimes with explosive consequences. There was something about 'saying it' and breaking a pattern in doing so, or consequences unimagined stemming from things said.

It seemed to be clearing the way for what occurred at the solar eclipse, which being in the sign of Libra involved things to do with relationships, ideals and principles of ethics, fairness and justice, and so on – it is an air sign – and the understanding of past relationships too. That was a consistent theme brought in by clients in almost every reading I did during those two weeks.

This eclipse season was also relevant for an entire generation of people with their Neptune in Libra. About three-quarters of them will have had either one or both eclipses conjunct their Neptune. I told you one story already, of the woman who had it in the 1st house, with the solar eclipse exactly on it, but this particular pair of eclipses must have had collective significance for this generation of people. Something about illusions ending, deceptions surfacing, boundary issues needing attention. So I would invite any of you who have this to think back over that period and see what transpired for you.

Audience: My progressed Moon is on that same degree.

Melanie: What was that like?

Audience: I sat up and watched the eclipse of the Moon, although that was earlier, not on my Moon. It was a very, very personal space, and I saw lots of cosmic images, like looking down onto the ocean which seemed somehow heart-shaped, and the Sun was there too, like flames bursting. It was an amazing process.

Melanie: Beautiful! I just thought of another practical point. There is controversy about how long the effect of eclipses will last, and from my exploration of this through various texts, there seems to be all manner of rules, which do seem rather arbitrary and theoretical, although I can't say I have tested them all empirically myself. For example, there is a tradition which apparently goes back to Ptolemy, which says that the effect of an eclipse lasts as long in years as the eclipse itself lasts in minutes. There's been no research done on that, as far as I know, so it must remain in the category of unproven 'received wisdom'. Another 'rule' is that the effect will last until the next Saturn transit passes over the eclipse degree. If that is true, you could have up to about twenty-nine years' worth of eclipse effect! Make of that what you will. In the spirit of Pluto in Sagittarius and Uranus in Aquarius, I must say I find these ideas less than helpful at best and, at worst, a recipe for creating a negative reality for yourself with your own fearful expectations.

Audience: In Ptolemy's time, waiting for Saturn to come round, thirty years, you would probably be dead!

Melanie: Wonderful! Maybe that's what is meant – once an eclipse, always an eclipse or something! However, with even a rudimentary knowledge of psychological process, an eclipse can be a prime opportunity for inner work. To do that, you have to be willing to go into the dark, and learn to see in the dark, otherwise everything can just happen outside you, out there, and you are not involved with it, not in relationship with it, and therefore it is very scary. In a participatory model, it is not quite the same. It may still be unpleasant and painful, but you have some means of working with it symbolically. I think this kind of work can also help you to know where the boundaries are. If you know what you are participating in, you are a better position to act creatively, rather than just react.

Audience: I actually had a lunar eclipse on my natal Moon a couple of years ago and it was pretty dramatic. I would say it was more like a switch going on. It was not so much what happened on that day, but it was a beginning of a whole new process.

Melanie: How many people really registered a theme, very strongly like that, on the last eclipse? At least half of us. Eclipses do demonstrate the primary symbolism of the Nodes – the inter-relationship of the Sun, Moon and Earth – in a very immediate way. They are a very interesting time to connect with these inner polarities. Nodal factors come out for real, they happen in life, they want to manifest. Indeed, they *do* manifest, like it or not. In terms of energy attunement, the eclipse times are valuable, because something may really open up during those two eclipse seasons that you can learn a great deal from.

For years, I have been in the habit of always trying to be up and awake to watch lunar eclipses. On that last one, I was very tired, came home late without my ephemeris, and went to bed, thinking 'Oh, well, I've missed this one.' Then I woke up in the middle of the night, and saw that the eclipse was just starting. I felt like something in me was attuned to it and said 'Tired, or not, you've got to get up and see this.' I watched it for hours. What I saw looked like a diamond ring, as it had a flare of light at the top – did you see that? It was really amazing. So, remember that eclipses are times when energy moves powerfully, and sometimes cycles reach their turning point. It is awe-inspiring to be consciously participating in that.

Audience: Melanie, it has just occurred to me that the big solar eclipse in 1999 is in Leo, and so it will pick up a lot of our Plutos.

Melanie: Yes, it will. And it will be visible here in England, especially in Cornwall, where apparently every hotel is already almost fully booked!

Audience: It also goes through Europe.

Melanie: Yes, it's really worth looking at this path. It starts about level with New York, goes across the Atlantic, exactly over Southern England, through central Europe, the Middle East, and ends over the middle of India, on the east coast.

Audience: Is it the end of Western civilisation as we know it?

Melanie: It's not only Western civilisation that is in trouble! I don't know what the eclipse will bring on that level. However, the chart itself is also very interesting – there is a Grand Cross in fixed signs. Uranus in Aquarius opposes Sun, Moon and North Node, and squares Mars in Scorpio and Saturn in Taurus. Any of you who have planets in the middle of the fixed signs, watch that space!

Prenatal Eclipses

Audience: What about the prenatal eclipse point?

Melanie: Yes, I had meant to mention that. Because our time in the womb is forty weeks long, about nine months, and there is an eclipse season every six months, that means that everybody experiences one eclipse season while in the womb. This is a very useful sensitive point on the chart, which definitely responds powerfully to transits, and particularly if a later lunar or solar eclipse should contact this point. It seems to have a quality of somehow taking us back to the 'before', the origins, the sense of what it is we came here with, or what we must release, and transits to that eclipse point can mean very important times when prenatal material is released, or when we are catapulted into a new stage of life. That can be useful to know, because this area of material, being completely non-verbal and very physically based, is likely to precipitate in events, symptoms and other signals which may need some interpretation in order to understand what feelings are being released. Our emotional experience is almost completely fused with our mother at this stage and so, when this point is stimulated, it can be an important time of separating and clarifying.

I have rather a dramatic example.

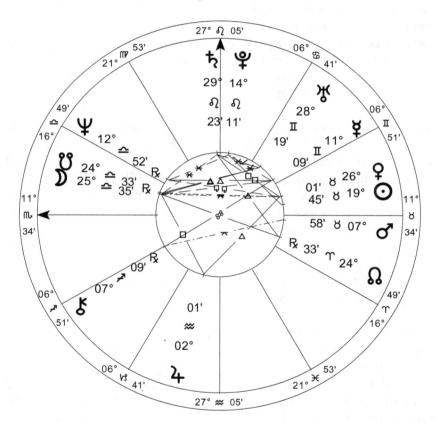

The prenatal eclipse point on this chart is at 9° Taurus, in the 6th house, just next to the Descendant, and there have been two further solar eclipses close to this point during this woman's life thus far. On the first one, she had been travelling abroad with her husband, and they could not get a return flight home on the same plane.

Various events had already occurred on the trip which made her feel the marriage was over, and although she was depressed and mourning this, she had not yet really faced it consciously. As the plane took off, she noticed the setting Sun eclipsing, and was filled with foreboding. The journey was broken for refuelling, which meant an overnight stop. That evening, walking in the market, she was attacked and robbed by a man who pounced at her from the window of a stationary taxi, grabbing her shoulder bag. The taxi then sped off down the road, and because she had wrapped the bag around her arm for security, she was dragged a considerable distance before managing to work herself free. Incredibly, the flight she had taken was right under the actual eclipse path, and the eclipse itself was conjunct her prenatal eclipse degree, close to the Descendant in the 6th house.

Almost twenty years later, another eclipse touched this point, and she remembered the whole experience in great detail. At the time, she said that the shock of it had catapulted her into an acceptance of the loss of her marriage, and in her own words 'It was like I had the choice whether to live or die. I could have gone under the wheels of the vehicle. I remember seeing my face reflected in the hubcap, as if from far away, and knowing that I had to make a choice. I was out of my body, and had somehow to snap back in. The next thing I knew, I was standing on my feet in the road, bleeding profusely, with my clothes in rags, my money, passport and everything else gone, but alive and conscious.'

The prenatal connection became apparent in the later remembering, when she was shown in dreams how, during this eclipse time, her mother was fearing that her own marriage was dying, and was feeling deep grief over this. She did not speak to anyone, and became inwardly quite desperate, but never showed it. In that sense, the experience while travelling could be seen as also discharging her mother's association of her presence in the womb with grief and loss in the marriage.

Audience: How can you tell ahead of time where an eclipse path will be?

Melanie: I'm not aware of any book which gives the geographical areas of eclipse visibility, but the Solar Maps computer program, and others, will show you these eclipse paths graphically on a map of the world. And of course you find it online. Also, my website has a section called 'Moon Talk' in which you'll find some links for that.

Audience: I had two solar eclipses conjunct my Venus in Scorpio, in 1994 and 1995. After the first crisis, it changed levels, and then it was nothing to do with personal relationships, in a way, although I had one encounter after another, with men and women. Not all sexual, but all Scorpionic. Sometimes erotic, sometimes full of rivalries and unpleasant feelings. But I had to start looking at the relationship between men and women, collectively, and what kind of evolution was happening. For the second one, I actually travelled to a place where it was visible, like a kind of pilgrimage.

Conclusion and Guided Imagery

At this point of the day, all I can say is that Fiona Griffiths was definitely right when she said you needed at least a week to do justice to the Nodes! I said to her 'But we've only got a day!' and that day is already nearly over. I'd like to leave some space now for last questions, anecdotes or comments. Then we will finish with a guided imagery exercise, but I'm afraid there will not be time for any in-depth processing of it. So we will end on a somewhat introspective note, quietly, and you can process the experience on your own, or you can always arrange to meet up with others from the group and spend time discussing your experience.

A Guided Imagery Exercise

Melanie: We need to move on to the last part of today, now, and begin to change gear and prepare for the guided imagery work.[49]

Audience: Can we close the curtains?

Melanie: Yes, of course ... I thought it might be too dark.

Audience: We can make our own eclipse ...

Melanie: Let's begin ...

I would invite you now to begin the process of turning your attention inside. To do that, get yourselves as comfortable as you can in your chair ...

Have your feet flat on the floor, your legs uncrossed, arms uncrossed ... although if you want to link your hands that's fine. Give your body a decent space on the chair so that energy can circulate in your body ...

And as you do that, just become aware of your breathing ... you don't need to change anything, but let your attention rest in becoming aware of your breathing.

Let yourself feel progressively more relaxed, and more settled, as you follow your breath in and out, and allow it to deepen and settle.

I would like you to imagine now that you are walking along a straight path ...

Just take note of the surroundings and let the image be clear for you. It is a straight path from somewhere to somewhere, and on this path you can't actually see the beginning or the ending, but you are on the walk, on the journey...

As you walk, pretty soon you are going to come to a resting place ...
Maybe there is a chair or a stone or a glade to one side of this path ... Somewhere to pause ...
Let yourself go to this resting place ...
In your imagination, allow yourself to settle there ...
From this vantage point to one side, you survey your straight path ... and you look to the left ... and you look to the right ... and although you can't see the end of the path, or the beginning of the path, that's OK ... you just let yourself settle in the middle.

In a short while, you begin to turn your attention to the beginning of the path ... this part of the path that you can't see ... and you invite an image to present itself, of this part of your path, your unseen beginnings.

Let this image become clear, and see if there is any way that communication needs to happen between you, between you and your own beginnings, your own legacy, what you bring and where you are.

Just take whatever comes ...

Let that process be focused and clear in your imagination ...

You might even like to explore what was there before this image, or what was there before that, or for how long this image has been there. Is it something you recognise? Is it familiar? What does it bring?

Then, concluding your communication with this image, turn your attention now to the other end of your line, your walk, your journey and focus on where you are going ...
Focus on that goal ... that destination ...
The 'Where to?' of your journey ...
And just allow an image to emerge from that unseen place of where you are going ... Explore this image ...
See how you respond...
Is this familiar to you?
What happens as you give your attention to this?
As you establish rapport with this end of your journey line, see how you feel.
Does it feel different?

Now bring to a close your sense of communion with this end of your journey and return to just settling yourself once more in your place of rest.

Now see if you can embrace, in your awareness, both of these ends. Your beginning and your destination.

What happens as you consider these two images, these two ends, at the same time?

Do you have a sense of what needs to happen?

Is it possible that the one image might like to be in contact with the other?

See what happens if you simultaneously really hold these two images ...

Do they change? Or not? Does something else happen?

Just track what is occurring now ...

Resettling yourself now, in this place of rest again, begin to let go of these images, just noting what has transpired thus far, and allowing it to register very clearly in your memory, and thanking your inner process for making itself available to you.

And finding yourself once more in your place of rest beside your path, your journey, just begin the process now of returning to present time and into the room ...

Do so by becoming aware of your breathing and by feeling the chair underneath you, supporting you, by beginning to focus on the sounds in the room and bringing with you anything that you need to remember or understand about this experience.

When you are ready, gradually return into the room and just make any notes that you need to in order to anchor the experience.

[Time allowed for personal writing.][50]

Well, we have reached the end of a very full day, and I want to thank you all for your participation, and for your staying with some very concentrated material. I have enjoyed today very much, and I hope you have too. And happy fairy tales if you do the exercise I spoke about!

APPENDIX I – Nodal Wonders

The Nodal Day and Year

Diagrams and inspiration courtesy of Robin Heath

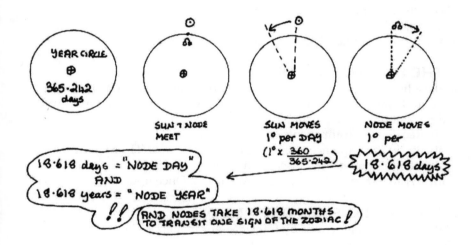

SUN & NODE MEET

SUN MOVES 1° per DAY
$(1° \times \frac{360}{365.242})$

NODE MOVES 1° per 18.618 days

18.618 days = "NODE DAY"
AND
18.618 years = "NODE YEAR"

!! AND NODES TAKE 18.618 MONTHS TO TRANSIT ONE SIGN OF THE ZODIAC !

The Eclipse Year

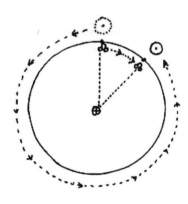

Draconic period of revolution =
Eclipse year = 365.242
                 − 18.62

            = 346.618 days

N.B. 346.618 = 18.618 × 18.618
                    or (18.618)² !!

– The solar year has 19.618 'Node Days'
– Solar year ≈ 18.618 × 19.618
– 19.618 − 18.618 = 1 (UNITY)

"The ☽'s orbit is directly affecting the length of the year. The nodes are the key to another cosmology."

APPENDIX II – A Life-Review Process

Deepen your understanding of your own life process by studying the Nodes, and release energy by focusing healing intention.

Bibliography
ALLI, Antero: *Astrologik*, Vigilantero Press, 1990 (o/p).
BORSTEIN, Agneta: *The Moon's Nodes*, Crescentia Publications, 2010.
HUBER, Bruno and Louise: *Moon Node Astrology*, Weiser, 1995.
SUTTON, Komilla: *The Lunar Nodes - Crisis and Redemption*, Wessex Astrologer, 2001.
VAN TOEN, Donna: *The Astrologer's Node Book*, Weiser, 1981.

1. THE TRANSITING NODAL AXIS
Make a list of all the conjunctions and oppositions created by the retrograde movement of the Nodes around your chart, from birth until the present time. Use North Node only.
    i) Recall significant events on those points
    ii) Study the sequence as a metaphor of your own 'Hero's Journey'. What patterns do you see? What comes to mind?
    iii) Write a story in the style of a folk tale ... Once upon a time ...

2. MAJOR TRANSITS TO THE NODES
Make a list of conjunctions by transit (outer planets + Chiron) to both North and South Nodes.
    i) Recall significant events around those points
    ii) Is there a pattern? (e.g. Is one end favoured? What happened?)

3. TURNING POINTS – THE BALANCING ACT
A. List all outer planet transits and also progressions which square the Nodal Axis
    i) What happened?
    ii) What did you learn?
    iii) See the image of a bow and arrow. Where is it going?

B. What else lies at these balance points (in the natal chart)?
    i) Fixed Stars
    ii) Sabian symbol of that degree
    iii) Midpoint structures
    iv) Centaurs, TNOs, etc. ... whatever interests you!

C. Note future times when the faster-moving planets will locate at the balance points, and track this.

4. FURTHER EXPLORATION

i) South Node

What most deeply supports your momentum in life?
What patterns of difficulty do you find here?
What comes easily? How do you hide? How do you handle loss?
What do you seek to release or renounce? What stops you?

ii) North Node

What do you need to let go of in order to feel supported?
What patterns of difficulty do you find here?
What rewards/successes? Your dreams? Your cutting edge?
How do you go forward? What stops you?
What drives you and towards what?

ENDNOTES

Part One – The Four Angles

1. The reader is invited to follow these exercises, using the instructions in the text, in order to experience the resulting sense of physical orientation and alignment. In the class the exercise was done slowly and contemplatively, in order to give the body time to sense the energy of the alignments being explored, and the mind time to grasp the conceptual model of it.

2. See *Vision of the Sun King*, Robin Whitlock, in *Quest* magazine, Vol.1, Issue 3, p.66. The main door of a Christian church usually faces west, where the baptismal font is situated, traditionally of octagonal design.

3. See for example *The Orion Mystery: Unlocking the Secrets of the Pyramids*, Robert Bauval and Adrian Gilbert (William Heinemann, London, 1994), concerning the alignment of the Great Pyramid to the stars in the constellation of Orion, said to represent Isis and Osiris. Also, for the well known alignment of Stonehenge with the Sun and Moon, see the work of Robin Heath in *Sun, Moon & Stonehenge*, Bluestone Press, Cardigan, 1998.

4. Robin Whitlock, *op.cit.*, p.66. See also *The Sun*, Richard Moeschl, in *The Mountain Astrologer*, Aug-Sept 1995, p.32ff.

5. *The Astrological Houses*, Dane Rudhyar, Doubleday and Co., New York, 1972.

6. *Beyond the Brain: Birth, Death and Transcendence in Psychotherapy*, Stanislav Grof, SUNY Press, 1985.

7. *A Student's Text-Book of Astrology*, Vivian E. Robson, B.Sc., Cecil Palmer, London, 1922, pp.68–84.

8. Dane Rudhyar, *op.cit.*, pp.121–2.

9. Emanuel Swedenborg (1688-1772) founded the New Jerusalem Church, inspired by a vision of the plurality of worlds, which was a departure from mainstream Christianity. His *magnum opus*

was titled *Arcana Caelestia*, translated into English in 1787. As late as the 19th century, men of science were asserting notions of extra-terrestrial beings, but this visionary dimension was gradually edited out of the common knowledge of what such men were thinking.

10. *Astrologik*, Antero Alli, Vigilantero Press, Seattle, 1990, p.28.

11. See *The Moment of Astrology*, Geoffrey Cornelius, Arkana, London, 1994. New edition published by The Wessex Astrologer, 2005.

12. See *Saturn, Chiron and the Centaurs: To the Edge and Beyond*, Melanie Reinhart, Starwalker Press, London, 2011, pp.184-91, and also *Interface*, Nick Kollerstrom, Ascella Publications, London, 1997, pp.45-55.

13. *Tables of Planetary Phenomena*, Neil F. Michelson, ACS Publications, San Diego, 1990.

14. See *Retrograde Planets: Traversing the Inner Landscape*, Erin Sullivan, Arkana, London, 1992.

15. To participate in the exercise described, consider recording the material so that the listening pace can be modulated by using the 'pause' function. As guided imagery work draws strongly on right brain (intuitive) functions, the recording should not be listened to casually, while driving, or in situations that require a predominantly left brain (logical and practical) modality.

Part Two – The Nodes of the Moon

16. My grateful thanks to Fiona Griffiths, Head Tutor of the Faculty of Astrological Studies, for an enjoyable discussion about the Nodes, and to Robin Heath, Editor of the *Astrological Journal* (1995-8), for his diagrams, helpful information and astronomical input.

17. In the UK, DIY is an abbreviation for 'Do It Yourself'.

18. Thanks to Robin Heath for offering helpful information on this question.

19. See http://content.time.com/time/health/ article/0,8599,2114544,00.html. Last accessed 19 April 2014.

20. See Appendix I, p.251.

21. *Sun, Moon & Stonehenge*, Robin Heath, Bluestone Press, Cardigan, 1998.

22. See also Part One of this volume, pp.14-21, for a description of the physicality of the symbolism of the four angles as depicted on the circular horoscope.

23. For a full exploration of this theme, see *Retrograde Planets: Traversing the Inner Landscape*, Erin Sullivan, Arkana, London, 1992.

24. This theme is explored in some depth in *Saturn, Chiron and the Centaurs: To the Edge and Beyond*, Melanie Reinhart, Starwalker Press, London, 2011, pp.151-6. The reader is also referred to the work of Francis J. Mott, specifically *The Nature of the Self* (2012) and *Mythology of the Prenatal Life* (2014), both published by Starwalker Press.

25. See also Part One, p. 23-4, where the symbolism of the Ascendant/Descendant axis is discussed.

26. *New Mansions for New Men*, Dane Rudhyar, Servire, The Hague, 1971, p.103ff.

27. At the time of revising this text, India was poised to create a new hypersonic weapon which has been specifically and deliberately linked to the mythic image of the Sudarshan Chakra. See http://defence.pk/threads/india-to-have-sudarshan-chakra-like-missile-soon.288229/ Last accessed 24 August 2014.

28. *Draconic Astrology*, Pamela Crane, Shoestring Publishing, Faversham, UK, 1994, pp. 35-6. (New edition by Flare Publications, 2013.) She quotes Cyril Fagan, *Zodiacs Old and New*, reprinted 2011 by Literary Licensing.

29. *A Collection of Emblems, Ancient and Modern*, George Wither, London, 1635, p.102. (Reprinted by Kessinger Publishing Co, 2003.) The picture is of a plate engraved by Crispin de Pass and

son, first used in Gabriel Rollenhagen's *Nucleus emblematum selectissimorum*, Arnhem and Utrecht, 1611-13.

30. See *The Sirius Mystery*, Robert K.G. Temple, Futura Publications, London, 1976.

31. *Sufi: Expressions of the Mystic Quest*, Laleh Bakhtiar, Thames and Hudson, London, 1976, p.45.

32. *The Astrology of Personality*, Dane Rudhyar, Servire, The Hague, The Netherlands, 1963, pp.316-22.

33. Thanks to Geraldine Hallett for this image.

34. *Astrologik*, Antero Alli, Vigilantero Press, Seattle, 1990, p.200-4.

35. *The Psychology of AstroCartography*, Jim Lewis with Kenneth Irving, Arkana, London, 1997.

36. See also Part One of this volume, p. 94-7, on 'sensitised degrees'.

37. *An Astrological Mandala*, Dane Rudhyar, Vintage Books, New York, 1973.

38. Rudhyar, *ibid.*, p.85ff.

39. Rudhyar, *ibid.*, p.145ff.

40. Rudhyar, *ibid.*, p.264ff.

41. Pamela Crane, *op.cit.*

42. Thanks to Joyce Hopewell of the English Huber School, Cheshire, UK, for computing this chart.

43. Bruno and Louse Huber, *Moon Node Astrology*, Samuel Weiser, Inc., York Beach, ME, 1995, p.135.

44. See Appendix II, p.252-3.

45. Matthew 16:18.

46. *Finding Our Way Through the Dark,* Demetra George, ACS Publications, San Diego, 1995.

47. See p.158, details at n30.

48. See *Saturn, Chiron and the Centaurs: To the Edge and Beyond,* Melanie Reinhart, Starwalker Press, London, 2011, pp.125-34, for a fuller exposition of this mythic image.

49. In order to participate in this exercise, it is recommended that the reader either record the instructions first, or enlist the help of a friend to do the exercise. The recording should not be listened to while driving or doing any other activity.

50. The personal sharing at the end of this seminar was not transcribed.

CPSIA information can be obtained
at www.ICGtesting.com
Printed in the USA
BVHW080205170921
616818BV00002B/182

9 780955 823138